Why Is Corporate America Bashing Our Public Schools?

Kathy Emery and Susan Ohanian

HEINEMANN
Portsmouth, NH

Heinemann
A division of Reed Elsevier Inc.
361 Hanover Street
Portsmouth, NH 03801–3912
www.heinemann.com

Offices and agents throughout the world

Library of Congress Cataloging-in-Publication Data

Emery, Kathy (Mary Kathleen)
    Why is corporate America bashing our public schools? / Kathy Emery and
Susan Ohanian.
        p. cm.
    Includes bibliographical references and index.
    ISBN 0-325-00637-7 (alk. paper)
    1. Business and education—United States. 2. Public schools—United States.
    3. Politics and education—United States. 4. Education—Standards—United States.
    I. Ohanian, Susan. II. Title.

LC1085.2.E388 2004
371.19'5—dc22

                                                            2004012229

Editor: Lois Bridges
Production management: Renée Le Verrier
Production coordination: Abigail M. Heim
Typesetter: Publishers' Design and Production Services, Inc.
Cover design: Catherine Hawkes/Cat & Mouse Design
Manufacturing: Steve Bernier

Printed in the United States of America on acid-free paper

07   06   05   04   EB   1   2   3   4   5

For Steve Orel, whose fight against a mean system makes a difference.
—S. Ohanian

To Don Arnstine
For giving me the opportunity to become more like myself.
—K. Emery

Contents

Introduction

McMerde Double Bacon Cheeseburgers, Steinway Pianos, and Standing Up for the Teaching Covenant

Cheese and Children

In 1999, after the United States imposed 100 percent import tariffs on Roquefort cheese, ten sheep farmers whose special Lacaune ewes produce the milk used in making the cheese climbed on their tractors and trashed the construction site of a McDonald's. McDonald's was chosen as a conspicuous symbol of America's drive for a global economy and because its ubiquitous golden arches are seen as a special threat to French cuisine and culture. Later that year, when Ralph Nader invited José Bové, farmer and trade unionist spokesman, to the demonstrations against the World Trade Organization in Seattle, Bové smuggled some unpasteurized cheese past American customs. He posed for cameras outside a Seattle McDonald's eating a Roquefort sandwich, declaring, "You are what you eat."

Now think about this: If we aren't what we teach, then who are we? Maybe we should take this up as a mantra: You are what you teach. You are what you teach. You are what you teach. You are what you teach.

As we find ourselves in education free fall, think of something else Bové said as he munched on his illicit Roquefort. "We are peasants and citizens, not shareholders, not servile slaves at the mercy of agribusiness."

Ask yourself: Whose bidding have *you* been answering of late? And how do you feel about it? This book describes the hijacking of American education; it spells out chapter and verse how the globalists are usurping public opinion—wiping out local school boards, hog-tying teachers, and terrifying children. Nothing short of the survival of democracy is at stake.

The ten farmers staged their resistance near Montpelier, France. Susan Ohanian would like to point out that in 2004, after protests and legal battles,

1

her state capital, Montpelier, Vermont, still hangs on to its position as the only state capital in the country refusing to allow McDonald's to open a franchise. First McDonald's; next No Child Left Behind (NCLB). Citizens *can* stand up and say "No!" to global agribusiness. They can say "No!" to standards and testing shipped in from a corporate-politico agenda. They can stand up and shout "Yes!"—yes to local cheese, yes to local children. A two-decade drive by The Business Roundtable to get schools lined up behind their plan has seen its fruition in NCLB, hog-tying teachers and terrifying children.

Pianos and Perfection

It is not as huge a leap as you might think from protecting the favorite cheese of Charlemagne to considering the qualities of pianos. As with Roquefort production, there is a specific, detailed process for making Steinway pianos. For an extra $50,000, one can opt for an ebony exterior, but the guts of every concert grand are the same—the same soundboard made of close-grained quarter-sawn spruce, the same strings, the same hammers that strike the strings, the same keys to which the hammers that strike the strings are attached, and so on through seventeen laminations of the hard maple rim. And yet, even though every piano is made from the same materials by the same work crews, every pianist will tell you that of the more than 563,000 Steinway pianos produced since the company's founding on March 5, 1853, every one ends up being different from every other. Some pianos are best suited to chamber music, others can overpower a full orchestra. Some concert pianists insist that two Steinways be brought to the concert hall, so they can choose which is more suitable. Horowitz, for one, wanted a light, responsive touch, Rubenstein, more resistance. When the music department at Oberlin Conservatory decided it was going to buy a Steinway, faculty members traveled to the factory in New York to get it right. They looked at five pianos and then made their choice.[1]

Writing in the *New York Times*, James Barron speculates, "Perhaps it is the wood. No matter how carefully Steinway selects or prepares each batch, some trees get more sunlight than others in the forest, and some get more water. Certain piano technicians say uncontrollable factors make the difference."[2] Uncontrollable factors. These days, such a notion will stop a teacher in her tracks. In these days of hyperaccountability and raising the academic bar, and driving high-stakes tests through children's souls as well as district finances, a teacher dare not mention uncontrollable factors when talking about student achievements. Never, never, never.

A Steinway grand has more than twelve thousand parts; a squirrelly third grader's brain has about one hundred billion neurons, but it's the third grader that teachers must standardize into what corporate America has defined as product. Any teacher will tell you how different is each third grader in her care. But the corporate-politico-media alliance long ago abandoned teacher judgment as only anecdotal, putting all its eggs in the granular-data basket. In these days of hyperaccountability, the Business Roundtable and its political cronies insist that all students must move along the same conveyor belt of skills. No variations allowed. *Uncontrollable factors* are for pianos and for Wall Street and for health care and for military assaults. Don't try it on standardized test scores. "No Excuses" is the corporate mantra shrouding the schools these days.

The Covenant

Concerned about issues of justice and equity that have become smothered by test-score hysteria, thirty parents and educators from all parts of the country traveled to Birmingham, Alabama, in March 2003. There could be no better place to organize for grassroots resistance to the corporate takeover of public education than the cradle of the civil rights movement and the site of the World of Opportunity (WOO). Under the leadership of longtime human and civil rights activist Steve Orel, the WOO shouts "Yes!" to diverse learners who are not always available to stand in line for the conveyor-belt skill delivery advocated by corporate America. Right before the administration of a high-stakes test, 522 African-American students were pushed out of local high schools facing state takeover if their test scores didn't improve. The easiest way to raise a school's test scores is to get rid of low scorers. And yet, WOO students have earned their GEDs; they've learned job skills and found jobs; they've earned college scholarships. They register to vote; they volunteer in the community; they write poetry, design websites, and write letters to McGraw-Hill, pointing out all the errors in its GED materials.

We presented the WOO with a check—and a stack of envelopes bearing postmarks of every state. Lots of envelopes held single dollar bills, sent by parents and grandparents worried about Birmingham students—and about their own children. One noteworthy envelope contained forty-seven one-dollar bills, sent by a Tennessee teacher in honor of each one of her fourth-grade students. She named each student, describing strengths unacknowledged by Standardistas.

This book is written to explain why and how schools and the children in them are under attack. This is important, because with this information, you can arm yourself. You can resist, and you can fight back. Here's a song we sang in Birmingham. It summarizes the attack on public education. Try singing it in the faculty room and at school board meetings. Sing it at city council meetings where the mayor wants to dictate school policy.

If you cannot find Osama, test the kids.
If the market hurt your Mama, test the kids.
If the CEOs are liars
Putting schools on funeral pyres,
Screaming, "Vouchers we desire!"
Test the kids.

If you have no health insurance, test the kids.
Your retirement's a game of chance? Test the kids.
If the GPA ain't growin'
And corporate greed ain't slowin'
And White House con is flowin'
Test the kids.

If your schools they are crumbling, test the kids.
And the Congress it is bumbling, test the kids.
CEOs want competition.
And public school demolition.
They're on a hunting expedition.
Test the kids.

Notes

1. Chipman, Michael. 1999. "Oberlin and Steinway: A 122-Year Partnership." *Oberlin Conservatory News*, fall. Accessed at *www.oberlin.edu/con/connews/fall99/steinway.html*.

2. Barron, James. 2003. "How Does a Piano Get to Carnegie Hall?" *The New York Times*, 11 May.

1
The Words That Bind

The trouble with words is that you never know whose mouths they've been in.

—Dennis Potter, British TV dramatist

Using deceptively simple, clear, appealing language, those who spawned No Child Left Behind took a page right out of Newt Gingrich's *Language: A Key Mechanism of Control*. Gingrich mailed this booklet to Republican leaders in 1990; the methodology lives on. Here are the words Gingrich tells Republicans to use when describing themselves:

> active, activist, building, candid(ly), care(ing), challenge, change, children, choice/choose, citizen, commitment, common sense, compete, confident, conflict, control, courage, crusade, debate, dream, duty, eliminate good time in prison, empower(ment), fair, family, freedom, hard work, help, humane, inventive, initiative, lead, learn, legacy, liberty, light, listen, mobilize, moral, movement, opportunity, passionate, peace, pioneer, precious, premise, preserve, principle(d), pristine, pro-flag/children/environment, prosperity, protect, proud/pride, provide, reform, sights, share, strength, success, tough, truth, unique, vision, we/us/our, workfare

Here are the words Republicans should use when speaking of Democrats:

> anti-flag/family/child/jobs, betray, coercion, collapse, consequences, corruption, crisis, decay, deeper, destroy, destructive, devour, endanger, failure, greed, hypocrisy, ideological, impose, incompetent, insecure, liberal, lie, limit(s), pathetic, permissive attitude, radical, self-serving, sensationalists, shallow, sick, they/them, threaten, traitors, unionized bureaucracy, urgent, waste

Note that Gingrich draws much more from the simple, direct words of advertising campaigns than from Latinate obfuscation. Writing in *Mother Jones*, George Packard refers to this technique as the *danger of clarity*, observing that these seemingly simple and tough-minded words blow out as much theatrical

5

smoke as the jargon of the Pentagon of decades past.[1] Nowhere is this smoke thicker than in the lingo the corporate-politico-media squad uses when talking about public schools. The phrase *failing public schools* has a lot in common with *war on terror:* get the media to parrot these phrases often enough so that you can't hear *terrorism* without thinking there's a need for war, and you can't hear *public schools* without thinking they are failing and need to be fixed.

This language works: ordinary people without an ax to grind, people who haven't set foot in a school for thirty years or more, will testify to failing public schools. This technique forestalls debate about what matters in public schools because the corporate and political elite have already defined both the problem and the solution. We have all become prisoners of their rhetoric, and it's time we break the chains that bind us. The beginning of education for democracy is to call things by their right name. And then to stand by those words.

In the hands of the U.S. Department of Education, the very title No Child Left Behind, hijacked from the Children's Defense Fund, has become the moral equivalent of the Pentagon's *pacification.* Of course, other verbal pyrotechnics are at work here—what Orwell called doublespeak. No Child Left Behind means the opposite of what it says. It is a plan not to help every school succeed but to declare public schools failures and accelerate the use of vouchers, turning public education over to private, for-profit firms. It is also a plan to blame the victim: the government declares it's leaving no child behind, so if a kid ends up on the streets after tenth grade, it must be his fault.

There's nothing new about politicians using slippery language to round up and herd the citizenry. The rhetoric of *school reform of the twenty-first century*—and watch the buzzwords pile up in *this* phrase—is filled with refrains repeated so often that people accept them as normal and even descriptive of reality. Here's an example from the *Raleigh News and Observer*:

> Wake County's dozen year-round elementary and middle schools will be the first in the state to learn whether their spring test results meet rigorous new federal standards for student performance.

Rigorous: the federal beacon for measuring up to the government's tough new rules. Think how the spin would be transformed by substituting *abusive.* Abusive isn't an overstatement to describe what's happening to third graders across the country. Those who think *rigor* is a terrific word to describe the education of children they care about should do what California teacher and mother of four Nancy Barr did and look it up in the dictionary.

> *Rigor:* a harsh or cruel act; a state of rigidity in living tissues or organs that prevents response to stimuli; death stiffening; inclemency; rugged sternness; relentless severity; cruelty; severity of life; voluntary submission to pain; inflexibility; something hard to endure.[2]

Rigor: Strictness or severity, as in temperament, action, or judgment.
A harsh or trying circumstance; hardship.
A harsh or cruel act.
Physiology: A state of rigidity in living tissues or organs that prevents response to stimuli.
Syn: Stiffness; rigidness; inflexibility; severity; austerity; sternness; harshness; strictness; exactness.[3]

It is hard to imagine parents giving permission for the state to apply *any* of these principles to their children.

Daily, the media bombards us with news of the movers and shakers. In this chapter we're going to ask, What about the moved and the shaken? We'll start by looking at the lingo of a few Standardistas, peeling away the onion-layered duplicity.

Refrain: I've walked in your shoes.

Example: "I've been a superintendent of a large city and I've walked in your shoes. . . . I think being a superintendent is one of the roughest jobs in America."

Speaker: Secretary of Education Rod Paige, in a speech approving the District of Columbia Accountability Plan under No Child Left Behind, June 9, 2003.

What It Means: In education, I'm a hero. In education policy, I'm a hero.

What It Hides: The shady practices in Houston, such as grossly underreported push-out rates.

Subtext: Did he mention he's a hero?

Refrain: preparing all students for the twenty-first-century economy

Example: "Today, more than ever, we live in a global economy where competition and technology are changing the workplace and impacting economic success for all Americans. U.S. schools must change if they are to prepare all students for the challenges and opportunities of the twenty-first century. This is not a partisan issue."

Speaker: Edward B. Rust Jr., chairman and CEO of State Farm Insurance Companies, former cochair of the Business Coalition for Excellence in Education, former chair of the Business Roundtable's Education Initiative, director of Achieve, Inc., former chair of American Enterprise Institute, member of President Bush's Transition Advisory Team committee on education, member of the National (Glenn) Commission on Mathematics and Science Teaching for the Twenty-First Century.

What It Means: When you and your kids can't find living-wage jobs, blame the schools.

What It Hides: We're shipping tons of jobs overseas.

Subtext: Don't try to figure out whether Rust is a Democrat or a Republican. Both political parties joined corporate America in selling out public education. Does any worker in the cutthroat competitive marketplace want his child's school to operate the way corporate America does?

Refrain: an opportunity to give them more credibility and status than they've ever had

Example: "One strength of the AFT [American Federation of Teachers] is that we are very good at walking and chewing gum at the same time. Our paraleaders, just like our teacher leaders, are fighting to save jobs and, at the same time, working to raise professional standards, which will lead to better outcomes for students and better pay for a group of people whose contributions have long gone unrecognized. Remember—early in the reauthorization process, there was an effort to eliminate paraprofessionals from Title I. Instead, we got an opportunity to give them more credibility and status than they've ever had."

Speaker: Sandra Feldman, president of the American Federation of Teachers, keynote address. QuEST Conference, Washington, D.C., July 10, 2003.

What It Means: Union members are helpless without their unions.

What It Hides: Paraprofessionals will have to obtain two-year college degrees to keep their jobs.

Subtext: The status of paraprofessionals comes from the communities to which they contribute invaluable services. Forcing them to learn calculus to keep their jobs, part of the corporate redefinition of *skill* in schools, is both unjust and immoral and may well be part of the ongoing plan to deprofessionalize and decertify teachers.

Refrain: You can't manage what you don't measure.

Example: "You can't manage what you don't measure. No executive can run a business without accurate, granular data that explains what's working and what's not. Our school systems should be no different. Better reporting of student performance will allow educators, parents, and policy makers to see where we need to improve and by how much."

Speaker: Joseph M. Tucci, president and CEO of EMC Corporation and chairman of the Business Roundtable's Education and the Workforce Task Force.

What It Means: Character traits like faith, hope, and charity count for nothing; talent in music, the arts, woodworking, or mechanics counts for nothing.

What It Hides: Learning for the sake of learning will be wiped out of the public school system. Everything must have a measured and measurable value.

Subtext: Data warehousing is the growth industry of our time. Public schools will be structured as businesses and treat the people in them as badly as businesses treat their employees.

Refrain: schools, just like any business . . .

Example: "In tough financial times, schools, just like any business or organization, must take a good hard look at why they exist and what are the critical steps necessary for fulfilling their primary mission. It may be appropriate for schools to eliminate past practices that no longer produce the kind of academic gains required in NCLB."

Speaker: Michigan Business Leaders for Educational Excellence (MBLEE) press release: "Tough Financial Times Offer Great Opportunity for No Child Left Behind," January 27, 2003.

What It Means: For the Business Roundtable, schools exist to serve the needs of corporate America. Increasingly, "eliminating past practices" means zapping recess, kindergarten nap time, libraries, the arts, and so on.

What It Hides: It hides the real agenda of schools' corporate partners.

Subtext: You're never good enough, you're never good enough, you're never good enough.

Refrain: clear, honest, bold data

Example: "This nation has a deep moral commitment to the principles of No Child Left Behind. Reporting achievement by student groups will be eye-opening for many people. We must be clear, honest, and bold about the data and use it to make changes to ensure that all students performing at high levels."

Speaker: John J. Castellani, president of the Business Roundtable.

What It Means: The BRT is going to use the data to screw public schools.

What It Hides: The Business Roundtable commissioned a national telephone survey to get an early signal about parent and voter understanding of the new accountability systems to help state leaders communicate effectively about the new changes.

Subtext: The proliferation of uncontrolled data would scare parents—if they knew about it.

Refrain: highly qualified teacher

Example: "Rod Paige has opted to define *highly qualified* in an eminently sensible way: knowing something about what one is teaching. In doing so, he has run up against the AACTE.[4] Traditional certification, as championed by this educators' guild, emphasizes the 'how' of teaching as much as, or even more than, the 'what.' Prospective teachers fill their days with courses in 'Educational Psychology' and 'Social & Philosophical Foundations of American Education.' By the time a new math teacher graduates, he may or may not know what calculus is, but he'll sure know every theory about how to teach it."

Speaker: Editorial in the *Wall Street Journal.*[5]

What It Means: The *Wall Street Journal* and its corporate allies have contempt for teacher-training institutions.

What It Hides: The transformation of schools of education into test-prep academies. The elimination of the history and philosophy of education, of different ways to teach reading and math, so teachers will be dependent on the test-prep materials handed to them by district officials who have contracts with McGraw-Hill et al.

Subtext: Media giants are readily available as mouthpieces for corporate policies.

Refrain: if a school is failing

Example: "The whole idea is that if a school is failing, the students that happen to be there ought not be doomed to attending that school for the rest of the academic year.[6]"

Speaker: Frances Marine, Florida State Department of Education.

What It Means: The "failing" label comes from a jerry-rigged federal formula that will have nearly every public school in America so labeled. Vermont, for one, anticipates 100 percent failure.

What It Hides: The label is not reality. Parents may be very well satisfied with the education their children are receiving. When given the opportunity to transfer to other schools—schools receiving a "successful" label—the vast majority of parents opt to keep their children where they are.

Subtext: Public school failure is being decided and decreed by forces not in the community and for purposes not linked to the school.

Refrain: strip away costly activities which drain resources and distract schools

Example: "NCLB is not just "another thing" that schools are being asked to do. It provides a structure and a challenge to schools that will help them strip away costly activities and practices which drain resources and distract schools from completing their central purpose, which is to educate kids."

Speaker: Jim Sandy, executive director of Michigan Business Leaders for Educational Excellence.

What It Means: Only tested subjects count in reports of school adequacy.

What It Hides: Art, music, and drama, regarded as "costly activities" and even frills by the business community, are being dropped by schools. Libraries, another frill, are disappearing. In states that don't test science, even science is vanishing.

Subtext: At the demand of corporate America, public schools are being standardized into sterile mediocrity.

Refrain: the noble profession of teaching

Example: "We're asking a lot of America's teachers, and they deserve our full support. We have a President in office who has repeatedly emphasized the need for action to encourage Americans to enter and remain in the noble profession of teaching. Republicans have taken major steps under President Bush to give teachers more freedom and resources to do their jobs—and even more help is on the way."

Speaker: U.S. House Education and the Workforce Committee chairman John Boehner (R-OH), in honor of Teacher Appreciation Week.[7]

What It Means: The Bush administration wants licensure and certification requirement eased so that other Americans can enter the profession. Funny that he specifies *Americans*. Several states are recruiting in India.

What It Hides: The Bush administration insists that any Tom, Dick, or Harry—retired military personnel, Wall Street analyst, or candlestick maker—can be a teacher and that professional courses offered by colleges of education are a waste of time.

Subtext: There's a move afoot to deprofessionalize teaching by instituting a tier system: master teachers will get upward of $100,000, and they will direct subteachers to dish out direct instruction. You don't need a professional to read a script, but you reassure parents by announcing someone making $100,000 is in charge of their children's education.

Refrain: stakeholders

Look at these examples—what's being said and who's saying it (indicated in endnotes). Think about the subtext.

Examples:

- Establish a decision-making process that ensures input from all affected stakeholders.[8]
- A Letter to Citizens and Other Stakeholders in the District of Columbia[9]
- 7.1.14 Communicate effectively with stakeholders via electronic mail (email, video conferencing, electronic newsletters, presentation software, etc.)[10]
- The Plan was developed under the leadership of the Maryland Business Roundtable for Education (MBRT) by key stakeholders throughout Maryland that represented not only the educational community but the public and private sectors as well.[11]
- Our membership—which includes the leading CEOs in Ohio—is excited about this opportunity and we will work vigorously with Battelle, Governor Taft, the Ohio General Assembly, the State Board of Education, education

stakeholders, and others in the business community to make Ohio's public schools the most improved in the nation by 2006, as measured by the National Assessment of Educational Progress.[12]

Refrain: global marketplace/economy/knowledge
Examples:

- In an era of ongoing transition where globalization is creating unprecedented world competitiveness, and redefining how society lives, works and plays, education is facing a myriad of challenges as it prepares students for the world of tomorrow. A significant challenge is in ensuring their ability to work effectively in a technically focused society, and use its tools in a productive and efficient manner to find, exchange and leverage information.[13]
- Pennsylvania's business leaders believe all high school graduates entering the workforce need to have the academic knowledge, skills and work habits required in the high-performance workplace. The challenges of global competition have changed business and industry conditions dramatically. We believe Pennsylvania's education system also needs to change to ensure that our students become the successful learners and workers of the future.[14]
- In order for MPS [Milwaukee Public Schools] to attain our goal of providing every student a world-class education that will allow them to be competent and competitive contributors in a global economy, District administrators and teachers must be able to immediately access information to monitor results, evaluate progress, plan for and act to implement improvements, and, finally, report back to stakeholders. (Milwaukee Public Schools superintendent Carol Johnson)[15]

Some word generators combine stakeholders and globals.

- The enhanced global perspectives brought on by exploding information technologies have precipitated dramatic changes in industry. Recognizing that suppliers and customers are stakeholders in the product realization process and bringing them onto the production team has resulted in significant improvement in quality and efficiency.[16]

Putting the Data Before the Kid

No question: the Business Roundtable and its bedfellows insist that schools become data-driven depots, or, as Frederick W. Smith, CEO of Federal Express, puts it on the Business Coalition for Education Reform website:[17] "If you can't measure it, you can't manage it."[18] One would point out to Smith and his allies that kids aren't packages to be delivered from one teacher to the next.

In November 2002, business leaders were invited *to hear leading thinkers on the power of data to drive educational change* at the Business and Education

2002 Conference: The New Era of Education Reform—Corporate Opportunities to Strengthen Tomorrow's Workforce. Codirected by the National Alliance of Business (NAB) and the Conference Board,[20] the conference featured a panel discussion titled "The Business Role in Pre K–16 Learning: Aligning the Knowledge Supply Chain," which was moderated by Robert T. Jones, NAB president and CEO. Panel members included Patrick M. Callan, president of the National Center for Public Policy and Higher Education; Kati Haycock, director of the Education Trust; Andrea Leskes, director of the Greater Expectations Project and vice president for education and quality initiatives for the Association of American Colleges and Universities; Gabriella Morris, president of the Prudential Foundation and vice president of community resources for Prudential Financial, Inc.; and Nancy Zimpher, chancellor of the University of Wisconsin–Milwaukee. Keynoting was Edward B. Rust, chairman of the board and CEO of the company of the year, State Farm Insurance Companies. If your eyes glaze over from reading the names, keep the corporate connections in mind.

In 1755, in the preface to his *Dictionary*, Samuel Johnson wrote, "I am not so lost in lexicography as to forget that words are the daughters of earth." The words of the National Alliance of Business are sons of the compost heap.

Every time we hear the ubiquitous ed-bizspeak—*schools as data-driven institutions, data-driven reform, total data control, data-driven decision making*—we must stop and challenge it. Stop and ask about the numbers game that obscures the very real needs of real children. Think of the historical uses of data without social conscience, asking yourself if following orders to produce more data can ever be justified. As we read that IBM is pushing "a data warehousing solution packaged with technology, services and critical intellectual capital that can help improve student achievement through better information management and data-driven decision making,"[21] we're reminded that there's a close relationship between the Auschwitz tattoo and IBM data sorters: IBM supplied the data solution to the Third Reich.[22]

Today, IBM is in the *solutions* business. It offers eight data solutions "to leverage your school district's technology investment to address and benefit from the NCLB legislation": Insight at School, Riverdeep Learning Village, Network Infrastructure Services, professional development tools and services, and more. For starters, people who think data collection is the answer to education's woes should ask themselves if a kid ever snuggled up to data. Or if data ever convinced him to read a book. Or listened to questions and concerns.

But data-mining entrepreneurs will shrug that off as so much romanticism, pointing to Wal-Mart's massive data warehousing as a model for schools. Just keep in mind that not only does Wal-Mart mine its own databases, but it allows its suppliers to mine them, too. The idea of school data moving out to the marketplace scares and offends lots of people. Conservatives have long been alert to the potentials for schools to collaborate on privacy invasion; it's past time for progressives to wake up. Maybe the U.S. Patriot Act sections 507 and 508, amending the Family Education Rights and Privacy Act (FERPA), which prohibited disclosure of student records without consent, will wake up a few people.[23] Under Patriot Act section 507, the attorney general or a designee may "collect education records in the possession of the educational agency or institution that are relevant to an authorized investigation or prosecution of an offense." No suspicion of wrongdoing is necessary, only relevance to an investigation. The Patriot Act absolves the educational agency from notifying parents of their rights; it also removes legal liability from the educational agency for producing the data. Section 508 specifies as an additional source for data the National Center for Education Statistics, whose handbook provides 475 data elements—starting with prenatal information, number of dental fillings, religion, family income range, and so on and so on.

Those who worship at the data collection altar should remember that although data never disappears, it sometimes goes awry. Take the Air Force Academy. A confidential list of forty to fifty cadets suspected of stealing, drunken driving, making fake ID cards, and downloading pornography was mistakenly emailed to everybody at the academy instead of to the intended recipients, the school administrators. The list included cadets being counseled for emotional problems. Then there's the security breach in the computer system that stored data for the HOPE Scholarship program in Georgia. The Georgia Student Finance Commission inadvertently released personal data about thousands of students; at the same time, passwords allowing access to computers at the agency were exposed on Google. This meant hackers could have used the passwords and codes to gain access to any file in the commission's computer. Any file. They could have used the doorway into the commission's network to enter other state databases, including those containing tax and medical records.

Another concern is that once data is collected, it can follow you forever. Take the Florida woman who, years ago, under a physician's care in Massachusetts, took Prozac. Then, out of the blue, she received, unsolicited and without consultation with a physician, a free one-month trial of the prescription medication Prozac Weekly—delivered to her current home in Florida. She wonders how somebody got into her medical records and started sending her dangerous medications.[24] A counsel for the Health Privacy Project in Washington observes that health care data is being bought, sold, and used like any other commodity.

In December 2003, *Wired* reported that one of the nation's largest commercial distributors of voter data sold voter registration lists featuring detailed personal information without verifying the identity or intent of buyers.

Aristotle International used a website to sell the lists, which contain details about registered voters from nearly every state. The data includes birth dates, home addresses, phone numbers, race, income levels, ethnic backgrounds and, in some cases, religious affiliations.[25]

Children's school data is just as vulnerable. Test scores, discipline reports, visits to the school psychologist—it will sit in the data warehouse until someone figures out how to make a buck off it.

Business Roundtable Threats and Braggadocio

When relating what he learned from his experiences in setting state standards in Georgia, Gary Lee, director of the United Parcel Service Foundation, offered advice to other employers should they encounter any opposition to the BRT's agenda. Lee told them to remind their communities that U.S.-based companies can find skilled workers for everything from manufacturing to software development overseas, adding that companies increasingly decide where to locate their operations both in the United States and abroad on the basis of workforce quality and the performance of local school systems.

Does anybody believe that the BRT's pricey lobbying for a permanent China free-trade policy had anything to do with the *schools* there? And funny thing: as we read about cities wooing Boeing during its relocation flirtation, it was tax breaks, not teacher qualifications, making the headlines. One newspaper dubbed it "the tax-breaks arms race." Chicago won, with Illinois kicking in $41 million in tax write-offs and the city ponying up another $19 million.

Standing by Words

In a document titled " 'Knowledge Supply Chain': Managing K–80 Learning,"[26] the National Alliance of Business describes teachers as *knowledge suppliers* and schools as *the knowledge supply chain*:

- I dream of the day when I can go to a knowledge systems integrator, specify my needs and have them put all the partners together to deliver the people I need.
- Applying the principles of the material supply chain to the process of lifelong learning is a cost-effective, efficient way businesses can ensure that worker knowledge is put to use to help companies' bottom line.
- Increased understanding by students and faculty at all levels of the education system of business and competitive needs of industry.

Teachers need to speak up, reminding the NAB and others of its ilk that *teacher* and *student* are honorable words, that their relationship is sacred; knowledge systems integrators and the competitive needs of industry be damned. Even so, we must acknowledge that there's plenty of evidence that *teacher* and *student* as honorable terms is merely a quaint notion—hence the nostalgia for the *Dead Poet's Society* or *The Emperor's Club* and the fantasy revenge on Professor Umbridges, who only get their comeuppance in the world of wizards and witches.

Notes

1. Packard, George. 2003. "Stop Making Sense." *Mother Jones*, May/June.

2. From *http://dictionary.reference.com*.

3. *The American Heritage Dictionary of the English Language*, 4th edition. 2000. Boston, Houghton Mifflin.

4. American Association of Colleges for Teacher Education.

5. "Teacher Liberation." 2003. Editorial. *Wall Street Journal*, 2 July. This editorial's wretched excess in attacking colleges of education and teachers who have made the profession their life's calling is a good example of a writer being unable to contain his bile. Here are the last two sentences: "Three cheers to the Bush Administration for picking this fight. Alternative certification will clear the way for intelligent, talented (and much-needed) teachers to head to the front of the classroom." The clear implication is that the stupid, untalented ones are there now. Accessed at *http://online.wsj.com/article/0,,SB105710414522406500,00.html?mod=opinion*.

6. Pinzur, Matthew I. 2003. "Miami-Dade Students Bailing on Failing Elementary Schools." *Miami Herald*, 11 June.

7. U.S. House Education and the Workforce Committee. 2003. "House Republicans Mark Teacher Appreciation Week." Press release. 7 May. Accessed at *http://edworkforce.house.gov/press/press108/05may/teachappreciation050703.htm*.

8. From Administrative Utilization Study, conducted for the Greenwich, Connecticut, Public Schools by SchoolMatch. Accessed at *www.greenwichschools.org/AboutDistrict/surveys.htm*.

9. Williams, Anthony A. (mayor). 2001. Policy agenda. 15 March.

10. Mississippi Online Technology Evaluation. Accessed at *http://mde.aws.com/results/statesum_sections.asp?CID=16&Q_Num=14*.

11. Maryland Business Roundtable for Education. Technology. Accessed at *www.mbrt.org/d-technolo.htm*.

12. *"Battelle for Kids" Sets Ambitious Goal for Ohio—Most Improved Public Schools in the Nation by 2006*. 2001. Battelle news release. 3 May. Accessed at *www.battelle.org/news/01/05-03-01Battelleforkids.stm*.

13. IBM. n.d. Case Study: Durham District Schools Board in Canada: Innovation in Education. Accessed at *www-1.ibm.com/industries/education/doc/content/casestudy/355668110.html*.

14. Pennsylvania Business Roundtable. Accessed at *www.paroundtable.org/about_priorities.html*.

15. From *www.mpls.k12.mn.us/news/news_release/eds_grant.shtml*.

16. Batty, J. Clair, and Karen O. Batty. 2001. "Bringing the K–12 Stakeholders onto the Engineering Education Team." Proceedings of the 2001 American Society for Engineering Education Annual Conference and Exposition. Accessed at *www.asee.org/conferences/search/00094_2001.PDF*.

17. See *www.bcer.org*. BCER members include American Business Conference; Business–Higher Education Forum; the Business Roundtable; the Chamber of Commerce of the United States; Committee for Economic Development; the Conference Board; Council of Growing Companies; Council on Competitiveness; National Alliance of Business; National Association of Manufacturers; National Association of Women Business Owners; U.S. Hispanic Chamber of Commerce, and Utility/Business Education Coalition. Affiliate members include Achieve, Inc.; National Association of Partners in Education, Inc.; and U.S. Department of Education.

18. This is a popular adage, employed at various times by Peter Rucker and Rudy Giuliani, among others. As noted earlier in this chapter, Joseph M. Tucci said pretty much the same thing.

19. National Alliance of Business. 1998. " 'Knowledge Supply Chain': Managing K–80 Learning." *Work America* 15 (5).

20. Conference sponsors were Merrill Lynch and Pfizer. Presenting assistance were Prudential Financial; ACT; Johnson & Johnson; Target Corp.; State Farm Insurance; GlaxoSmithKline; AOL Time Warner Foundation; and Thomson DBM.

21. IBM Press Room. Accessed at *www-1.ibm.com/press/PressServletForm.wss*.

22. Black, Edwin. 2001. *IBM and the Holocaust*. New York: Crown.

23. The authors wish to thank Peggy Daly-Masternak, a Toledo, Ohio, parent activist in issues affecting education and neighborhoods, for making her valuable research available.

24. Liptak, Adam. 2002. "Free Prozac in the Junk Mail Draws a Lawsuit." *New York Times*, 6 July.

25. Zetter, Kim. 2003. "For Sale: The American Voter." *Wired*, 11 December. Accessed at *www.wired.com/newsevote/0,2645,61543,00.html/2n_ascii*. Also see "Mining the Vein of Voter Rolls," accessed at *www.wired.com/news/business/0,1367,61507,00.html?tw=wn_story_top5*.

26. National Alliance of Business. 1998.

2

College Entrance

Universal Measure of Public School Success, or a
Straw-Man Setup of Business Roundtable Cronies?

Whenever you hear a politician carry on about what a mess the
schools are, be aware that you are looking at the culprit.

—MOLLY IVINS

In fall 2003, in Massachusetts, 20 percent of incoming ninth graders at Revere
High School wanted to attend a vocational school, but since there weren't
nearly enough spaces, they had to take a college-prep curriculum instead. Revere High School principal Scott Lumsden reports that the money once used
for the popular culinary arts program is now needed for MCAS-prep courses
(Massachusetts Comprehensive Assessment System). *Boston Globe* reporter
Laura Pappano talked to Malden High School principal Peter Lueke about
what the push for academics has meant in his school.[1] As he's watched enrollment in college-prep courses rise 20 percent in four years, Lueke has witnessed
the flip side: there are fewer vocational classes for students hoping to get a job
or pursue technical training after high school. Malden students have the choice
of college-prep, honors, or Advanced Placement classes.

Setting Straw Men on Fire

In a National Public Radio commentary, Tom Magliozzi, a college professor for
thirty years and cohost of *Car Talk*, asked, "Why did I and millions of other kids
spend valuable educational hours learning something we would never use?"[2]
While sitting in his son's high school classroom at a back-to-school night,
Magliozzi experienced a revelation:

> And on the board was the following description—Get this—Calculus is the
> set of techniques that allow us to determine the slope at any point on a curve

18

and the area under that curve. And all of my being wanted to cry, "So who gives a rat's patootie?"

Magliozzi concluded that "[t]he purpose of learning math, most of which we will never use, is to prepare us for more advanced math courses, which we will use even less frequently." Magliozzi made a list of subjects he wished he'd been exposed to in place of algebra, geometry, trigonometry, and calculus, and he concluded:

> Education really ought to help us to understand the world we live in. This includes flora, fauna, cultures, governments, religions, money, advertising, buildings, cities and especially people. Then it should help us to cope with that world. And in the process, it would be nice if it helped us to become good, kind, empathetic people. Algebra doesn't do any of these things.

In "The Malevolent Tyranny of Algebra," noted researcher Gerald Bracey says the whole nation has been algebra-scammed.[3] Algebra, insists Bracey, "has no value for most people." Education Trust, a nonprofit advocacy group whose functionaries crisscross the country with their *No Excuses* mantra, cites the National Association of Manufacturers website, which describes the qualifications of tool and die makers: four or five years of apprenticeship or post-secondary training, usually in a community college. They can earn more than $40,000 per year. "The courses they need to enter include algebra, geometry, trigonometry and basic statistics."[4]

Dennis W. Redovich, retired as director of research, planning, and development for the Milwaukee Area Technical College, conducts research on jobs at the Center for the Study of Jobs and Education in Wisconsin and the United States and denounces this claim. "Higher math skills are not required. Technology makes these jobs easier. Machines do the calculations and measurements. There is absolutely no shortage of workers for the small number of tool and die jobs available. The fact is that tool and die work is now being exported to low wage countries."[5]

Educating Kids for Jobs for the Twenty-First Century

Take a look at the U.S. Bureau of Labor Statistics and you will see that our new economy creates many more unskilled than skilled jobs—at the same time that it creates even more horrific income differences between the wealthy and the working classes. Saskia Sassen's analysis of the U.S. Bureau of Labor Statistics (BLS) paints quite a different picture from Business Roundtable and Education Trust scenarios.

> [The] BLS projects a massive growth of low-wage service jobs, including service jobs catering to firms. Three service industries alone will account for

about half of total U.S. employment growth between 1992 and 2005: retail trade, health services, and business services. Using [223 categories], the largest increases in terms of numbers of jobs are, in descending order: retail sales workers, registered nurses, cashiers, truck drivers, waiters and waitresses, nursing aides, janitors, food preparation workers, and systems analysts. Most of these jobs do not require a high school education and they are mostly not very highly paid. Nor does the BLS expect an increase in the median weekly wage of workers. At the other extreme are jobs requiring a college degree. Their share was twenty-three percent in 1992 and is projected to rise only by one percent to twenty-four percent by 2005.[6]

Putting these figures up against the BRT claims that all kids must take a rigorous college-prep course of study in high school, you have to ask why the corporate elite is so hell-bent on pumping up the pool of skilled workers. For starters, having more workers than jobs increases corporate America's bottom line. On Labor Day 2003, National Public Radio's *The Connection* aired a program titled "The Democratization of Unemployment," documenting that the white-collar worker, the person with a college degree, is "every bit as vulnerable as others with less education." Barry Bluestone, professor of political economy at Northeastern University and director of the Center for Urban and Regional Policy, explained that during the deep recession of the 1980s, high school dropouts were four times as likely to be unemployed as college graduates. But these days, you have higher probability of facing unemployment if you have some college education—or are a college graduate—than if you have none. Even with a bachelor's degree or more, Bluestone emphasized, you are as likely to face unemployment as a high school graduate. In *A Working Stiff's Manifesto: A Memoir of Thirty Jobs I Quit, Nine That Fired Me, and Three I Can't Remember*, Iain Levison observes that "the conventional wisdom is that you are unemployable without a college degree. That you are often unemployable with one is something a lot of people spend a lot of money to discover."[7]

Writing in *Fortune* in June 2003, Nelson D. Schwartz noted, "Of the nine million Americans out of a job, 17.4% are managers or specialty workers."[8] They should ask the Business Roundtable, Education Trust, Progressive Policy Institute, and all the other outfits pushing algebra as the gateway to success why their high-skills diplomas haven't kept them safe from global pirates. Standardistas continue to blather about schools preparing kids for highly skilled jobs for the twenty-first century at the same time they are outsourcing jobs faster than we can count. The truth that the corporate fat cats refuse to speak is that there are more highly skilled workers than there are jobs—and that's the way they like it. When you have lots of people competing for few jobs, workers are scared and compliant.

Nonetheless, Education Trust executive director Kati Haycock intones, "It's a new century. It's time to set aside our Industrial Age curriculum and agree on a common core curriculum for the Information Age."[9] Education Trust might just as well have subtitled its *A New Core Curriculum for All* paper *Denying a High School Diploma to Other People's Children*. In her introduction, Haycock chides *educators* (emphasis in original) for being comfortable with the fact that many minority children do not go on to college. Maybe we should ask her if it's better to be comfortable with the fact that now that she and her Business Roundtable cronies are in power, young people who fail a test based on a college-prep curriculum are denied a *high school* diploma. *Star Tribune* columnist and master Internet blogger James Lileks advises, "When your opponent sets up a straw man, set it on fire and kick the cinders around the stage. Don't worry about losing the Strawperson-American community vote."[10] It's past time for teachers and parents to smash the corporate-politico Standardista icons for the straw men they are. Our silence is destroying childhood.

Like its corporate allies, Education Trust dismisses the high school diploma as pretty much worthless:

> The benefits of a high school diploma alone turn out to be slight, especially when compared to the employability and earning power that college brings.

Parents and teachers worry that kids who struggle hard to satisfy the requirements of a high school diploma are now being denied those diplomas—while Education Trust shrugs and says, "Oh well, those diplomas aren't nearly so good as a college degree anyway."

Let's look at a few facts. State job banks indicate jobs requiring a high school diploma: automobile mechanic; baker; broadcast technician; cardiology technologist; communications dispatcher; electro-neurodiagnostic technologist; fingerprint classifier; forklift operator; graphics designer; heating, air-conditioning, and refrigeration mechanic; hotel desk clerk; land surveyor; legal secretary; medical transcriptionist; numerical control machinist; optometric technician; paramedic; plumber; robotics technician; sheet metal worker; shorthand reporter/court reporter; solar energy system installer; small appliance repairer; surgical technician; tool and die maker; translator/interpreter; veterinary technician; ward clerk (medical); webpage designer. And so on.

Read the list again. How many of these occupations would you like to eliminate as not necessary or useful in your life? And how about chefs, carpenters, gardeners, stone wall builders? Poet Jane Hirschfield writes that she envies those who make something useful, "Or those who fix, perhaps / a leaking window: / strip out the old cracked putty / lay down cleanly the line of the new."[11] If we keep denigrating the jobs of people who know how to make things and fix things, we're likely find ourselves living quite desperate lives.

Degree qualifications aren't available for the position of page turner at Carnegie Hall or golf ball diver at the Davis Golf Ball Company in Florida. Or the crack filler at Mount Rushmore.[12] A woman who judges her husband's writing and math skills as poor to fair writes, "My husband, a high school graduate, works as a CAD designer. The job requires outstanding spatial abilities. For the past 5 years my husband has made over $100 thousand a year and has supported me through grad school."[13] Not bad for a young man with just a high school diploma. These days, he'd be denied a high school diploma because he couldn't write a persuasive essay or solve quadratic equations.

Why Is the MCAS Math Test Tougher than the SAT?

In June 2003, the state of Massachusetts denied one-fourth of the seniors at the Joseph P. Keefe Technical School in Framingham high school diplomas.[14] Keefe just happens to have both the second highest number of bilingual students and second highest number of special education students among vocational schools in Massachusetts. But let's remember: *No Excuses.* This means the young man who plans to become an auto mechanic is out of luck, even though he satisfied all course requirements set by his teachers. As a senior, half his coursework was spent in on-the-job training, but he can't pursue this work without the diploma.

The fact is that young adults whose high school work has been judged acceptable by scores of teachers—and who have career plans—are denied a high school diploma because of an arbitrary test experts judge invalid. People disputing this system aren't just lazy kids and their lazy teachers, as business and media moguls would have the public believe. Take John E. Cawthorne, assistant dean for students and outreach at Boston College, for one. He wonders why the state demands that a high schooler outbest college applicants to qualify for a high school diploma. Cawthorne discovered while tutoring students that the Massachusetts Comprehensive Assessment System is tougher than the SAT.[15] Visit University of Massachusetts professor Eugene Gallagher's website.[16] After analyzing two math tests, Gallagher concluded that MCAS is a state-mandated intelligence test, not an appropriate math measure.

In a statement of remarkable mendacity, Heidi Perlman, spokeswoman for the Massachusetts Department of Education, told the *Boston Globe,* "We believe that a high school diploma needs to mean something. It doesn't make sense to give diplomas to students who haven't met that standard, because we feel it belittles the meaning of that diploma to everyone else."[17] What student headed for the Ivy League could possibly care whether every diploma recipient is proficient in algebra?

Lieutenant Governor Kerry Healy insists that pleas for requiring vocational students to meet standards different from the college-prep material man-

dated by the state shows prejudice. One size must fit all. Standardistas operate in the world of all or nothing, labeling alternative curricula "low expectations." They demand: Pass college-prep requirements or you don't get a high
school diploma. This travels under the heady banner of *No Excuses*.

These rhetorical sleights of hand are deliberate: You can call someone ignorant, ill informed, and irritating, and she'll stand her ground on the argument at hand. But label her prejudiced and you're home free. And outfits like
the Massachusetts Department of Education claim this all-or-nothing policy
is working. Trumpeting the news that 86 percent of the 12,005 seniors in
ninety-five vocational or technical programs statewide have passed the exam,
Lieutenant Governor Healey insisted the data discredits arguments in favor of
separate standards for vocational students. What the statistics deliberately con-
ceal, in the name of high standards and excellence, is how many high schoolers were pushed out before their senior year. The *Boston Phoenix* reports that
in Boston, fully 60 percent of Latino and black ninth graders are held back—
because they are judged not ready for the MCAS, the rigorous state test given
to tenth graders. Unable to make it to the upper grades, these students drop
out of school.[18]

Anne Wheelock, the author of several publications on dropout prevention
and alternatives for students placed at risk of dropping out, keeps close track
of the young people the state would like to forget. In "How the Class of 2003
Got to a 95% Pass Rate,"[19] Wheelock refutes Massachusetts Department of Education data presented in its *Progress Report on Students Attaining the Compe-
tency Determination Statewide and by District: Classes of 2003–2004*,[20] which
reports that 95 percent of the class of 2003 passed the MCAS as of September
2003. This MCAS pass rate is based on 56,967 students passing the MCAS, divided by the 60,249 students who remained with the class through June 2003.
The trouble with such a calculation is that it doesn't account for the students
who started with this class four years earlier. Wheelock reveals that the class of
2003 lost 16,817 students between grade 9 and grade 12. Between the beginning of grade 12 and June 2003, the class lost another 667 students. This loss of
17,484 students represents 22.5 percent of the class. Here are the revised MCAS
pass rates:

- *All students:* 56,967 students passing/77,733 originally enrolled: 73.3%
  (not 95%)
- *White students:* 46,024 students passing/58,903 originally enrolled:
  78.1% (not 97%)
- *African American students:* 4,262 students passing/7,003 originally enrolled: 60.9% (not 86%)
- *Latino students:* 3,838 students passing/8,313 originally enrolled: 46.2%
  (not 83%)

- *Asian students:* 2,710 students passing/3,301 originally enrolled: 82.1% (not 95%)
- *Native American students:* 133 students passing/213 originally enrolled: 62.4% (not 96%)

Wheelock points out that "[t]he odds of passing MCAS and graduating on time with one's class vary considerably by community income. Consider the following.

- In Duxbury (median household income in 2000 $97,124), students have a **10 out of 10** chance on passing MCAS and graduating with their class.
- In Northboro-Southboro ($79,781/$102,986) or Lexington ($96,825), student chances are 9 out of 10.
- For Malden ($45,654) or Easthampton ($45,185), student chances are 8 out of 10.
- In Quincy ($47,121) or Haverhill ($49,833), student chances are 7 out of 10.
- In Worcester ($35,623) or Pittsfield ($35,655), students chances are 6 out of 10.
- In Chicopee ($35,672) or Winchendon ($43,750), student chances are 5 out of 10.
- In Holyoke ($30,441) or Springfield ($30,417), student chances are 4 out of 10.
- In Lawrence ($27,983), student chances are just over 3 out of 10."

Aurora, Illinois, elementary principal Karen Hart told the *Chicago Tribune*, "It's scary. Sometimes I feel like answering the phone, 'Rollins Test Center' instead of Rollins School. We're dancing as fast as we can. But we're not all Lake Woebegone, and we're not all going to be above average."[21]

White House Spin

At a July 30, 2003, press conference, President Bush was asked about jobs being shipped overseas. He replied:

> Sure. Listen, I fully understand what you're saying. In other words, as technology races through the economy, a lot of times worker skills don't keep up with technological change. And that's a significant issue that we've got to address in the country.[22]

Nobody reported the president's nose suddenly growing longer. Unfortunately, nobody asked a follow-up question either. Nobody asked the president when he and his cronies would stop blaming the victim. It's the profits, stupid. The U.S. labor force is suffering from what is now known as *offshore outsourcing*, not because U.S. workers aren't competent but because a top electrical or chemical engineering grad, say, expects eight times the $10,000 a year a graduate from Indian Institutes of Technology will work for. Aeronautical engineers, software designers, and stock analysts are finding their jobs outsourced to China, Russia, and India.[23] Paul Saffro of the Institute for the Future in Menlo Park, California, observes, "Now Indians are taking the lead in colonizing cyberspace."[24] Huge numbers of U.S. information technology staffers find themselves out of work. And medical technology offshore outsourcing is a new growth market. In early December 2003, Reuters carried a small announcement: Ford Motor Company expects to source about $1 billion in automotive parts from China next year.[25] And IBM is shipping thousands more programmers' jobs overseas. They call it *global sourcing*. Cute. Teachers are directed to train kids for the global economy—so their jobs can be global sourced. According to the *Wall Street Journal*, by the end of 2004, one in ten jobs within U.S.-based computer services companies will have moved overseas.[26]

Too bad the president doesn't talk to Ed Marx, a former computer programmer who found himself stocking shelves on the graveyard shift at Target after his job (of twenty-seven years) was shipped overseas. According to a May 2003 segment on MSNBC highlighting the toughest white-collar job market in twenty years, with a Ph.D. in information technology, you can get a job at Starbucks. Starbucks jobs are considered premium because with twenty hours a week, you get medical coverage. And Bush tells the press, "Let them eat globaloney!"

But it isn't just Bush. Responding to business leaders' demand that the federal government expand the H-1B guest worker visa quota because of a supposed shortage in computer programmers, in October 2000, President Clinton signed a law increasing the annual cap (and don't forget the North American Free Trade Agreement [NAFTA]). The U.S. didn't have a shortage of experienced programmers; it had a shortage of industry willing to pay top wages. A month before Clinton signed the bill, economic policy analyst Richard Rothstein titled his *New York Times* article "How to Create a Skilled-Labor Shortage,"[27] in which he argued that in 1995, corporate CEOs reduced programmers' wages, making the jobs less attractive and thus creating a shortage. Importing workers is one way Silicon Valley can avoid offering better working conditions.

High-skills jobs in financial services and information technology, those jobs so venerated such a short time ago, have been hit hard. Take information technology: We've lost 11 percent of the jobs that existed in this category in February 2001. Outfits like IBM used to call it outsourcing, but in late 2003 they updated the term to *global sourcing*. A more honest name would be *pad-the-company-profits*. Companies increase their profits by shipping the jobs to

India or the Philippines. If we had labor sections in our newspapers the way we have business sections, maybe such practices would be tagged as *un-American*. Consider this: since George W. Bush took office, 2.5 million manufacturing jobs and about 600,000 service jobs have moved offshore.

When corporate moguls shop the world for cheap labor, a mean economy becomes even meaner. As Jeff Gates (no relation to Bill) points out in *Democracy at Risk: Rescuing Main Street from Wall Street*, in 1998, the top-earning 1 percent of Americans raked in as much income as the lowest-earning 100 million Americans. This is way beyond that adage "The rich get richer."

The Jobs for the Twenty-First-Century Scam

The screaming headlines about the high skills needed for jobs for the twenty-first century are delusional at best and at worst, the daily atrocities continue to pile up. In reality, most jobs of the twenty-first century are not different from those of the twentieth century. All one has to do is check the projections of U.S. Bureau of Labor Statistics for 2010: 22 percent of jobs will require four years of college; 9 percent of jobs will require an A.A. degree—some technical training. So if 100 percent of our children pass algebra and go to college, as the U.S. Department of Education and most of the state education departments insist, there sure will be heavy competition for those college-required jobs. A CEO's dream. And there are plenty of people who think that's what all the pumped-up push for high standards and testing and raising the bar and turning kindergarten into skill-drill zones has been about from the get-go. Make kids—and future workers—feel inadequate. Make them feel they're never good enough. Convince them that it's a dog-eat-dog world out there—with everybody competing in a musical chairs game.

The crime is not that there isn't a workforce able and willing to do the jobs that need to be done; the crime is that so many of these jobs we need to make our country work don't come with a living wage. The blatant hypocrisy and ugly reality never acknowledged by the Massachusetts state education department—or the business consortium drafting its education policy—is that more than 60 percent of the jobs created in Massachusetts don't pay a living wage.[28] And 42 percent of the total jobs pay less than $18,970 a year. That's for full-time work. To put things in perspective, Dennis Picard of Raytheon, to name just one top CEO, is compensated $110 per minute. The National Priorities Project determines the Massachusetts living wage for a family of three to be $19.34 an hour.[29] Here are the figures for a few other states:

Alabama	$14.05
Florida	$15.72
New York	$18.33

Vermont	$16.53
Texas	$15.00
Mississippi	$14.05
Connecticut	$18.39

Look around and take note of how many jobs in your community pay this wage. Beth Shulman writes that one out of every four jobs in the U.S. is low-wage work—less than $8.70 an hour—and this is expected to grow in the next decade.[30] Many people working at jobs that help us daily are not getting even close to a living wage. And if you think these jobs are low-skilled, just try taking care of an aging parent or processing meat or landscaping.

Job Distribution

Richard Rothstein has observed that we distribute jobs by social class, that a kid's chances of getting hired can depend as much on his name sounding black or white on a job application as they do on his academic achievement, and that kids would be better off if we put the money spent on high-stakes testing into fighting discrimination.[31] The dirty little secret is that if we qualify all students with a college degree, then 100 percent of students will be competing for the 22 percent of jobs that require college degrees. The answer here is not to push more kids into college but to pay better salaries for those jobs not requiring college. Instead, we get the phenomenon of parents in affluent districts raising thousands, even hundreds of thousands, of dollars to fund everything from extra-teacher salaries to field trips, to make sure the differential between their kids' school and other schools is maintained. For example: The Parent-Teacher Association at the 240-student McGilvra Elementary in North Seattle raises $200,000 annually to pay for three full-time teachers and a part-time computer science teacher, and parents have provided items such as a new refrigerator for the staff lounge and fifty-five new iMac computers. Talking to the *Seattle Post-Intelligencer*, the PTA president said, "Our parents take great responsibility for the education of their kids." Well lah-de-dah. What about the rest of the kids in their community? The newspaper pointed out that Beacon Hill Elementary, located "in a more modest neighborhood" a few miles away managed to raise $22,000 by selling cookie dough and organizing a read-a-thon. This fall it is asking each family to pay for a ream of paper to help compensate for budget cuts.[32]

It's a neat little trick: instead of taxing the community to provide good resources for all children's schools, keep taxes low and then pay the extra money so just *your* kids benefit. It's past time for the parents at McGilvra Elementary to stop bragging about all the good things they do for their kids' education.

It's time for the parents at McGilvra Elementary to take great responsibility for the education of *all* kids. And it's past time for everyone in the country to do this. These are our children. All of them.

Workers and Wordsworth

The Commission on the Future of the American Workforce titled its 1990 report *America's Choice: High Skills or Low Wages!* Robert Kuttner, cofounder and coeditor of *The American Prospect*, says a better title would have been *America's Choice: High Skills AND Low Wages!* Kuttner points out, "The skills gap is largely a mirage . . . millions of people who are literate and numerate and offer good work habits still receive dismal wages . . . except at the very top, workers are being compensated less generously for the skills they have."[33] Iain Levison observes, "If you ask the rich why you're not capable of supporting yourself, they'll tell you it is your fault. The ones who make it to the lifeboats always think the ones in the water are to blame."

There is plenty of evidence that the free market always seeks a workforce that is desperate and cheap, not to mention hungry. Laissez-foul.

But the minion Standardistas plying their trade in state departments of education and consulting think tanks continue to ratchet up their frenetic sales pitch that kids who aspire to be automobile mechanics must pass state tests on a full college-prep curriculum. This is justified on the grounds that these future mechanics will need to be able to read the manuals for repairing $25,000 cars. Right. In Massachusetts, in order to be qualified to repair a car, fledgling mechanics must prove their proficiency by deconstructing Wordsworth's sonnets on a high-stakes test. Think about it: William Wordsworth as the gatekeeper to becoming an auto mechanic. He's probably rolling over in his grave.

Standard Setting

One way to put all this into context is to look at other aspects of society that get regulated for the common good. Oops! The government is deregulating public utilities; the energy plan privatizes profits; environmental protection is in free fall. It sure looks like the only things that are getting regulated up the wazoo are illegal aliens and schoolchildren. Let's take a look at the federal regulation of the standards placed on automobile manufacturers through the lens of No Child Left Behind rules. Whether or not the Iraq venture is about oil, plenty of experts worry that America's love affair with gas-guzzlers is ecological suicide. And yet, as the *Wall Street Journal* observed in May 2003, "Average fuel economy in 2002 was lower than in any year since 1980." Experts speculate the stats will be worse for 2003. This item was buried back in the paper. Detroit's failure to meet standards doesn't rate the front-page headlines or editorial breast-beating of schools ranked as failing. Think back to the Cold War rhetoric the *Nation at Risk* used to describe public schools: "If an unfriendly foreign power had attempted to impose on America the mediocre educational performance that exists today, we might well have viewed it as an act of war."

Where are the apocalyptic rants in Washington, D.C., about the harm automobiles wreak on the environment? Or the threat our dependence on oil poses to our national security? Our current national policy is to mandate what books primary graders must read and to pass legislation giving rich taxpayers up to a $100,000 loophole for buying a Hummer, with a wink and a nod to Detroit. It's called educating children for the global economy and offering taxpayers an economic stimulus package. To get the tax break, one had to buy a gas-guzzler weighing more than 6,000 pounds.

The federal government's Corporate Average Fuel Economy, or CAFÉ, rules were first set in the 1970s. The standard for cars is 27.5 miles per gallon and 20.7 mpg for trucks, not increased since the 1986 model year. Vehicles over 8,500 pounds are exempt from all federal fuel economy standards. Probably that's why at the official website of the 8,600-pound Hummer, one can't find out how many miles it gets to the gallon. Obviously, if you have to ask, it's not the vehicle for you. To avoid automotive trickery on what's a car and what's a truck, Senator Dick Durban suggests changing designations to passenger vehicles and nonpassenger vehicles and setting standards accordingly. With this plan, by 2015, passenger vehicles would have to get 40 miles per gallon.

We suggest that the feds make Detroit operate like schools: automakers must come up with a plan of action for reaching 100 percent fuel proficiency by 2015. What a plan: the perfect kids produced by federal fiat in 2014 can ride around in perfect cars in 2015.

Meanwhile, as Detroit is working its way along the road to perfection, newspapers can publish annual charts of those cars that meet the Adequate Yearly Progress (AYP) target and those that "need improvement." Two years in a row of not meeting target, and auto personnel will need retraining. Some may need to be vacated and new staff brought in. Probably the industry needs people who have proven their expertise in other fields: retired generals, for example. Automakers need to come up with a plan of action, which must be approved by a panel of experts. To expedite matters, just use the seventy-three members of the No Child Left Behind Reading First panel. They probably know as much about cars as they do about kids.

Four years without meeting target, and the company executives and employees can be removed and the company subject to state takeover. What is the state going to do with auto plants? That's as good a question as what the state is going to do with the schools declared to be failing.

A Happiness Index

People who care about children and about public schools need to ask why the policy makers care less about happiness than does the chicken research sponsored by McDonald's. While GE's retired CEO Terminator Jack Welch is brought in to train principals in New York City and the Broad Foundation spreads a corporate model nationwide, McDonald's and Kentucky Fried Chicken are sponsoring research to find out answers to such questions as Are cows ever happy? Do pigs feel pain? What do chickens really want?

Put aside for the moment the question of whether McDonald's and KFC are being disingenuous. Just consider the new territory they are entering: asking about animals' feelings. Consider that these questions are no longer asked about children in school. The fact that it is inconceivable to imagine the current U.S. Department of Education sponsoring research to find out answers to such questions as Are schoolchildren ever happy? and What do schoolchildren really want? should give parents and teachers pause.

Why isn't a kindergartner's Happiness Index taken as seriously as his phonemic awareness score? Why don't we ask high schoolers, What do you really want? Ask that—and shut up and listen to the answer. These questions are neither frivolous nor rhetorical. The cruelty of No Child Left Behind puts childhood at grave risk, setting schools on a course that will produce very angry children who grow up to be adults whose values are skewed and who are mad as hell to boot. A *New York Times* article detailing the research about animals' feelings indicates that "[s]ome food retailers have introduced labels indicating that an animal was raised with care."[34] Can schools do any less? Every teacher, every year, must be able to testify that every child was educated with care. Childhood is short; it is our obligation to make sure it is also sweet.

Notes

1. Pappano, Laura. 2003. "Debate Simmers over Schools Who Failed MCAS on Graduation." *Boston Globe*, 18 May.

2. Magliozzi, Tom. 2001. "Who Gives a Rat's Patootie About High School Calculus: School Should Be More Than Preparation for More School." *All Things Considered*, 4 April. You can hear Magliozzi deliver his spiel at *http://cartalk.cars.com/About/ATC/*.

3. Bracey, Gerald. 2000. "The Malevolent Tyranny of Algebra." *Education Week*, 25 October.

4. Education Trust. 2003. "Double the Numbers." Accessed at file://C:/WINDOWS/Temporary%20Internet%20Files/Content. IE5/SOKN5HSP/696, 22, Requirements for Tool and Die Makers.

5. Personal communication. June 2003.

6. Sassen, Saskia. 1998. *Globalization and Its Discontents*. New York: New, 143.

7. Levison, Iain. 2002. *A Working Stiff's Manifesto: A Memoir of Thirty Jobs I Quit, Nine That Fired Me, and Three I Can't Remember*. New York: Soho.

8. "Down and Out in White-Collar America." 2003. *Fortune*. 9 June.

9. Haycock, Kati. "A New Core Curriculum for All : Aiming High for Other People's Children. 2003. *Thinking K–16* 7(1). Accessed at *www2.edtrust.org/NR/rdonlyres/26923A64-4266-444B-99ED-2A6DF1406IF/0/K16_winter2003.pdf*.

10. Lileks, James Oz. "The Bleat." Accessed at *www.lileks.com/bleats/archive/02/1102/110201.html#110402*.

11. Hirschfield, Jane. 2001. "Mathematics." *In Given Sugar, Given Salt*. New York: HarperCollins.

12. Schiff, Nancy Rica. 2002. *Odd Jobs: Portraits of Unusual Occupations*. Berkeley: Ten Speed.

13. Personal communication with the authors.

14. Pappano. 2003.

15. See *www.eyeoneducation.tv/about/cawthorne.html*.

16. See *www.es.umb.edu/faculty/edg/files/edgwebp.htm#MCAS*.

17. Saltzmann, Jonathan. 2003. "MCAS Hits Some Vocational Schools Hard." *The Boston Globe*. 8 May.

18. David S. Berstein "Adios Escuela." *Boston Phoenix*. 12–18 March. Accessed at *www.bostonphoenix.com/boston/news_features/other_stories/multipage/documents/03666295.asp*.

19. From the author. 2003. 23 October.

20. Accessed at *www.doe.mass.edu/mcas/2003/results/0903cdprogrpt.pdf*.

21. Dell'Angela, Tracy. 2003. "School Says Exam Leaves Unfair Mark." *Chicago Tribune*, 31 October.

22. White House Press Conference of the President. Accessed at *www.whitehouse.gov/news-releases/2003/07/20030730-1.html*.

23. Uchitelle, Louis. 2003. "A Missing Statistic: U.S. Jobs That Went Overseas." *The New York Times*, 5 October.

24. Kripalani, Manjeet, and Pete Engardio. 2003. "The Rise of India." *Business Week*, 8 December.

25. Reuters. 2003. "Ford to Source $1 Bln in Parts from China in 2004." 2 December.

26. Bulkeley, William M. 2003. "IBM to Export Highly Paid Jobs to India, China." *The Wall Street Journal*, 15 December.

27. Rothstein, Richard. 2000. "How to Create a Skilled-Labor Shortage." *The New York Times*, 6 September.

28. National Public Radio special. 2003. WAMC News, 12 June.

29. From *www.natprior.org/sos2001/sosSources.htm*.

30. Shulman, Beth. 2003. *The Betrayal of Work: How Low-Wage Jobs Fail 30 Million Americans*. New York: New.

31. Oliver, Ed. 2003. "MCAS Debated at Mock Hearing." Massnews.com, 15 January.

32. Beck, Deborah. 2003. "PTA Plugs Budget Holes—Unevenly." *Seattle Post-Intelligencer*, 2 September.

33. Kuttner, Robert. 1998. *Everything for Sale: The Virtues and Limits of Markets*. New York: Knopf.

34. Barboza, David. 2003. "Animals Seeking Happiness." *New York Times*, 29 June.

3

One Size for All

The Business Roundtable Brings the Global Economy to Your Neighborhood School

They'll privatize your hopes and they'll privatize your fears. If they catch your children crying, they'll privatize the tears.

—BRIAN MCNEILL, *SELL YOUR LABOUR, NOT YOUR SOUL*

Some will rob you with a six-gun, and some with a fountain pen.

—WOODY GUTHRIE, *PRETTY BOY FLOYD*

The editorial pages of the *Wall Street Journal* often entreat schools to be more like business. At least since 1999, when Education Trust began peppering the pages of its publication *Thinking K–16* with references to Standardista school superintendents as CEOs, the national push to align school reform in a corporate model has been out in the open. "Why can't schools be more like business?" business whines. Market research conducted in 2001 by Denver-based Quality Education Data gives a short answer to that question: Teachers spend more than $1 billion a year on supplies for their classrooms—for such basics as pencils, paper clips, and paper. Some bring in soap and toilet paper. There you have it: people who work in the offices of corporate America pilfer the pencils and paper clips that teachers must buy for their students. Can you picture the CEO of IBM, Boeing, or State Farm spending some $800 annually to stock his office?

The Long-Playing Message

From the hand-holding embraces at the 1989 corporate-politico education summit in Charlottesville through the passage of the No Child Left Behind Act in

January 2002, the Business Roundtable (BRT) has been turning up the volume on its long-playing message that pounds out the beat for systemic school reform. Corporate fat cats are determined to deform the schoolhouse, to poke a huge hole in the very notion of what it means to live in a democracy. In the name of preparing workers for the global economy, we get hyperacademics: kindergarten twisted from a children's garden into a high-skill zone, with blizzards of worksheets and threats of failure; we get third graders vomiting on the tests that will determine whether they move on to fourth grade; we get high schoolers weak in bibliographic reference skills and trigonometry denied a diploma.

After talking for decades, by 1989, CEOs had reached consensus on what school reform should look like. Soon the BRT was cranking out materials and strategies enabling its members to speak with one voice.[1] The BRT took the lead in establishing the Business Coalition for Education Reform, now a thirteen-member group that serves as a unified voice for the corporate community.[2] Roundtable companies are at the forefront of a national effort to "stimulate academic progress by aligning their hiring, philanthropic and site location practices with the education reform agenda."[3]

For a glimpse of the extensive Business Roundtable education links, see Appendix A, "Six Degrees of Separation Cut in Half." Using a common education agenda as a springboard for action, each BRT company takes responsibility for at least one state. In Maryland, the CEOs of Lockheed Martin, Potomac Electric Power, and Citigroup established the Maryland Business Roundtable for Education; in Washington it was Boeing. And so on across America. The BRT's deep pockets aid the effort: with its $51.3 million lobbying effort from January 1999 through December 2002, the BRT offered members of Congress "a direct pipeline to big-business CEOs."[4]

The BRT was founded in 1972 as "an association of chief executive officers who examine public issues that affect the economy and develop positions which seek to reflect sound economic and social principles."[5] In 1989, CEOs of the nation's largest 218 corporations met to figure out how to promote the National Education Goals developed by the nation's governors. They insisted then and continue to insist now that their decision to bring the resources of corporate America behind a specific educational reform agenda stemmed from the threat to the United States' premier economic status in the world.

Pumping Up the Heat

Edward Rust, CEO of State Farm Insurance and chair of the BRT Education Task Force, provided the spin on the economic motive behind the BRT's education agenda, a spin that pops up in newspaper headlines frequently.

In a global economy built on knowledge and technical skills, employees must be able to do more now than they did a generation ago. And these demands will continue to increase. In 1950, 60 percent of jobs for new workers were classified as unskilled; by 2000, only 15 percent will be. . . . The percentage of U.S. companies reporting a lack of skilled employees as a barrier to growth continues to rise—from 27 percent in 1993 to 69 percent last year.[6]

Edward Rust's prominent role in systemic education reform cannot be overemphasized (see Figure 3–1). Called a bulldog for standards, this member of the National Wrestling Hall of Fame used his powerful web of corporate cronies to push for the business model of school management, which emphasizes testing and hierarchy, at the same time that his company was found guilty of fraud in five separate class action lawsuits—big suits, as in a $1.2 billion settlement for one of them.[7] Here we see the business model: using generic re-

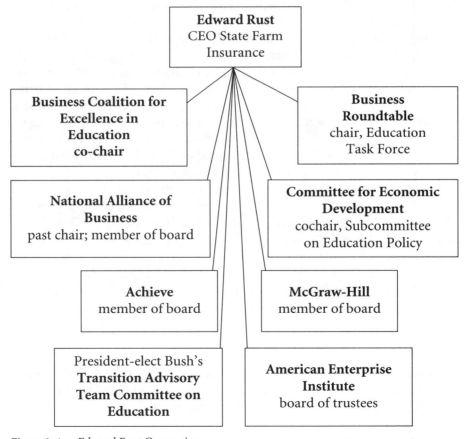

Figure 3–1. *Edward Rust Connections*

placement parts, misleading customers, covertly cutting some clients, destroy-ing documents—at the same time you are decrying teacher excellence. But all that was another day, another dollar. Now, Rust crisscrosses the country talk-ing about why schools need to be overhauled. According to Rust's argument, schools have been laggardly about educating the number of skilled workers nec-essary for corporate growth. We saw in Chapter 2 just how bogus these claims are. As desperate college graduates deliver pizza and computer programmers serve coffee in Starbucks, the deceit of BRT claims becomes transparent.

The BRT's reform strategy, embodied in the Nine Essential Components of a Successful Education System (1995) came out of a process that started at the 1989 Business Roundtable summit—along with the ten-year commitment to hype these principles:[8] say it loud, say it often. The chart in Figure 3–2 shows that education reform comes from the blueprint drawn up at that meet-ing. Governors fell over each other rushing to adopt this corporate agenda. Al-though the nine educational goals sound innocuous enough, we'll see that the devil is in the details.

In assessing the progress of the BRT's ten-year commitment, Rust noted that the intimate relationship between business and state government officials has made progress possible. In Washington State, "Boeing's Frank Srontz worked with Governor Booth Gardner to draft comprehensive reform legislation that passed in 1993. In Kentucky, John Hall of Ashland, David Jones of Humana, and Oz Nelson of UPS personally intervened to save school-improvement legislation."[9] And so on.

For the last fifteen years the BRT's bully pulpit has pushed state govern-ments to establish rigorous and measurable standards in core academic sub-jects for *all* students (emphasis in original) and adopt statewide testing to find out whether students are meeting the standards. The BRT focuses on standards because "standards drive curriculum, teacher training and assess-ment." When you wonder why the number of state standards exceeds the population of Liechtenstein, thank the Business Roundtable, who insists that, as night follows day, "when standards are high and assessments are geared to such standards, teaching improves and student achievement rises."[10]

BRT's *A Business Leader's Guide to Setting Academic Standards* provides case studies to show how business leaders have taken charge of state standards. In Fort Worth, Texas, for example, three hundred companies analyzed the tasks and knowledge needed for nine hundred different jobs and then asserted that 72 percent of all jobs required a high level of math to be successful (e.g., an entry-level job of putting telephone poles in the ground required geometry). As a result, low-level math was deleted from the high school curriculum, and algebra was mandated for every ninth grader.[11]

Not one to hide his ego in a barrel, Edward Rust offered his reflections on lessons learned in ten years of leading the BRT charge on school reform, asserting, "In setting our course, the founding members of the BRT's Education

Evolution of Corporate Education Goals over Time

Summer 1989—BRT Educational Reform Goals	October 1989—National Education Goals Summit (President Bush and the National Governors Association joint communiqué)	1995—BRT's *Nine Essential Components of a Successful Education System*	2001—No Child Left Behind Act
• Outcome-based education • High expectations for all children	• Performance goals, if achieved, guarantee that we are internationally competitive • The level of training necessary to guarantee a competitive workforce	• Standards	• All students to meet high academic standards established by each state; Title I—Improving the Academic Achievement of the Disadvantaged
• Strong and complex assessments of student progress	• Performance of students on international achievement tests, especially in math and science; improvement of academic performance, especially among at-risk students	• Performance assessment	• Every state to create annual assessments for grades 3 through 8 in reading and math
• Rewards and penalties for individual schools	• Establishment of clear lines of accountability	• School accountability	• Rewards and sanctions attached to annual yearly progress
• Greater school-based decision making	• Establishment of clear lines of authority	• School autonomy	• Title VI—Flexibility and Accountability

Figure 3–2

• Emphasis on staff development	• The supply of qualified teachers and up-to-date technology	• Professional development	• Title II—Preparing, Training, and Recruiting High Quality Teachers and Principals
• Establishment of pre-kindergarten programs • Provision of social and health services	• The readiness of children to start school	• Learning readiness	• Early Childhood Educator Professional Development Program; Early Reading First Program; Ready-to-Learn Television
	• The functional literacy of all Americans	• Parent involvement	• Title V—Promoting Informed Parental Choice and Innovative Programs
• Greater use of technology in schools	• Up-to-date technology	• Technology*	• Educational Technology State Grants Program; Distance Learning
	• The establishment of safe, disciplined, and drug-free schools	• Safety and discipline	• Each state must report on school safety on a school-by-school basis; funding for after school programs; Title IV—21st Century Schools

*A recent survey by the Progressive Policy Institute (an affiliate of the Democratic Leadership Council) used sixteen "indicators" to create a "new economy index" by which to evaluate an "area's ability to take advantage of the 'new economy.'" One of the sixteen indicators was "computer use in schools." The report is expected to be used to "promote the tech policies of elected [Democratic] officials, and help mayors and city managers adopt tech-friendly policies to boost the income of their residents" (*San Francisco Chronicle*, 4/19/01).

Figure 3–2. *Continued*

Task Force demonstrated exceptional wisdom and foresight."[12] Rust also admitted that the BRT is committed to beating up on public schools:

> It is said that large organizations such as schools "don't change because they see the light; they change because they feel the heat." Business Roundtable CEOs have successfully applied the heat on state policy makers, while state coalitions help the public and educators see the light about the need for change. We need to keep it up. . . .

In his testimony before the Committee on Education and the Workforce on March 8, 2001, Rust called for aligning assessments systems to standards; annual state testing, professional development in standards and assessment literacy; basing state accountability on increased student performance ("Accountability systems should have clear rewards for increasing achievement and consequences for persistently failing schools"); and high-quality, research-based data supplied by the federal government.[13]

Rust's recital before the House committee can be regarded only as a warm-up for the No Child Left Behind main event. Lest anyone had any doubts, Rush told the committee flat out that "the current Elementary and Secondary Education Act needs to be rebuilt to include increased accountability for student achievement." Here's his final recommendation:

> States should establish accountability systems with clear consequences for schools, principals, and teachers who persistently fail over time to meet standards. Consequences may include replacing personnel, restructuring or closing schools, and providing options for students to enroll elsewhere.

Getting the Word Out: Meetings with Journalists and McDonald's Place Mats

The BRT document *Building Support for Tests That Count* is a thirty-three-page handbook offering tips from business leaders on overcoming opposition to high-stakes testing.[14] Significantly, the guide advises, "First things first. State policymakers first need to be persuaded that stronger tests should be aligned to challenging academic standards." So much for politicians responding to the will of the people. The BRT regards political deal making as the crucial step in establishing policy: make the deal and then sell the public on it.

Here's one example of how the BRT gathers bipartisan political support for its agenda. When the Florida Comprehensive Assessment Test (FCAT) was first given in 1998, then-Governor Lawton Chiles, a Democrat, and then-State Education Commissioner Frank Brogan, a Republican, joined with legislators and business leaders to explain to the public that scores would be low. In the words of the BRT booklet, "Members of the business community have adopted what amounts to a mantra when discussing the FCAT: 'Don't flinch.' "[15] They don't blink either. Or stop for tears. Since its beginnings, Florida's FCAT fallout has been ratcheted up to such a degree that a kindergarten teacher responded to a reporter who asked about a little boy spending his third year in kindergarten: "Too old? Too bad. What good is it to move him on if he cannot read?"[16]

When John Puerner was publisher of the *Orlando Sentinel*, he was also a member of the Governor's Commission on Education and "active in reviewing standards and assessments." He was credited with making sure "his newspaper [gave] education improvement initiatives front-page coverage"; he also encouraged the state education commissioner to meet with editorial boards, teachers, and parent organizations to introduce the FCAT.[17]

Across the country, Business Roundtables put a lot of money into public relations campaigns stressing the importance of high-stakes tests. Take the Maryland BRT. When its focus groups of parents, teachers, and principals revealed widespread concern about the new tests, MBRT had the state delay the introduction of these tests and then used funds from the Annie E. Casey Foundation to create a forty-five-member speakers bureau to stump for public support of the test.

Members of Washington's BRT coalition, Partners for Leadership (PFL), met with newly elected state legislators every two years and served on cut-score committees. When the PFL encountered public concern over the reform agenda, it, too, launched an extensive media campaign, creating a video and a handbook to explain the need for high standards to parents. The PFL held workshops for editorial writers, members of the chamber of commerce, and community movers and shakers on *how to get the word out to the community*. It also worked with McDonald's to put sample test questions on place mats at franchises throughout the state. (See Figure 3–3 for the scope of the Washington BRT's public relations campaign.)

In Massachusetts, Mass Insight Education describes itself as "information synthesizers and providers . . . a catalyst for informed state policymaking on education-related issues . . . a provider of practical, research-based technical services, professional development programs, and consulting services to schools and school districts."[18] It uses public outreach, school leadership training programs, and consultant services to further its agenda. Mass Insight published a newsletter promoting "high standards and rigorous assessment" that CEOs mailed to their employees, with a cover letter affirming support for higher standards.[19]

The Ohio Business Roundtable conducted a survey documenting the gap between what high school seniors know and what they should know in the workplace. Having located their defined gap, it now exploits it, using the results for its survey "to sustain the business community's push for higher

Washington State's 1998 Schedule of Business Roundtable Communication Activities*

Activities	Audience		
1. Broad Public Information	Opinion Leaders	Parents	Educators
PUBLICATIONS			
Thematic quarterly newsletter	•	•	•
Parents' and teachers' guides: fourth-grade and seventh-grade test scores		•	•
Easy-to-read parents' brochure		•	
Fliers to parents		•	
Comparison guide to old versus new tests	•	•	•
One-page overview of education reform	•	•	•
Businesspersons'/employers' guide to education reform	•		
Explanations of certificate of mastery and new accountability	•	•	•
Postcard to "supporters" on PFL mailing list	•	•	•
TARGETED ADVERTISING			
Public Service Announcement campaign for Spanish-speaking parents		•	
MEDIA			
Meetings with editorial boards	•		
Assorted op-eds: fourth-grade test scores and seventh-grade tests	•	•	•
Newsletter articles to community groups and businesses	•	•	•
VIDEO/INTERNET			
Video explaining fourth-grade and seventh-grade tests		•	•
Maintain and update website	•	•	•
RESEARCH			
Follow-up 1996 poll with three to four questions on standards and testing	•		•

Figure 3–3.

Activities	Audience		
	Opinion Leaders	Parents	Educators
Focus groups on communicating about accountability	•	•	•
2. Community Support and Grassroots Development			
COMMUNITY OUTREACH			
Community breakfasts (Everett, Spokane, Yakima, Tri-Cities)	•	•	•
Summer workshop for school district communicators		•	•
Fall workshop for new legislators	•		
Briefings to community leaders on accountability recommendations	•		
Meetings/follow-up with thirty chambers of commerce	•		
"Business sector" meetings with state superintendent of public instruction	•		
"Brown bag" lunches with employees on tests	•		
COMMUNITY ADVISERS (EIGHT CITIES)			
Local events to explain new tests	•	•	
Speakers bureau	•	•	
Outreach to local churches/minority groups	•	•	
Support for locally developed communication plans	•	•	•
*Business Roundtable. 1998. *Building Support for Tests That Count*. Washington, DC: Business Roundtable, 30.			

Figure 3–3. *Continued*

standards and increased accountability." After creating a partnership with the Ohio Department of Education and the State Board of Education, the Ohio BRT developed a series of report card prototypes. Actual report cards soon followed—with immediate buy-in and acclaim from the business community. Nobody is saying how teachers and students and parents reacted.

The Partnership for Kentucky's Schools was founded by David A. Jones, chairman of Humana, Inc.; Kent C. "Oz" Nelson, chairman and CEO of the United Parcel Service (retired); and John R. Hall, chairman and CEO of Ashland, Inc. The partnership ran weekly newspaper ads and funded an eight-page advertisement insert in the major newspapers in Kentucky; it also distributed 1.5 million copies through a direct mailing. The advertisement was adapted to a video which aired on television. Using grants from the Pew Charitable Trusts and the Annie E. Casey Foundation, the partnership funded research on professional development practices.

Notice how some foundation names supporting standards and testing keep popping up?

Why professional development for teachers? Read *indoctrination*. Nationwide, veteran teachers are required to attend courses on so-called reform curriculum. No dissent allowed. BRT's *Building Support for Tests That Count* admonishes, "If teachers do not support the new assessments, parents are likely to be concerned as well." This is why, insists BRT, quality professional development is so critical. If teachers can be persuaded to buy in to reform, parents will follow. And so veteran teachers who meet every standard of excellence are forced to sit through indoctrination sessions on behaviorist methodology. And when they ask tough questions, they are reprimanded.

Response to Resistance

In spite of the BRT's ability to rally such powerful political and media forces, the opposition to high-stakes standards and testing doesn't quit. Many of the twenty-four governors who gathered at an education summit in Palisades, New York, in October 1999 conceded that their new policies had produced "demoralizing effects."[20] Public hostility caused the postponement of some state graduation tests. In urging the crew to stay the course, Lou Gerstner, then-chairman of the International Business Machines Corporation and organizer of the meeting, asserted: "We understand the pain. And we're going to have to deal with it. But we're not going to deal with it by backing off."

In the spring of 2001, the BRT acknowledged the resistance again, publishing *Addressing the "Testing Backlash": Practical Advice and Current Public Opinion Research for Business Coalitions and Standards Advocates*. Although conceding that those working to implement state standards and tests "are challenged by concerns and questions from increasingly vocal parents and teachers," the booklet leads off with condescension:

> This "backlash" to higher standards and increased accountability is not a surprise. It is a natural reaction to change and to tougher consequences for poor student performance.[21]

This, of course, is a common tactic: Accuse your opponents of having attitude problems; call resistance an inability to adapt to change. Never acknowledge that any of the issues raised are substantive.

Claiming that testing opponents dominate the media, which presents a lopsided view in front-page headlines, the BRT tells members to pull up their socks and assert "the leadership and credibility of the business community." The business community. Just the sound of it presents an image of importance, not to mention solidarity, especially when one considers there is no teaching community solidarity—or anything close.

The BRT booklet offers strategies for handling parents and teachers who oppose the testing agenda. *Handling* is the BRT's word. Here's a sampling of strategies for "addressing the backlash":

1. Anticipate organized opposition.
2. Take advantage of the superior organization and resources of the BRT network.
3. Be very aware of the undecideds, improving communications.
4. Make sure standards are matched to the curriculum—and hold focus groups to explain to parents and teachers that they are matched.
5. Don't confuse support for reform principles with issues of the implementation of these policies, where parents and teachers share certain misgivings.
6. Consider creating an alternative appeals process for students who do not pass the tests but can show they nevertheless have mastered the material.
7. Don't back down, but don't rush either.
8. Offer support for teachers: identify and share promising practices from other schools.
9. Make sure teachers get data in a timely manner and help them learn how to manage it and act on it.
10. Target key audiences—people who are seen as the most credible sources of information about standards and tests. Don't rely on "better spin" to change public opinion.
11. Keep the focus on student learning, not testing.

12. Remind people why states are raising standards. Too many students are leaving high school without "the knowledge and skills they need to succeed in college, at work, and in their communities."

Of particular note is how the BRT divides and conquers the anticipated teacher opposition—by offering sample lessons(!) and time to plan and learn from colleagues. It's quite a notion: Edward Rust writing a lesson on, say, the Incas or long division. There's no suggestion of what these corporate lessons might look like, but the Business Roundtable adjunct Achieve seems to be moving in this direction. On its website, it proclaims, "FOR PUBLISHERS: Align Your Content ONCE and Be Aligned to ALL State Standards!"[22]

For educators, Achieve offers the Align to Achieve Academic Standards elibrary (A2A): "*Meet your growing needs as a teacher* for lesson plans, unit themes, and assessments to align to state standards."[23] Achieve promises that the A2A + McREL Alignment System provides a common thread or classification system for state and selected national academic standards, "similar to the Dewey Decimal System, which can be used to catalog any educational content."[24] Get that? *Any.* As teachers know only too well, when a school signs up for alignment, be it Achieve or some other setup, then the pressure is on for teachers to eliminate anything that doesn't fit in the alignment box. An upstate New York teacher was ordered to scrap the six thousand–volume classroom library he'd amassed over the years—and stick to Open Court.

The result is administrators expecting to see the alignment classification on the board for what's going on in the classroom every minute of every day. And now, with classroom camera surveillance becoming the new growth industry in schools, districts can hire an alignment checker to verify that teachers are in line—and are keeping kids there. Various reporters interpret *in line* literally, extolling outfits like Knowledge Is Power Program (KIPP) for the neat and tidy lines of single-file kids that fill their hallways.

Achieve gratefully acknowledges the following foundations and companies that support its efforts: Agilent Technologies Foundation; the Annenberg Foundation; the Atlantic Philanthropies; AT&T Foundation; BellSouth Foundation; Bill and Melinda Gates Foundation; the Boeing Co.; Bristol-Myers Squibb Foundation, Inc.; Citicorp Foundation; Eastman Kodak Co.; E. I. DuPont de Nemours and Co.; IBM Corp.; the Pew Charitable Trusts; Phillips Petroleum Co.; the Procter & Gamble Fund; the Prudential Foundation; State Farm Insurance Co.; State Street Foundation; the UPS Foundation; the Washington Mutual Foundation; the William and Flora Hewlett Foundation; Williams; and the Xerox Foundation.

Oh, the friendliness of it all—reaching out to teachers with lots of resources. More important, the BRT policy of focusing on strategies and tactics is a very deliberate system for controlling people as well as programs: Talk about the means to improve test scores without allowing any debate over the validity of using test scores to enforce state standards—or any debate of the standards themselves. Talk about improving test scores and avoid any discussion of the BRT motives for pushing the high-standards/high-expectations agenda. When dissension occurs, there's always the BRT clincher argument, the mantra of systemic reform: high standards are needed to increase the number of students who can "succeed in college, at work, and in their communities." As though forcing a kid to take algebra or write a term paper would increase the chances of his growing up to be an adult who donates blood, volunteers to coach a youth team, serves on committees, helps at the food pantry, picks up litter, writes letters to the editor, reads aloud to his kids, and does all the other things that keep a community vibrant. By putting the emphasis on the schools' supposed failure to produce successful citizens, the BRT deflects attention from its own policies of putting millions out of work and leaving communities in shambles. The success of the BRT strategies and tactics is documented in Appendix B, "Evidence of Coordination by The Business Round Table." This Appendix tracks the progress made by each state toward The Nine Essential Components as well as revealing how integrated the systemic reform network has become by 2004.

Task Completion and Problem Solving

The corporate demand for workers who can do more now than they did a generation ago exerts pressure on school folk to deform classrooms into skills conveyor belts and to further pervert the whole notion of a public school education. People are attracted to and co-opted by the rhetoric of systemic reform because it promises both to level the playing field and to offer a more challenging curriculum. But the promises are empty. For starters, task completers and problem solvers are two different kettle of fish. To complete a task, one needs to rely on habitual activity, rarely needing the kinds of thinking involved in problem solving. Completing tasks has taken on the sacred mantra of *time on task* in many schools: *continuous work on a teacher directed task without interruption.*[25] Here are the seven components of task completion: (1) begin work immediately, (2) work quietly, (3) remain seated, (4) ask good questions, (5) complete work, (6) work carefully, and (7) follow instructions. Such strictures may keep a classroom orderly; they do not produce problem solving.

Take Daryll, a boy repeating first grade whose official records labeled him as having "[a] short attention span, difficulty sticking to a task." One day Daryll worked for three hours straight on his proof that sixteen bottle caps on one side of a balance weighed the same as sixteen bottle caps on the other side. He set up this proof and then tested it and tested it and tested it. Along the way he weighed other things. Lots of other things. After taking a two-day break from bottle caps, Daryll weighed them again—just to make sure. Then he wondered what would happen with one hundred bottle caps. Messy stuff, just verifying that one has one hundred of something, and not the sort of thing people who talk of benchmarks, rubrics, and efficiency can tolerate. There's no room for such problem solving in a schedule filled with state edicts of skill alignment and piles of accompanying worksheets. But once he'd verified the number of his one hundred bottle caps, Daryll wondered what would equal their weight—a book, his shoe, the teacher's lunch. Three days later, Daryll got the idea of putting one hundred bottle caps on the other side of the balance. This was a very profound moment. Daryll discovered that, just as 16 bottle caps = 16 bottle caps, 100 bottle caps = 100 bottle caps. He recounted every bottle cap to verify this discovery. He stared at the balance. He counted again. He stood contemplating the balance. There had been brief conversations during the three days. There would be more conversation later, after Daryll had time to think about his accomplishment. This is what it means to be a teacher—knowing when to move in, when to keep hands off.

Even though the Business Roundtable declares, "The only way we can assure that the skills and abilities of our young people will keep pace with the rapidly advancing, technology-based world marketplace is by setting standards for our schools, putting in place the processes to meet those standards and then testing to ensure that the standards are in fact being met,"[26] Daryll and his teacher know differently. For the Business Roundtable, it is an issue of control. For Daryll and his teacher, it is an issue of independence.

From time to time, other children watched Daryll work; then they'd wander off, finding their own problems to solve. Telling a student what to learn and when to learn it is the surest means of preventing that student from becoming engaged with the material. Without engagement, no problem-solving skills are developed. As Donald Arnstine points out,

> Solving problems isn't just a mechanical procedure; it calls for more than a set of skills. It requires attitudes and dispositions—like the courage needed to acknowledge the existence of a problem that has to be dealt with; the patience and persistence required when a problem isn't easily resolved; a willingness to risk, to seek help and to give it, to accept personal responsibility, and to admit error.[27]

In that same ungraded classroom, Jeannie, a fifth grader, seemed to be spending more time checking in on other kids' projects than pursuing her own work on sound experiments. She watched a film being shown to kids working on structures about a bridge collapsing because of resonance. Like her classmates, Jeannie loved that film. She watched it five times. And then, she commented, "Isn't that like the rice experiment?" Not written in the teacher's plan book, it was an incredible moment of problem solving. If a teacher has one such moment in her career, she's blessed.

Weeks before, Jeannie had taken an oatmeal carton, cut a hole in the side, stretched tissue paper over the top, and put grains of rice on the paper. She noted that when some children shouted into the hole, the rice jumped, but other voices, no matter how loud they yelled, could not make the rice jump. Her experiment card directed her to readings that explained how the frequency of some sounds matches the natural frequency at which the air in the box vibrates, causing the rice to jump. Jeannie asked dozens of kids to shout into her oatmeal carton before she wrote up the experiment, further evidence that when kids are truly involved in a problem, they need to do it over and over and over. They aren't wasting time; they are getting from that messing around what they need to get. Weeks later, Jeannie was prepared to make the association between the convoluting bridge and the jumping rice.

Jeannie needed the kids shouting and its attendant tomfoolery; she needed the repetition; she needed the freedom to explore, to play, to work, all in preparation for that impressive intellectual leap. No assessment could measure Jeannie's discovery. And no teacher who witnessed it could ever let big business gain control of her classroom.

Standardistas carp that not all teachers are as knowledgeable and talented as Daryll and Jeannie's, and so standards and scripts are necessary. Tracy Kidder's conversation with Harvard professor, renowned infectious-disease specialist, anthropologist, and MacArthur genius award winner Paul Farmer provides the answer.[28] When Kidder carped, "But some people would ask, 'How can you expect others to replicate what you're doing here?' What would be your answer to that?" Farmer replied, "Fuck you."

When Standards and Assessments Fall Off a Cliff

Standards cause bad things to happen. Maybe Holocaust lessons are actually no worse than most standards-based lesson plans, but when you see Nazi data on concentration camps presented as a worksheet on map and chart skills, the result can only be termed grotesque.[29] This lesson is aimed at grades 4 and up.

> DIRECTIONS: This chart lists just ten of more than two dozen known concentration and death camps created by the Nazis during the Holocaust. The chart lists the location of each camp, the date it was established, and the estimated number of people who were killed there.[30]

The teacher can write on the board and in his plan book that students who successfully read the chart and answer the questions will satisfy national social studies standard NSS-WH.5-12.8, national geography standards NSS-G.K-12.6 and NSS-G.K-12.1, and national mathematics standards NM.5-8.8, NM.5-8.10, and NM.9-12.10. One of the mathematics standards has to do with pattern and function: "Analyze functional relationships to explain how a change in one quantity results in a change in another." Another is statistics:

"Systematically collect, organize, and describe data." Isn't this what the Nazi functionaries did? Objectify horror? Count it, code it, summarize it?

This kind of offal results when standards rule, when teachers are ordered to do nothing in their classrooms that can't be defined as standards-based. So when they want to teach, say, *Anne Frank: The Diary*, very bad things happen.

KAMICO Instructional Media publishes a lesson titled "Critical Thinking Through Literature" and asks students in grades 5 through 8 to read *Anne Frank: The Diary of a Young Girl*.[31] As hard as this is to believe, students are given a spelling-activity guide based on Christmas-themed questions about Santa, Frosty, and Rudolph. The answer spells out *Diary*. This is an integrated unit, so we have vocabulary and math problems:

- Anne's diary weighed 925 grams. . . . How many milligrams did the diary weigh?
- All Jews were forced to wear a yellow 6-pointed star. How many vertices are on a 6-pointed star?

A diagram is provided of the secret annex and students are asked to figure out the area. Here's the writing prompt, which is classified as "informative classificatory":

Anne Frank is forced to move away from her home and into a new one. . . . There are good things about moving and bad things about it, as well. Write an entry in your diary in which you explain both what is good and what is bad about moving into a new home. Try to be as thorough as possible when explaining each point.

This publisher's material is recommended by Patricia Davenport, who does staff development nationwide.[32] California Teachers report being reprimanded for questioning her instructional directives. Davenport's website notes that although there are other publishers of standards-based material, "Pat stands by the company that aided Brazosport I.S.D. in its dramatic improvement of student test scores when Pat served as curriculum director there."

When so much emphasis is placed on standards and testing, even good teachers can lose sight of what matters. Then teachers and students ignore the real lessons of the past and focus on the weight of Anne Frank's diary. This kind of willful distraction produces citizenry not able to analyze and oppose current government policy.

Promoting On-the-Job Learning

After explaining how important benchmarking is, the BRT cautions that since benchmarking requires time and expertise, business leaders "may prefer to consult two organizations that are leading the way in comparing American standards to their counterparts abroad." One is the National Center for Education and the Economy's New Standards Project, the other the American Federation of Teachers.

That the Business Roundtable would choose to feature a sample from the National Center for Education and the Economy's (NCEE) New Standards' Applied Learning Standards is significant: Here, problem solving is reduced to task completion within a group. Although the projects NCEE suggests—working with others on a weekly school news service and sharing responsibility for collecting information for a weather station and preparing daily reports—may well be laudable activities, they contain no sense of students *finding* a problem. And too often the performance tasks range from the silly to the gargantuan. At one end of the performance assessment scale, one finds students in third-year Spanish classes constructing Mexican government buildings out of graham crackers. The other extreme is illustrated in this spoof that traveled the Web:

GRADUATION EXAM—AUTHENTIC ASSESSMENT

Read each question thoroughly. Answer all questions. Time limit: four hours. Begin immediately.

History: Describe the history of religion from its origins to the present day; concentrate specifically but not exclusively on its social, political, economic, religious, and philosophical impact on Europe, Asia, America and Africa. Demonstrate your understanding by creating your own religion and describing its likely impact on world affairs.

Literature: Compose an epic poem based on the events of your own life; footnote allusions from T. S. Eliot, Keats, Chaucer, Dante, Norse mythology and the Marx brothers. Critique your poem with a full discussion of its metrics.

Music: Write a piano concerto. Orchestrate it and perform it with flute and drum. You will find a piano under your seat.

Biology: Create life. Estimate the differences in subsequent human culture if this form of life had developed five hundred years earlier, with special attention to the probable effects on the English Parliamentary system. Prove your thesis.

Medicine: You have been provided with a razor blade, a piece of gauze, and a bottle of Scotch. Remove your own appendix. Do not suture until your work has been inspected. You have fifteen minutes.

If you think this quiz is much of an exaggeration, go to the website for the New Standards Performance Standards for Applied Learning for New York City.[33] At the site, you can choose elementary, middle, or high school examples of applied learning. Here's a brief sample from the elementary level, aimed at fourth grade, where students must conduct at least two projects involving the following types of problem solving:

- *Design a Product, Service, or System:* Identify needs that could be met by new products, services, or systems and create solutions for meeting them.
- *Improve a System:* Develop an understanding of the way systems of people, machines, and processes work; troubleshoot problems in their operation and devise strategies for improving their effectiveness.
- *Plan and Organize an Event or an Activity:* Take responsibility for all aspects of planning and organizing an event or an activity from concept to completion, making good use of the resources of people, time, money, and materials and facilities.

The plan seems to stop short of requiring fourth graders to conduct appendectomies. Stay tuned.

If those fourth-grade tasks sound corporate-, rather than kid-oriented, that's no mistake. According to NCEE, in developing the tools and techniques for working with others, elementary school students can: "Work with others to achieve a shared goal, to promote *on-the-job learning* and to respond effectively to *the needs of a client.*"

NCEE intones that the student works with others to complete a *task*; that is, the student "reaches agreement with group members on what work needs to be done to complete the *task* and how the work will be tackled . . . consults with group members regularly during the *task* to check on progress in completing the task, to decide on any changes that are required, and to check that all parts have been completed at the end of the *task*" (emphasis added).[34]

Somehow, this doesn't sound like Edison at work. Or Einstein. *Respond effectively to the needs of a client* is the kind of goal that has put NCEE on the hit list of countless conservative groups who resist any hint of a school-to-work (STW) agenda. Conservatives point immediately to the heavy hand of corporate involvement in such goals, noting the exclusion of local school boards. For example, here's Robert Holland of the Lexington Institute: "The STW locomotive proceeds through executive orders at the federal and state levels, and unaccountable corporate partnerships—with state legislatures and state/local school boards excluded from exercising their constitutional powers."[35]

Unaccountable corporate partnerships. One can wonder why liberals aren't making the same protestations. For at least a decade, conservatives have been issuing high-pitched calamitous tirades about the corporate-politico conspiracy to wrest control of public schools from local authority, while liberals maintain their navel-gazing silence. Not wanting to attack outcomes-based education or their cherished performance assessments, liberals don't fight the corporate takeover that embeds these policies. Liberals seem frozen into quietude by the fear of ever agreeing with the Eagle Forum. Just because some crackpot conservative critics label School-to-Work and its planned economic link between schooling and jobs a communistic plot set up by the United Nations[36] shouldn't mean that liberals can't also denounce School-to-Work. And just because, with a new administration in the White House, the federal School-to-Work website has been removed doesn't mean the corporate-politico agenda is also removed. As more states institute high-stakes graduation requirements and big numbers of students fail the tests in tenth grade, some form of Tucker's idea of a Certificate of Initial Mastery is likely to regain currency.

Marc Tucker left his position as executive director at the Carnegie Forum on Education and the Economy to found the National Center on Education and the Economy in 1988.[37] On November 11, 1992, immediately after Bill Clinton was elected, Tucker wrote an eighteen-page letter to Hillary Clinton,[38] who served on the board of the NCEE. Tucker opens the letter with the news that he's just met with David Rockefeller, John Sculley, Dave Barram, and David Haselhorn, "and the subject we were discussing was what you and Bill should do now about education, training and labor market policy."

Much of Tucker's ambitious plan outlined in the infamous "Dear Hillary" letter became law: the Goals 2000 Act, the School-to-Work Act, the reauthorized Elementary and Secondary Education Act, and No Child Left Behind. Touted as *reform*, these acts set up the apparatus with which to restructure public schools: schools as training grounds for the global economy. The features of this dismantling of public education as we know it include:[39]

- Sending federal funds to each state governor and his appointees on workforce development boards, thus bypassing local school boards. Funds become a quid pro quo for alignment with federal agenda.

- Creating a database, called a labor market information system, which includes all student information. The computerized data will be available to the school, the government, and future employees.

- Using the new slogan *high standards* to cement national control of tests, school honors and rewards, financial aid, and the Certificate of Initial Mastery.

- Controling the vocabulary ("Standards are what the people in power say they are.").

Phyllis Schlafly writes, "The Tucker-Clinton plan would change the mission of the public schools from teaching children knowledge and skills to training them to serve the global economy in jobs selected by workforce boards."[40] Liberals need to bite the bullet: does Schlafly's loathsome positions on Title IX and illegal aliens disqualify her from being at least 70 percent right on School-to-Work?

Education Trust: On the Road for Parsimony and Rigor

Established in 1990 by the American Association for Higher Education to encourage colleges and universities to support K–12 reform efforts, Education Trust's major funders are Atlantic Philanthropies, Inc.; the Annie E. Casey Foundation; the Carnegie Corp. of New York; the Edna McConnell Clark Foundation; the Bill and Melinda Gates Foundation; the James Irvine Foundation; the MetLife Foundation; the John D. and Catherine T. MacArthur Foundation; the Pew Charitable Trusts; the State Farm Co. Foundation; and the Washington Mutual Foundation. The Education Trust is working to align state high school graduation tests with state university admission and placement tests. The stated purpose of such alignment is "to promote high academic achievement for all students at all levels." Presumably, this will guarantee equity and excellence in the educational system.

In a most curious statement, Education Trust tries to claim some higher moral ground by outdoing the standards experts, declaring, "For standards to succeed, however, they must not only have the qualities normally set forth by the standards gurus, including clarity, parsimony and the like. They and the assessments based on them must also be unyielding in their rigor."[41] Parsimony and rigor. What a combination with which to nurture the nation's children.

Education Trust's team of analysts pronounced the New York Regents exam, along with the Massachusetts state exam (MCAS), to be the best in the land. Ed Trust evaluators complained that most tests were on a "much lower level than either the college admissions or placement examinations." Get that? A student must pass a college admissions exam to receive a high school diploma. Ed Trust complains that most state tests for high schoolers contain "such practical day-to-day texts as tax forms, data presentations, technical instructions, etc."[42] In contrast, college admissions tests contain primarily academic and literary texts—no practical, real-world documents, no straightforward human interest narratives.

"In contrast," intones Ed Trust, "[t]he New York Regents' Examination in English was an exception to most of the high school tests in that it integrated sophisticated and varied reading passages with written open-response questions."[43] Translation: This means that high schoolers were instructed to write "a unified essay about the power of nature" as revealed in a passage written by Roger Ascham and another passage written by Jack London. They were instructed to use evidence from each passage, develop a controlling idea, and show how the author used specific literary elements or techniques to convey that idea. They were to show how each author used specific literary elements (for example: theme, characterization, structure, point of view) or techniques (for example: symbolism, irony, figurative language) to convey the controlling idea. You remember Roger Ascham, of course, the sixteenth-century essayist who wrote about archery. People with graduate degrees in English literature quake when faced with Ascham's text. A key word in understanding the passage is listed as *obsolete* in the *Oxford English Dictionary*. What is such prose doing on a high-stakes test to determine high school diploma worthiness? Ask Education Trust.

This inquisition came on the second day of a two-day exam. On the first day, testees listened to an examiner read a long selection by the coach of the Pittsburgh Steelers—then they used that passage to write a report on management techniques in the workplace.[44]

In a *New York Times* front-page story, Jeanne Heifetz, indefatigable member of the Parents Coalition to End High-Stakes Testing, exposed the Regents tests for changing authors' words in literary passages. As fun as the public embarrassment of the New York Department of Education was, the real crime is not its editorial fiddling but the premise with which it put the test together, the premise that Education Trust likes so much. Writing in the *New York Times*, Moira Mosco, one of the teachers grading the Regents exam, points out that the recycling prompt for writing a persuasive essay was one students should have been able to handle—if they'd been given a fair break. But within sixty to ninety minutes, they had to read and figure out a 1,400-word *Consumer Reports* article steeped in technical jargon and crammed with facts. To compound the information overload, there was also an accompanying statistical chart, described by Mosco as "only slightly more engaging than the New York State tax code." They had to answer multiple-choice questions about the article and the chart and *then* "plan and draft an articulate, well-developed, grammatically sound piece of rhetoric that drew support from both documents."[45] All in an hour and a half.

The S Scale

This S Scale instrument, a self-checking device, yields an estimate of standards receptivity at the personality level. Answer true or false for each statement.

1. The most important thing we can teach children is to work hard.
2. A person who doesn't pass algebra and calculus can hardly expect to get a good job.
3. If children would fool around less and work harder, they would do better.
4. Jobs for the twenty-first century require increased skills over jobs of the past.
5. The arts have their place, but mathematics is more important to today's workforce.
6. Teacher unions have degraded public schools.
7. Students who don't read on grade level should be retained until they master the skills.
8. What schools need most are high standards.
9. No sane, normal, decent person who cares about children could ever think of allowing social promotion.
10. Nobody can succeed in the twenty-first century workforce without first mastering more complex curriculum than was required a generation ago.
11. Students today don't know as much as they used to.
12. American students score abysmally low on international comparisons.
13. The fact that many students can't locate Florida or Iraq on a map is evidence of school failure.
14. Rapid globalization means that curriculum reform is imperative.
15. States that have not instituted tough new academic standards aren't asking enough of their students.
16. High-level critical thinking skills are the birthright of every child.
17. Students who want to succeed in life need high standards that promote cultural and technical sophistication to compete economically with citizens from around the world.
18. States need to align their standards and tests.
19. The fact that Japan practices social promotion has probably been a key factor in its recent economic troubles.
20. Employers must have confidence that a high school diploma means something.
21. Social promotion is an educational fad that harms children.
22. All children can achieve at high levels.
23. The Four Horsemen of the Apocalypse are still at large.

24. States can strengthen their academic expectations for students by benchmarking their standards against those of the highest-performing nations.

25. America's schools need better-qualified teachers.

26. Pouring more money into the schools won't solve the problems.

27. America's teacher education institutions need an overhaul.

28. The quality of a high school can be measured by the percentage of students taking Advanced Placement courses.

29. The public education system should, as its primary goal, prepare students to enter the future workforce.

30. Those who don't believe all children can achieve at high levels are cheating children with low expectations.

31. New York City is lucky to have retired General Electric CEO Jack Welch as chief adviser to its Leadership Academy for principals.

Score two points for each true answer. Score zero points for each false answer.

If your score is 2 or lower, you qualify to write editorials for the *Anarchist Weekly*.

If your score is between 4 and 6, maybe you need to lighten up.

If your score is between 8 and 18, you are a hard-core Standardista.

If your score is between 20 and 40, you are eligible to be president of the local Business Roundtable.

If your score is between 42 and 50, blame your mother for obsessive toilet training.

If your score is between 52 and 62, you are eligible for a job writing press releases for the U.S. Department of Education.

Notes

1. Cornell Maier, a business lobbyist in California, explained the evolution of business interest in the following way: "When they first read *A Nation at Risk*, the 1983 report, . . . businessmen charged into partnership with the schools. Companies, in their thousands, hurried to adopt schools. These partnerships, which included things like buying chic uniforms for school bands and school basketball teams, make local people happy. But business leaders began to realize that they did nothing for true educational reform. But the Boston Compact, and the copy-cat programs that followed, are today regarded as a disappointment. In Boston the number of students failing to complete high school has actually increased. The partnership programs now tend to be dismissed as no more than 'temporary palliatives.' " This is why, in the summer of 1989, "the Business Roundtable devoted their entire annual meeting to the subject." Maier, Cornell. 1989. "American Survey." *The Economist U.K. edition*. 26 August.

2. Among its members are the Business Roundtable, the National Alliance of Business, and the U.S. Chamber of Commerce.

3. Rust, Edward. 1999. *No Turning Back: A Progress Report on the Business Roundtable Education Initiative*. Business Roundtable. Accessed at *www.brtable.org/pdf/312.pdf*.

4. Jacobson, Louis. 2003. "The Roundtable's Turnaround." *National Journal*, 28 June. Accessed at *www.brt.org/pdf/njroundtableturnaround.pdf*.

5. Business Roundtable. 1995. "Continuing the Commitment: Essential Components of a Successful Education System." Business Roundtable. Accessed at *www.brtable.org/pdf/130.pdf*.

6. Rust. 1999.

7. France, Mike, and Andrew Osterland. 1999. "State Farm: What's Happening to the Good Neighbor?" *Business Week*, 8 November. Accessed at *www.businessweek.com/1999/99_45/b3654189.htm*.

8. One can trace the reform agenda back to the *Nation at Risk* report or President Reagan's promulgation of his Six Fundamentals: (1) give more authority to teachers to demand that students take tests, hand in homework, and "quiet down" in class; (2) remove drug and alchohol abuse from schools; (3) raise academic standards; (4) establish merit pay for teachers; (5) restore parents and local governments to their rightful place in the educational process; and (6) teach the basics.

9. Rust. 1999.

10. Business Roundtable. 1995.

11. Business Roundtable. 1996, 21. *Building Support for Tests That Count*.

12. Rust. 1999.

13. From *http://edworkforce.house.gov/hearings/107th/edr/account3801/rust.htm*.

14. Business Roundtable. 1998. *Building Support for Tests That Count*. Washington, D.C. Accessed at *www.brtable.org/pdf/225.pdf*.

15. Ibid., 14.

16. Weber, Dave. 2003. "FCAT Scores May Flunk 10,000 Area 3rd Graders." *Orlando Sentinel*, 24 February. We would observe that the research on the devastating effects of being held back in school is so one-sided that one cannot term it controversial. There is no study showing benefits of retention.

17. Puerner, now publisher and president of another Tribune Company paper, the *Los Angeles Times*, received special acknowledgment for his work in the Business Roundtable's 1998 publication *Building Support for Tests That Count*.

18. From *http://66.102.11.104/search?q=cache:MTHvYrZgwC0J:www.buildingblocks.org/consulting/artifacts/BOS2002_Program_Book.PDF+%22Mass+Insight+Education%22+%22information+synthesizers%22&hl=en&ie=UTF-8*.

19. Mass Insight. n.d. *About Mass Insight Education: Working to Improve Student Achievement in Public Schools*. Accessed at *www.buildingblocks.org/about.htm*.

20. Steinberg, Jacques. 1999. "Academic Standards Eased as a Fear of Failure Spreads." *New York Times*, 3 December.

21. Here the BRT refers readers to "organizations like Achieve, Inc." They "have developed expertise in reviewing state standards and tests; they can help you make revisions to improve quality." Achieve, of course, was cofounded by Lou Gerstner, who called the first education summit to denounce public schools.

22. From *www.aligntoachieve.org/publishers.html*.

23. From *www.aligntoachieve.org/educators.html*. Emphasis on originals.

24. From *www.aligntoachieve.org/e_library.html*.

25. From *www.foothill.net/~moorek/timeontask.html*.

26. Business Roundtable. 1996.

27. Arnstine, Donald. 1955. *Democracy and the Arts of Schooling*. Albany: State University of New York Press.

28. Kidder, Tracy. 2003. *Mountains Beyond Mountains: Healing the World*. New York: Random House.

29. Hopkins, Gary. n.d. "Nazi Concentration Camps." Education World. Accessed at *www.education-world.com/a_lesson/00-2/lp2016.shtml*.

30. Ibid.

31. KAMICO Instructional Media. Austin, TX. Accessed at *www.kamico.com/samples/web-lit-anne.pdf*.

32. See *www.equityineducation.com/faq/*.

33. See *www.nycenet.edu/dis/standards/applied*.

34. Ibid.

35. Holland, Robert. 1998. "Illegal End Run." *Richmond Times-Dispatch*, 16 September.

36. Here are a few samples of such claims:

Caruba, Alan. 2001. "The Subversion of Education in America." Accessed at *www.anxietycenter.com/subversion.htm*.

———. 2002. "It's Not 'Leave No Child Left Behind'; It's Leave No One Alone." *The Fan Mountain Almanac and Trout Wrapper*, February. Accessed at *www.troutwrapper.com/archive/feb2002-warningsigns.htm*.

Cuddy, D. L. n.d. "Warnings from D. L. Cuddy." *World Newsstand*. Accessed at *www.worldnewsstand.net/msc/DLCuddy.htm*.

Eagle Forum. 1998. "Education Conference Explores Standards and School-to-Work." *Education Reporter*, March. Accessed at *www.eagleforum.org/educate/1998/mar98/conference.html*.

Education List. n.d. "The Communist/Socialist/UN takeover of American Education Falls into Four Parts." Uhuh.Com Exposing Corruption. Accessed at *www.uhuh.com/education/list-ed.htm*.

Farrell, Dick. 1997. "School to Work—A Stupid Idea." *The Times Reporter*, 16 March. Accessed at *www.fessler.com/SBE/listen.htm*.

Flanagan, Kathleen. n.d. "Straight A's Deserves an F." *Learn US Education Reform*. Accessed at *www.learn-usa.com/er031.htm*.

FORCES Deluth. 2002. "School to Work." Accessed at *www.forcesduluth.com/stw.html*.

"Government Education." n.d. Restoring America. Accessed at *www.restoringamerica.org/archive/education_index.html*.

Harmon, Theresa. 2002. "A New and Improved Socialism??" *Federal Observer*, April. Accessed at *www.federalobserver.com/archive.php?aid=2304*.

Hyde, Henry. 1997. "School to Work; Goals 2000; Outcome Based Education." *Congressional Record*, April. Accessed at *www.cptexas.org/articles/OBEGoals2000.shtml*.

Iserbyt, Charlotte Thomson. n.d. "No Child Left Behind, No American Left Alone." Property Rights Research. Accessed at *www.propertyrightsresearch.org/no_child_left_behind.htm*.

———. 2002. "Cold War Myth: An Exercise in the Use of Dialectic." 23 November. Accessed at *www.newswithviews.com/iserbyt/iserbyt2.htm*.

Larson, Joseph R. n.d. "Countdown to Socialism in America." Restoring America. Accessed at *www.restoringamerica.org/archive/larson/countdown_to_socialism_p2.html*.

McLamb, Jack. n.d. "Bush Signs on to Speed Up Indoctrination of Our Children." Accessed at *www.patriotamerica.com/News%20Items/BUSH%20SIGNS%20ON%20TO%20SPEED %20UP%20THE%20INDOCTRINATION%20OF%20OUR%20CHILDREN.htm*.

Ryan, Clarice. 2002. "Comments on 'A New and Improved Socialism?'" 22 April. Accessed at *www.bitterroot.com/grizzly/socialism.htm*.

Sanders, Charlene. 2002. "School-to-Work and Ralph Tyler." 12 August. Accessed at *www.citizenreviewonline.org/august_2002/school_to_work.htm*.

37. NCEE's board of trustees included David Rockefeller Jr. (vice chairman of Rockefeller Family and Associates), Mario Cuomo (honorary chairman), John Sculley (former CEO of Apple Computer), James B. Hunt Jr. (former governor of North Carolina), Vera Katz (known as Portland's Bella Abzug), Adam Urbanski (president of the Rochester Teachers Association), and Hillary Rodham Clinton (partner in the Rose Law Firm and first lady of Arkansas).

38. See *www.eagleforum.org/educate/marc_tucker/marc_tucker_letter.html*.

39. This summary of the Tucker-Clinton plan is adapted from Schlafly, Phyllis, 1997, "The Clinton Master Plan to Take Over Education," Eagle Forum, 10 February. Accessed at *www.eagleforum.org/column/1997/feb97/97-02-19.html*.s

40. Ibid.

41. Education Trust. 1999. "Ticket to Nowhere." *Thinking K–16*, 3 (2): 5.

42. Most citizens living in the real world would probably think anybody who can decipher a tax form deserves a high school diploma.

43. Education Trust. 1999, 21.

44. See *www.nysedregents.org/testing/engre/engs1100.pdf*.

45. Mosco, Moira. 2000. "How Albany Failed English." *The New York Times*, 5 February.

4

Not-So-Strange Bedfellows

The Business Roundtable Power Network

If they can get you asking the wrong questions, they don't have to worry about the answers.

—THOMAS PYNCHON, *GRAVITY'S RAINBOW*

The first part of the education agenda proposed by the corporate-politico alliance at the 1989 Charlottesville summit—state standards, state-mandated tests, and rewards and sanctions—was successfully implemented in nineteen states by 1998. In 2004, twenty-four states have high school exit exams in place, with six of these not yet withholding diplomas. Business leaders have been able to create an interlocking corporate-government-foundation-nonprofits network, all pumping for high-stakes standards and testing. Looking at the funding sources and links provides a glimpse of this interconnectedness. As you read, keep in mind that several organizations foster interplay between state governors and corporate CEOs. One of the oldest and most important is the Education Commission of the States. Started in 1966, ECS currently provides governors with practical resources with which to implement systemic reform in their respective states. One of these resources is the Institute for Educational Leadership (IEL). Another organization of CEOs and governors is Achieve, Inc. Both ECS and Achieve partner with the Annenberg Institute, which in turn has partnerships with Public Agenda, as well as dozens of other institutes and research centers, all promoting standards-based, systemic reform.

Education Commission of the States

The 1966 National Governors' Conference voted unanimously to create the ECS as a vehicle to "improve education with the active leadership and personal participation of the governors."[1] The 1999–2000 executive committee included three governors, the chair of the U.S. Budget and Taxation Committee, the vice chair of the U.S. Senate Education Committee, an assistant superintendent of public instruction in Utah, a retired superintendent, the educational policy adviser to the governor of Colorado, and Carl Takamura, executive director of the Business Roundtable of Hawaii. Takamura also served on the ECS Steering Committee. The 2003 senior fellows included Raymond Cortines, former executive director of the Pew Network for Standards-Based Reform at Stanford University; Christopher Cross, senior fellow with the Center for Education Policy, consultant to the Broad Foundation and the Stuart Foundation, and a member of the advisory board for the School Evaluation Service program of Standard and Poors (from 1994 to 2002, Cross was CEO of the Council for Basic Education and before that he was director of the Education Initiative of the Business Roundtable); Milton Goldberg, executive vice president of the National Alliance of Business; James Guthrie, director of the Peabody Center for Education Policy at Peabody College, Vanderbilt University; Janet S. Hansen, vice president and director of education studies at the Committee for Economic Development (CED); Sharon Lynn Kagan, Virginia and Leonard Marx professor of early childhood and family policy at Teachers College, Columbia University, and a senior research scientist at Yale University's Child Study Center; and Stephen R. Portch, chancellor emeritus for the Board of Regents of the University System of Georgia.

Whew! Is there a teacher in the house?

The blueprint for action by ECS is laid out in a document called *ECS Priorities*, and it provides a good summary of the goals and aims of all of the organizations discussed in this chapter. High standards and assessments are at the heart of the agenda. According to the party line, standards and assessments provide the data to which teachers, students, and individual schools can be held accountable through a system of incentives, rewards, and sanctions. Complex assessment of measurable standards will provide, the ECS says, credible and reliable data to "communicate to people what they need to know, when they need to know it, and in a form that is understandable and useful to them."

Hubris enshrined: *what they need to know and when they need to know it.*

Committed to the principles of lean production—also known as total quality management (TQM), total quality control (TQC), and deregulation—ECS works with state governments to promote flexibility among school systems through decentralized, decision-making charter schools. ECS' position is that since research has shown that the quality of the teacher is the "single most important variable in determining student achievement," we must improve teacher quality. But then, employing a circular argument that takes into account neither the teacher nor the student, ECS narrowly limits what it means to be a quality teacher. In defining a quality teacher as someone trained on how to use data (test-score results) to make decisions to improve student performance (higher test scores)[2] ECS encourages the standardista penchant for promoting data as wisdom.

Institute for Educational Leadership

The Institute for Educational Leadership provides a window into how educational researchers, school boards, and administrative and teacher unions have been successfully co-opted by the wide network of programs and partnerships funded by corporate America. A major player, the IEL supplies programs and partnerships offering structural support for the Business Roundtable's standards and assessment agenda. From its modest beginnings as a nonprofit institution established in 1964 in Washington, D.C., to run a Washington Internships in Education program, IEL has grown to sponsor a wide array of programs, publications, and networks funded by sixteen major foundations and forty-four corporations. Here's how IEL describes itself:

> Improving education requires a nationwide commitment that transcends institutional and partisan loyalties. For more than three decades, IEL has helped build that commitment. By establishing broad-based leadership networks and by creating innovative approaches to complex issues, IEL has brought forth change and produced striking results. With more than twenty programs and partnerships in place, IEL is a national institution that reaches deep into states and communities throughout the country.[3]

IEL's School Board Effectiveness Program helps school boards "focus on the critical issue of student performance."[4] Six major foundations helped IEL establish Superintendents Prepared. This program provides training and on-the-job support for aspiring urban school superintendents "to strengthen the pool of individuals . . . in an era characterized by declining public support and funding, by growing diversity among students and by raising awareness for the need to focus more attention on student achievement in order to develop and prepare students for the twenty-first century."

IEL programs provide structural support for the development of an "interlocking directorate" that promotes the Business Roundtable's standards and assessment agenda. IEL's Education Policy Fellowship Program (EPFP) has produced "4000 plus alumni who now lead in K–12 and higher education, foundations, education policy groups, nonprofits, government and the private sector." (See Appendix C for an extensive list of the organizations affiliated with IEL.) Once the leaders are in place, EPFP provides ongoing workshops and national forums. One of the two national meetings takes place in Washington, D.C., and "connects Fellows to national policy processes and personalities." In North Carolina, the Public School Forum, the BRT's administrative nerve center in the southeast, "takes a cohort of mid-level professionals through a series of seminars on how educational policy is made in North Carolina and on the national level."[5] The California site, located in Downey, serves researchers from the Southwest Regional Laboratory (SWRL), producing research to guide teacher training. Such training and professional development models are designed to help teachers adapt to their new roles in the developing TQM system that promotes the BRT agenda of high standards and assessment. The following selection, from the foreword to an SWRL publication, illustrates this development.

> While the changing student population presents numerous challenges to teachers and other persons involved in teacher development, future agendas for school improvement/restructuring also hold heavy expectations for changes in teacher responsibility and performance. For instance, new approaches to student performance assessment, including application of national standards and use of alternatives to standardized achievement tests, call for teacher participation in development and interpretation of performance measures as well as application of them. New models of schooling that incorporate high technology and school-business collaboration ask teachers to expand their instructional processes to include an enlarged array of human and technical resources. . . . Reconceptualization of both teaching and the teacher development process is required if persons who assume this professional role are to be both effective teachers of diverse student populations and effective contributors to reform of the schools in which the students are enrolled. . . . The ideas advanced in this occasional paper suggest some ways to accomplish this.[6]

Maybe the vague language indicates some ambivalence toward the BRT agenda. Or maybe it's just obfuscation. The heavy use of words that are either codes to disguise the real intent or lazy jargon makes it hard to tell. A document that relies on such words should raise red flags: *changing student population, diverse student populations, performance measures, teacher development process, persons who assume this professional role, effective teachers, reform,* and so on. In either case, it doesn't seem likely that future teachers trained in the *teacher development process* or current teachers judged *effective* will be allowed to implement—or even consider—alternatives to state-mandated standards and standardized achievement tests. In the context of such reform, effective teaching of *diverse student populations* can only mean developing methods to train all students for one test. Notice that when Standardistas preach what they call the teacher development process they never mention chasing hamsters or interrogating kids about the toilet paper wads on the lavatory ceiling.

Public Agenda

Public Agenda is a nonprofit organization whose apparent purpose is to provide information to reporters investigating education issues.[7] To that end, Public Agenda asserts that four *alternative perspectives* on educational reform exist:

- Higher academic standards and well-defined goals are essential.
- Student-centered schools should be created to teach problem-solving skills.[8]
- Parents should have a choice where their kids go to school.
- There is not enough funding for schools.

Public Agenda concedes that these four perspectives "are not necessarily mutually exclusive" but insists that "each leads to a distinctive prescription about what is to be done."[9] Thus, the debate is kept neatly within the boundaries of the agenda as defined by the Business Roundtable's Nine Essential Components of a Successful Educational System—the TQC management model. Those straying outside these narrow boundaries, of course, find many other possibilities for bringing about change in schools, but Public Agenda, IEL, and the BRT want to keep the debate within the confines of high standards and high-stakes testing. It is to their purpose to ignore altogether some twenty-five hundred years of debate about the means and goals of education.

Public Agenda is best known for its opinion polls relating to current education issues, most particularly those having to do with standards and standardized testing. Not surprisingly, its polls are characterized by loaded questions with impossible choices. As Sean Gonsalves, *Cape Cod Times* writer, observed on AlterNet.org: "*Opinion Poll, n.* A propaganda device used to conform public opinion into the shape elite opinion leaders see fit; a survey in which many respondents side with the ready-made opinion they think the pollster wants to hear."[10] Sam Smith, alternative journalist and founding editor of the *Progressive Review*, observes that "[p]olls are the standardized test used by the media to determine how well we have learned what it has taught us."[11]

On March 9, 2002, the *New York Times* published a letter by Deborah Wadsworth, Public Agenda president, that should disabuse anyone of the idea that this is an independent research setup operating without an agenda. In the letter she splits hairs over the *Times* report that large numbers of teachers and parents said that too much emphasis was put on testing. Wadsworth says it wasn't testing at all but test scores that upset people. And then she concludes with this paragraph: "While teachers and parents are clearly attentive to the complaints raised by critics of standardized testing, our survey made it equally clear that there is no desire to turn back the clock on the effort to raise standards." Sneaky. Suddenly the argument is switched to standards, creating a deliberate confusion between high-stakes standardized testing, to which even Public Agenda's own data shows growing opposition, and high standards, which few dare oppose. Sneaky but not surprising: You don't have to have been bleating for years that it's the standards, stupid,[12] to recognize that as soon as someone starts yammering about high standards, alarm bells should ring— she's selling something. In this case, Public Agenda is selling high-stakes testing.

Like its previous Reality Check polls, Public Agenda's fifth annual Reality Check survey is a joint project with *Education Week*.[13] Pew Charitable Trusts and the GE Fund pay for the research; *Education Week* publishes these reports with support from the Pew Charitable Trusts. After asking middle and high school students about their experiences with achievement testing, Reality Check 2002 trumpeted the results with the attention-grabbing headline "Few Students Are Unsettled by Testing" and a conclusion asserting "public school students nationwide appear to be adjusting comfortably to the new status quo." So the party line was: More testing? Ho hum. Playing tag team, IBM CEO Louis V. Gerstner immediately jumped in with an op-ed in the *New York Times*, citing Public Agenda's survey as evidence that "the great majority of middle and high school students are comfortable with the increased testing in public schools." Interesting, isn't it: A member of the Business Roundtable can get that coveted op-ed position any time he wants. A progressive organization like TomPaine.commonsense has to pay for it.

Writing in *Education Week*, Eric Schaps, president of the Developmental Studies Center, takes issue with the Public Agenda–*Education Week* Reality Check data.[14] Schaps dug up the actual wording of a key question:

Which best describes how nervous you get when you take standardized tests?

    a. I don't get nervous at all.
    b. I get nervous but I can handle it.
    c. I get so nervous that I can't take the test.

What a choice. Nearly three-fourths of six hundred students sampled chose option b. What else could they do? When the other choices were total cool and total meltdown, then what other choice did they have? And their forced choice allowed Public Agenda to conclude that "few students are unsettled" by standardized testing.

Schaps also observes that when Public Agenda dismissed as "only a handful" the students who said they "'get so nervous' that they can't take the tests," it was ignoring 5 percent of the responders. In California alone, that's 135,000 students—so anxious that they can't function. There you have the difference between Standardistas and educators: Standardistas are willing to dismiss a handful here and a handful there; these are the kids educators agonize over.

Annenberg Institute for School Reform

Headquartered at Brown University in Providence, Rhode Island, the Annenberg Institute was established in 1993 with a $500 million grant from longtime Reagan pal and Nixon ambassador to Great Britain Walter Annenberg.[15] Warren Simmons, the executive director, calls the institute a "standards-based, practice-centered policy research and technical assistance organization."[16] The organization is also one of the central hubs in the vast network of standards-based reform. As a central hub, the institute coordinates a network that is attempting to replace school boards as the governing agency of local schools. This network is called the Task Force on the Future of the District and includes the Education Commission of the States, the Consortium for Policy Research in Education, the Cross-City Campaign for Urban School Reform, and the New American Schools.[17] Another program is the Annenberg's Tools for Accountability Project, which is pursuing a key component of the BRT strategy: data-driven reform.[18]

Annenberg devotes big resources to developing *public engagement*—co-opting members of the community to support standards-based reform. The institute has contracted with Public Agenda to determine what are "the attitudes of school board members, administrators, teachers, and the general public on the challenges and impediments to effective, sustained public engagement around the issue of education."[19] One Public Agenda poll published by the Education Commission of the States reveals "85 percent or more of parents approve of their local school district holding students to high academic standards and involving the business community in changing schools." As we saw earlier, examining what questions were posed is crucial to understanding the significance of the conclusion.

Be that as it may, with this and other data, the institute is confident that it has developed engagement techniques that are "channeling a community's concern, apathy or anger into informed and constructive action."[20] These techniques include house meetings, neighborhood canvassing, focus groups, and meetings among local business owners. Further, Annenberg announces that business and community groups are launching parent institutes, and radio and TV stations and newspapers are establishing civic journalism projects to help communities "make tough decisions" about education reform.[21] Annenberg trumpets the success of these techniques: "many groups can already point to substantially improved student performance" and there is evidence of "involvement of the public in formulating new standards for student achievement." And there's more: the future challenge is to figure out "how to bring in senior citizens, small business owners, or citizens without school age children" to the discussion of how to improve test scores.

Nobody said Standardistas aren't relentless. Wherever you are, they'll find you.

Annenberg insists that it isn't enough to get standards and to get state benchmarks. The public still needs to be browbeaten—whoops, its term is *engaged*—to sustain political and popular support for standards over time.[22]

The Annenberg Institute casts a wide net. It partners with the Public Education Fund Network,[23] Achieve,[24] the Cross-City Campaign for Urban School Reform, the Providence Public Schools, the University of Pittsburgh's Institute for Learning, and the Consortium for Policy Research in Education. Sharing resources and information with its partners, the institute has spent $500 million to fund eighteen "locally designed school reform projects" assessed by university-based researchers. Among the institute's Program Advisory Group are university education professors, several Local Education Fund (LEF) representatives, as well as representatives from each of the following: Achieve, Inc., Public Agenda, the Disney Learning Initiative, the Education Trust, the U.S. Department of Education, and the Bay Area School Reform Collaborative (BASRC). Without such a network, it is unlikely that so many parents and educators would have been misled into believing that systemic reform can deliver on its promise to make the educational experience successful for all students.

Public Education Network

The Public Education Network (PEN) is, in its words, "a national association of local education funds (LEFs) and individuals working to advance public school reform in low-income communities across our country." These LEFs are the vehicles through which local business groups pursue standards-based reform in their cities. The Ten Point Framework, which guides the work of these LEFs, looks remarkably like the Business Roundtable's nine-point plan. Among the big players in national reform on the board of directors are the executive director of the Pew Forum on Standards-Based Reform (who is also chair of the Massachusetts Education Reform Review Commission), the president of the Alliance for Education, the deputy chair of the New York City Board of Education, and a former superintendent of Philadelphia Public Schools. With public resistance against No Child Left Behind growing, PEN stepped forward to support the legislation. On July 18, 2003, PEN president Wendy Puriefoy appeared on a panel addressing the House Budget Committee Democratic Caucus and the Senate Democratic Policy Committee, thanking them for passing No Child Left Behind. "It is a tool to dramatically raise performance in communities that want to regain confidence in schools but have not known what to do or how to leverage the system to change." She asked Congress to fully fund NCLB, promising that PEN "will be blitzing the media and elected officials with information about what underfunding of NCLB and the tax cut are doing to classrooms."[25]

PEN works with LEFs in more than twelve hundred school districts—including the Charlotte-Mecklenburg Education Foundation (CMEF), founded in 1991. CMEF members are "active members" in NC Partnerships, "involved in annual legislative briefings of EEBC [Education: Everybody's Business Coalition] on all legislative alert and updated mailing lists" and can be called upon by EEBC to "support specific issues like the recent successful $2 billion bond package for higher education."[26] Locally, CMEF is active on many fronts. It gives out grants to teachers, helps parents become their children's coaches, conducts annual surveys, coordinates high school application processes with the state's university system, instructs the public on finance issues and school board elections, and honors those who show a "dedicated interest in education."[27]

During the 1980s, Charlotte corporate leaders began to complain about the shortage of entry-level workers. These leaders blamed the city's public school system for not contributing to a pro-business climate as well as not producing the kinds of workers business needed. When John Murphy became superintendent in 1991, he set out to establish a close working relationship with the business leaders, many of whom belonged to CMEF. He convened a panel of experts to advise him on systemic reform; business leaders served on education task forces and adopted schools. At the end of Murphy's first year, the CEO of First Union Bank lobbied the school board for a substantial pay raise for Murphy. And an anonymous group of corporate leaders handed him $30,000 as a bonus.[28]

In 1992, Charlotte's historic desegregation plan was replaced with a parental-choice plan centered on magnet schools, increasing the segregation in the school system (which is ironic, given that federal desegregation money was used to fund the pilot magnet schools). Although many middle-class African Americans supported the creation of magnet schools, many from the working class did not. Critics of the new choice plan worried that the new magnet schools had diverted resources from older inner-city schools. In August 1994, in response to this criticism, Murphy presented the school board with results of the first year of Project First. Funded by IBM and Americorps in partnership with PEN and CMEF, this project promised to provide technology and expertise to ten nonmagnet elementary schools. Roslyn Mickelson's absorbing study, "International Business Machinations: A Case Study of Corporate Involvement in Local Education Reform," questions how a program could rectify the imbalance of funds between magnet and nonmagnet schools. For example, in 1993, one magnet school received $750,000 in technology resources, while a Project First school received an Americorps volunteer and several IBM computers. The volunteer neither was a technology expert nor had been trained in technology. The IBM computers were never used because the existing infrastructure could not support them.[29] From talking to those who put together Project First, Mickelson concluded that IBM executives were motivated by the "increased share of the IBM computer market" and the greater legitimacy such a project gave to a business role in education. This is consistent with Point 9 of Public Education Network's Ten Point Framework for LEFs: "Technology must be included in teaching, special education, and information management."[30] (See Appendix D for all ten points of PEN's framework.)

Just for the Kids®

At first glance, it was a Florida story. Dateline Tallahassee, August 16, 2003.[31] Governor Jeb Bush is contracting with what's termed a *politically connected* Texas company called Just for the Kids to do a computer analysis on the state's FCAT scores and make recommendations for how Florida schools might do better. Tom Luce, a Dallas attorney with well-connected Republican ties, started the company in 1995 to develop "comprehensive, data-driven school data reports for Texas that analyze student achievement data to determine benchmarks for individual schools. They also identify and investigate the highest-performing schools in the state to determine what is causing their success and provide training sessions to help educators across the state replicate those practices."[32] Ostensibly a nonprofit working for children, Just for the Kids, of course, has a corporate-politico agenda.

A little digging shows that Just for the Kids is on the move. Note the corporate-politico alliance that funds this particular number crunching. Its real point is to make mandatory testing look legitimate. As Bob Schaeffer, education director for FairTest, observes, "There is some political value in having an outside group that looks neutral ratify your work, particularly when your program is controversial."

Another outfit, the National Center for Educational Accountability, is a joint venture of Just for the Kids, the University of Texas at Austin, and the Education Commission of the States. The company's nonprofit tax returns for 2002 show government grants made up nearly $500,000 of its $2 million in revenue.[33]

Here are the states where Just for the Kids was established as of August 2003—and who financed each group:

- Arkansas thanks the Arkansas Department of Education; the Office of Research, Management, and Evaluation at the University of Arkansas; and the Arkansas Business and Education Alliance.

- Colorado thanks the Colorado Partnership for Educational Renewal; the Public Education and Business Coalition; the Colorado Forum; the Education Commission of the States; the Colorado Association of School Boards; the Research and Development Center for the Advancement of Student Learning in Fort Collins; the Colorado Department of Education; the Rose Community Foundation; the Donnell-Kay Foundation; and Governor Owens' office.

- In Florida, Just for the Kids is an initiative of the Council for Educational Change (established by the Florida Annenberg Challenge). Its goals include partnering with business, mobilizing parents and the community, engaging in research and development, and serving as a catalyst for public policy.

- In Massachusetts, Just for the Kids is an initiative of the Massachusetts Business Alliance for Education.

- In New Jersey, Just for the Kids was established and is maintained by the Business Coalition for Educational Excellence at the New Jersey Chamber of Commerce in cooperation with the New Jersey Department of Education.

- Tennessee thanks the Michael and Susan Dell Foundation; the Atlantic Philanthropies Foundation; the Education Commission of the States; the Tennessee Department of Education; and Governor Sundquist.

- The Texas thank-you list for funding the development of Just for the Kids is very long, with many names familiar only to Texans. The usual corporate representatives are there. (See Appendix E for list.)

- Washington thanks the Bill and Melinda Gates Foundation and Washington Mutual.

Progressive Policy Institute

Just a brief note about the Progressive Policy Institute, which positions itself somewhat apart from the intertwined collaborators in the rest of this chapter. Part of the Third Way and the Democratic Leadership Council, PPI describes itself as a catalyst for political change, its mission being to modernize progressive politics and government for the Information Age. Leaving behind what it terms the stale left-right debates of the industrial era, PPI is "a prolific source of what it terms the Third Way thinking that is shaping the emerging politics of the 21st century."[34]

PPI's 21st Century Schools Project "works to develop education policy and foster innovation to ensure that America's public schools are an engine of equal opportunity in the knowledge economy."[35] That phrase *knowledge economy*, which PPI uses frequently, is a tip-off to its agenda. Truth in disclosure:

In the June 21, 2003, *21st Century Schools Project Bulletin* director Andrew Rotherham characterized one of this book's authors as paranoid:

> In "Capitalism, Calculus, and Conscience,"[36] Susan Ohanian repeats the common paranoid charge that efforts to increase standards are really a corporate plot to force kids to drop out and hence provide low-skilled workers for the "global economy." Never mind that here in the real world corporations are demanding skilled rather than low-wage workers (but ignore that, it's just part of the clever concealment of the true plot!) and that actual data on standards-based reform and drop-out rates is quite mixed among the states.
>
> That's just the tip of the iceberg and we can't hope to do the article justice here, you can't caricature a caricature, so you'll have to take our word that it's worth reading. All the usual suspects—Achieve, the Business Roundtable, and so forth—are cited as card-carrying conspirators.

PPI finds lucre by keeping company with what many progressives would find strange bedfellows. Since 1996, PPI has received funding from the ultra-conservative Bradley Foundation. The Lynde and Harry Bradley Foundation of Milwaukee is well known for its support of far-right-wing causes, most notably, the Heritage Foundation. The Bradley grant to PPI is to support general program activities. According to Bruce Murphy, writing in *Milwaukee World*, "Joyce [then-head of the Bradley Foundation] says his goal in funding this group was to help move the Democratic Party 'away from the left and toward the center. It's in everybody's interest to have a less radical politics in the nation.'"[37]

And the strategy is working. A policy forum held April 9, 2003, titled Implementing the No Child Left Behind Act, was sponsored by the National Center on Education and the Economy, the Thomas B. Fordham Foundation, and the 21st Century Schools Project/Progressive Policy Institute. Fordham and PPI also produced *Rethinking Special Education for a New Century*, Individuals with Disabilities Education Act intended to influence the debate for the reauthorization of the IDEA.

Asia-Pacific Economic Cooperation

If you've never heard of APEC, it's time you did. APEC is the Asia-Pacific Economic Cooperation, twenty-one economies with borders on the Pacific, both in Asia in the Americas. Global economy, get it?[38] Denis Doyle presented a paper on New American Schools at the first APEC meeting, held August 5–6, 1992, in Washington, D.C. Bruno Manno, then-acting assistant secretary for policy and planning, for the U.S. Department of Education, took notes for the United States. Manno's other affiliations have links throughout this chapter: Design

Team member of the Modern Red Schoolhouse; senior fellow of the Hudson Institute; trustee of the Thomas B. Fordham Foundation; and senior program associate of the Annie E. Casey Foundation. Here's what Manno reported on APEC: "At this meeting Secretary Alexander described work on a voluntary national examination system in the United States."

At their 2000 meeting, the APEC education ministers "acknowledged that the world is now truly the global village it was once envisaged to be. Economies have become more inter-connected and interdependent, and this will continue to be more so in the future. In the new millennium, technology and information networks will continue to re-orientate how economies communicate with each other." They also acknowledge that "[t]he Ministers observed that the new century will be marked by rapid social and economic change, brought about largely by advances in science and technology. The knowledge-based economy will see the rise of new businesses and industries. In such a world, knowledge and its effective application will become the important assets for economic and social advancement. Education must equip the workforce with relevant knowledge and skills for the new economy and society of the 21st century." And so on and so on. It all sounds very familiar, everybody reading from the same script.[39] One of the topics discussed: Best Practice Workshop of School-to-Work Transitions in APEC Member Economies for Youth at Greatest Risk of Unemployment.[40]

The Asia-Pacific Economic Cooperation was formed in 1989 as a new mechanism for multilateral cooperation among the economies of the Asia-Pacific region. Its members were Australia, Brunei Darussalam, Canada, Chile, the People's Republic of China, Hong Kong, Indonesia, Japan, the Republic of Korea, Malaysia, Mexico, New Zealand, Papua New Guinea, the Republic of the Philippines, Singapore, Chinese Taipei, Thailand, and the United States. Since then, Peru, Russia, and Vietnam have joined.

In 1994, in Jakarta, APEC issued a Declaration: A Human Resources Development Framework for the Asia Pacific Economic Cooperation, in which it affirmed "the value of, and need for, concerted development of human resources by member economies, the region's business/private sector enterprises, and research, education, and training institutions."[41]

In May 1997, the Ministry of Labor of the Republic of Korea published a paper for a Human Resources Development Ministerial meeting of APEC. This paper, *The Provisional Themes for the 2nd APEC Human Resources Development Ministerial Meeting*, summarizes the consensus reached by APEC on what education is about. One of the themes of the Korean paper is that globalization is inevitable and that education must prepare workers for the business needs of this globalization. Once schooling's purpose is defined as preparing future workers, then it follows that business should grab a central role in deciding the content of schooling. The APEC paper could not be more explicit, stating that "decisions must be taken by a school system for good business reasons with maximum business intervention." APEC declares schooling as "a transition from school to work." For parents who wonder why high-stakes testing has been imposed on schools, APEC explains that the governments "create a complementary educational environment and system [for] industrial restructuring due to technology advancements, a new international order with increased competition, and a distinct world trend of globalization."

The paper attacks "the emphasis on education for itself or on education for good members of a community." Further, children should not grow up to think that work is only an instrumental part of one's life. Instead, "students should acquire a breadth of knowledge, skills, and attitudes necessary for adjustments into [a] work environment. Academic achievement should correlate with potential for ample job opportunities."

For APEC, learning for learning's sake is to be stamped out. What it wants is the work ethic, as defined by the Business Roundtable. "Schools should provide a comprehensive skills-based achievement record." APEC calls this "need-based education." Not children's needs, but the needs of big business. APEC complains that some people respect general high schools more than vocational schools. That's because "curricula have been traditionally developed by intellectual elites with emphasis on learning for the sake of learning without much emphasis on outcomes." Such thinking must be stamped out. And the way to do this is by insisting that "decisions must be taken by a school system for good business reasons with maximum business intervention. A government should actively support or facilitate links with business." APEC explains that this is important so that the government can build a positive training culture to ensure that education and training "meet the needs of business, labor markets, and changing economic environment." No more frivolities like art, music, gym, recess, or the teacher reading chapter books aloud. If APEC has its way, learning for learning's sake will disappear from the globe.

APEC touches on the need for teacher education institutions to prepare future teachers to teach this way, subsuming any love of learning into an awareness of the needs of the marketplace. Newspaper articles screaming that teacher education colleges are falling down on the job, failing to prepare the sort of teachers the business community wants, are part of the strategy.

Maybe APEC decided it had been too candid. Formerly available online, this paper is no longer listed in the papers at APEC's website or available for purchase from its bookstore. A query to the headquarters in Singapore brought vague summaries but not the real thing.

For more news of APEC, here are two places to start: APEC Assessment Conference: New Directions in Student Testing and Technology, October 2000 at UCLA, cosponsored by the U.S. Department of Education and the Ministry of Education of China.[42] The APEC Education Ministerial 2000 meeting in

Singapore established international policy agreements, called Areas of Cooperation.[43] In this context, education for a global economy takes on a new meaning.

Postscript

The first chair of APEC's Education Forum, serving until 1996, was Dr. Alan L. Ginsburg. Some of Dr. Ginsburg's other activities bring the power network full circle. Director of the Planning and Evaluation Service for the U.S. Department of Education, Ginsburg coordinates development of the department's Strategic Plan and program evaluation activities. With Susan Thompson-Hoffman, Ginsburg coordinated the *School-Home Links Reading Kit* in the Compact for Learning Series, a joint project of the U.S. Department of Education, the Corporation for National Service, the *Los Angeles Times*, and Little Planet Learning. The *School-Home Links Reading Kit* is organized around a skills framework provided in the National Academy of Sciences report *Preventing Reading Difficulties in Young Children* and a reading framework developed by Edward Kame'enui and Deborah Simmons of the University of Oregon Direct Instruction and DIBELs (Dynamic Indicators of Basic Early Literary) fame. For those who think the government interference of No Child Left Behind is a Republican conspiracy, note that former U.S. Secretary of Education Richard W. Riley introduced the Compact for Learning, complete with contracts for teachers and parents to sign.[44]

The contract parents sign includes the promise to "[k]now what skills our child is learning in reading and other language arts classes each day. Do activities at home, like the School-Home Links, that continue our child's classroom learning at home." The principal signs a contract promising to "hold workshops on standards in reading and ways to set the standards into practice at school and at home." If the government imposing pedagogical standards on the home seems far-fetched, take a look at this September 2003 *Philadelphia Inquirer* headline: "Parents to Get 'Grades' from Phila.'s Teachers."[45] Philadelphia report cards contain a checklist on which teachers assign "home support" grades to parents. According to Paul Vallas, the school district's chief executive officer, "The feeling was, we should have a checklist of gentle reminders that would be helpful and instructive to parents." In seeking leaders to join its Urban Superintendents Academy, the Broad Foundation singled out Vallas as one of several "accomplished leaders from outside the education sector . . . taking on the challenge of leading our nation's largest school districts." Andrew Rotherham, director of the 21st Century Schools Project, testified before the Committee on Education and the Workforce, United States House of Representatives, paying homage to the Vallas model of superintendency. With the Vallas CEO-style superintendency being pushed from all corners, parents across the country shouldn't be surprised to learn they may well be next in line to be graded by the schools their children attend.

Notes

1. Education Commission of the States. 1999a. "ECS History: Education Commission of the States." Accessed at *http://ecs.org/ecs/ecsweb.nsf/23e9e2e59ebf38b4872565c5007831*.

2. Education Commission of the States. 1999c. "ECS Priorities: Education Commission of the States." Accessed at *http://ecs.org/ecs/ecsweb.nsf/23e9e2e59ebf38b4872565c5007831*.

3. Accessed at www.iel.org.

4. J. P. Danzberger is the director of Governance Programs at IEL and coauthor of the 1986 and 1992 school board reports as well as contributor to the Danforth Foundation's Task Force report on school governance. Michael Usdan is president of IEL.

5. Public School Forum. 2000. Public School Forum of North Carolina. Programs. Accessed at *www.ncforum.org*.

6. Tikunoff, W., and B. Ward. 1994. Foreword. In *Teachers, Students, and Language: Multiple Language Settings*, ed. G. Griffin, vi–vii. Southwest Regional Laboratory. The paper was prepared under subcontract with Far West Regional Laboratory for Educational Research and Development and has a Department of Education code number.

7. The subtitle to Public Agenda's webpage is "The Journalist's Inside Source for Public Opinion and Policy Analysis."

As a matter of record, Public Agenda's recent funders include AT&T; BellSouth; Annie E. Casey; Edna McConnell Clark; Danforth; Ford; Thomas B. Fordham; William Caspar Graustein; William and Flora Hewlett; IBM International; Henry J. Kaiser Family; W. K. Kellogg; Charles F. Kettering; John S. and James L. Knight; Markle; Charles Stewart Mott; Rockefeller; Surdna and UPS Foundations; the Pew Charitable Trusts; the Advertising Council; the Business Roundtable; Fidelity Investments; GE Fund; the American Federation of Teachers; and the National Education Association. Here are the links provided by the Public Agenda website: American Federation of Teachers; Association for Supervision and Curriculum Development; Brown Center; Center for Education Reform [school choice]; Character Education Institute; Citizens for Education Freedom [vouchers]; the College Board; Council for Basic Education; Council of Chief State School Officials [sic]; Education Commission of the States; Education Writers Association; Ethics Resource Center [Ethics fellows are associated with Business Roundtable and big corporations]; Home School Legal Defense Association; Impact II— the Teachers Network; Institute for Educational Leadership; National Assessment Governing Board; NAACP; National Association of State Boards of Education; National Center for Education Statistics; National Coalition for Sex Equity in Education; National Dropout Prevention Center; National Education Association; National School Boards Association; National School Safety Center; Phi Delta Kappa; Progressive Policy Institute: 21st Century Schools Project; Thomas B. Fordham Foundation; U.S. Department of Education.

8. For Engaging Americans in Educational Reform, "problem-solving skills" means the completion of tasks assigned by others. It is difficult to ascertain whether, when doing its survey, Public Agenda pollsters clarify what they or their respondents meant by "problem-solving."

9. Public Agenda. 1999. "The Perspectives in Brief." Accessed at *http://publicagenda. org/issues/debate.cfm?issue_type=*.

10. Gonsalves, Sean. 2003. " 'The Devil's Dictionary' Revisted." AlterNet.org, 14 July. Accessed at *www.alternet.org/story.html?StoryID=16393*.

11. Engel, Adam. 2003. "A Conversation in Medieval America with Sam Smith." Counterpunch, 14 November. Accessed at *www.counterpunch.org/engel11142003.html*.

12. Ohanian, Susan. 1999. *One Size Fits Few: The Folly of Educational Standards.* Portsmouth, NH: Heinemann.

13. These annual reports are not available at Public Agenda but are archived at the *Education Week* website: *www.edweek.org/ew/newstory.cfm?slug=25realitycheck.h21*.

14. Schaps, Eric. 2002. "High-Stakes Surveys." *Education Week*, 5 June. Accessed at *www.edweek.org/ew/newstory.cfm?slug=39schaps.h21*.

15. Even Annenberg's friends acknowledge that he ran the *Philadelphia Inquirer* as his personal fiefdom, keeping a blacklist of those whose names and photos could not appear in the paper. Coming up with the ideas for *Seventeen* and *TV Guide* brought him gazillions of millions. For a fairly balanced account of his life, see *www.post-gazette.com/books/reviews/19990704 review281.asp*.

16. Annenberg Institute for School Reform. 1998a. "New Directions." Providence: AISR, 1. Accessed at *www.aisr.brown.edu/publications/pubops.html*.

17. Ibid., 4.

18. Ibid., 6.

19. Ibid., 7.

20. Annenberg Institute for School Reform. 1998b. *Reasons for Hope, Voices of Change.* Providence: AISR, 3. Accessed at *www.aisr.brown.edu/publication/pubops.html*.

21. Ibid., 9.

22. Ibid., 32.

23. The Public Education Fund Network is a corporate-funded organization that coordinates and supports the activities of Local Education Funds in many major cities in the United States. These LEFs are organizations of local business leaders who promote standards-based reform in their city. One indication of the weblike structure of networking among business and educational leaders is the résumé of Paul S. Reville. Reville is on the board of directors of the Public Education Network. As a Harvard faculty member, Reville teaches a course on standards-based reform and coordinates state relations at the Harvard Graduate School of Education. Reville is also the executive director of the Pew Forum on Standards-Based Reform and chairman of the Massachusetts Education Reform Review Commission, which oversees the implementation of the Massachusetts Education Reform Act of 1993. If that did not make him busy enough, Reville is also the cofounder and executive director of the Massachusetts Business Alliance for Education, the state's Business Roundtable organization (see *http://publicagenda. org/aboutus*).

24. Achieve, Inc., is an organization of the nation's top CEOs and state governors that provides states with assessments of their standards and testing programs (for a fee) and supports an online database and links to help state governments develop and implement standards and assessments. As of June 2000, Louis Gerstner of IBM and Tommy Thompson, governor of Wisconsin, were the cochairs of the board of directors. Governor Gray Davis of California was among the other ten members of the board (see *www.achieve.org*). Achieve has a partnership with the American Federation of Teachers.

25. From *www.house.gov/budget_democrats/hearings/dem_ed_hrg/puriefoy.pdf*.

26. Dornan, J. 2001. Personal email communication, 30 December.

27. From *http://publiceducation.org/lef/nc.htm.*

28. Mickelson, Roslyn. 1999. "International Business Machinations: A Case Study of Corporate Involvement in Local Education Reform." *Teachers College Record* 100 (3): 481.

29. Ibid., 135.

30. From *http://publiceducation.org/lef/nc/charlotte.htm.*

31. Mahlburg, Bob. 2003. "Firm to Crunch FCAT Scores." *Orlando Sentinel*, 16 August.

32. From *www.nc4ea.org/index.cfm?pg=about_us&subp=fo.*

33. Ibid.

34. From *www.ppionline.org/ppi_ci.cfm?contentid=1125&knlgAreaID=110&subsecid=204.*

35. From *www.ppionline.org/ppi_sub.cfm?knlgAreaID=110&subsecID=204.*

36. Ohanian, Susan. 2003. "Capitalism, Calculus, and Conscience." *Phi Delta Kappan*, June. Accessed at *www.pdkintl.org/kappan/k0306oha.htm.*

37. Murphy, Bruce. 2001. "How Michael Joyce Sold Himself to George W. Bush." *Milwaukee World*. Accessed at *www.milwaukeeworld.com/html/mlaw/ml010625front.php.*

38. APEC Education Forum. 1992. "Education Standards for the 21st Century." M, August, 56. Accessed at *www.apec.edu.tw/ef3.html.*

39. Joint Statement from the 2nd APEC Education Ministerial Meeting. 2000. 7 April. Accessed at *www.apecsec.org.sg/apec/ministerial_statements/sectoral_ministerial/education/2000_education.html.*

40. From *www.edu.tw/bicer/c22/c22381.htm.*

41. See *http://usinfo.state.gov/regional/ea/apec/jakhrd.htm.*

42. See *www.cse.ucla.edu/CRESST/pages/apec.htm.*

43. See *http://216.239.41.104/search?q=cache:WXVobxZR_AYJ:aemm.moe.edu.sg/asp/asp_aemmpaper/paper/6a)_EdNet_report.PDF+%22Alan+Ginsburg%22+education&hl=en&ie=.*

44. See *http://216.239.41.104/search?q=cache:5ldxdMfAKxAJ:www.literacynet.org/ar-ca/compact/compact/compact1.pdf+%22Susan+Thompson-Hoffman%22&hl=en&ie=UTF-8.*

45. Snyder, Susan. 2003. "Parents to Get 'Grades' from Phila.'s Teachers." *Philadelphia Inquirer*, 18 September. Accessed at *www.philly.com/mld/inquirer/living/education/6797322.htm.*

5

Hijacking Democratically Elected School Boards—and Why We Should Care

Reform committees . . . were morning glories. Looked lovely in the morning and withered up in a short time, while the regular machines went on flourishing forever, like fine old oaks.

—TAMMANY HALL FIXER GEORGE WASHINGTON PLUNKITT

Mission Statement
The School Board of Palm Beach County is committed to excellence in education and preparation of all our students with the knowledge, skills and ethics required for responsible citizenship and productive employment.

—THE SCHOOL DISTRICT OF PALM BEACH COUNTY,
FLORIDA, APRIL 2003

100 Percent or Bust

The Palm Beach mission statement appears on page 2 of the district's *Academic Business Plan*.[1] Every word of the mission is straight from the Business Roundtable agenda. The fifty-seven-page business plan is crammed with charts—just like a stockholders' annual report—projecting what 100 percent of Palm Beach County students will achieve by 2014: 100 percent students scoring C or better in algebra, 100 percent taking at least one AP class, and so on. One hundred percent. All school graphs reach 100 percent by 2014, except for dropouts and suspensions, which dip to zero. You don't need to hire an accountant to see that these must be Enron numbers.

It looks like Palm Beach County gets its 100 percent figures from the federal No Child Left Behind 100 percent demands. According to the federal formula, in 2003, 31 percent of North Carolina students should have been reading on grade level and 38 percent should have been doing math on grade level. According to the plan, these percentages will increase each year until 100 percent of students reach the target in 2014. In August 2003, the public learned that 88 percent of the Palm Beach County schools fell short of that year's goal. Nonetheless, the School Board of Palm Beach County and the federal government agree that by 2014, 100 percent of the goals will be achieved. This isn't just smoke and mirrors: when a school board mission statement becomes an academic business plan, kids' school days are filled with test prep and their futures are put into the hands of global economists.

The No Child Left Behind mandate that "all schools must be proficient by 2014" legitimizes the growing polarization of wealth, the increasing dropouts and push-outs, the obvious lack of social mobility—caused by stagnating wages and the looting of the public sector. Heads up: Schoolteachers aren't doing the looting. Big business needs someone to blame for the end of the Horatio Alger era, and schoolteachers are handy. The corporate-politico alliance proclaims the new myth of our times: every student can and must learn the common-core, college-prep curriculum. Students must do this to take their place in the global economy. Then, when the schools fail to produce 100 percent common-core products, these schools are, by federal definition, failures, making vouchers and other privatization schemes more politically acceptable. By blaming teachers for failing to teach NCLB subgroups, the power brokers create a new myth: if everyone doesn't learn the common core, it's because (racist) teachers lack high expectations. The truth is that there *is* a long-standing problem of children in these subgroups failing to thrive in school, but business interests, instead of working to solve the problem, redefine it to their own ends. The business plan is to declare schools failures, vacating the principals and teachers. Pit teacher against teacher, school against school. Get conservatives fighting liberals over vouchers and charters so they don't join together against their common enemy—the Business Roundtable and the global economy.

Molly Ivins puts it this way: the fish rots from the head down.[2] Every recent business scandal, starting with Enron, has displayed the same features— investors ripped off, pension holders ripped off, employees often left with nothing, and executives walking away with millions. What if we applied the favorite words of NCLB—*transparency* and *accountability*—to corporations? What if?

In reading school board mission statements, one needs to get beyond the hot air and ask the same questions as when reading corporate business plans: Whom do they serve?

Mission Statements: What Do They Mean and What Do They Hide?

These days, everybody from dentists to doughnut makers must proclaim mission statements. Mostly, school boards are no exception, though Houston and New York City's missions aren't apparent on their websites, and they don't answer queries. Houston does have a purpose: "The Houston Independent School District exists to strengthen the social and economic foundation of Houston by assuring its youth the highest-quality elementary and secondary education available anywhere." Houston's Declaration of Beliefs was coauthored by school board member Rod Paige. It became the foundation for outsourcing school services and insourcing input from business. Traveling under various guises, *economics* pops up in lots of mission statements. Not as the actual word but as an underlying theme. Watch for its permutations: *productive employment* and *productive lives*, or, in billionaire Eli Broad's words, *future knowledge workers*. Such language reveals the extent to which the Business Roundtable agenda and myth making dominate school boards.

With mission statements, you have to figure out what's driving the sales pitch. Take a look at the Cambridge, Massachusetts, mission in all its high-toned malarkey. There is a whole lot of corporate malfeasance and subterfuge behind a phrase like *educate all of its students at high levels*. Not to mention a whole lot of ruined lives.

> Mission: The Cambridge Public Schools will work with families and the community to successfully educate all of its students at high levels. The school system will provide all students with a safe and nurturing environment and with a core curriculum that is rich and rigorous and which respects diversity in student's [*sic*] learning styles.

Across the river, Boston calls its statement Unifying Goal of Focus on Children II: "Accelerate the continuous improvement of teaching and learning to enable all students to meet high standards." Nothing here about a rich curriculum or a nurturing environment. In comparison, Cambridge is warm and cozy. The Boston code words reveal an intent to turn children into pawns of the twenty-first-century global economy: *all students* and *high standards*.

Some say why get agitated: nobody believes mission statements any more than we believe ads for beer commercials, those email promises of organ enlargement, or the promises of financial windfalls from Nigeria. Mission statements are high-minded: the flag, Mom, and apple pie transmogrified into all kids doing it all. But even if we concede that these pretentious statements are public relations pitches, surely the boards of education who issue them have something in mind. Not all board policy is driven by a corporate-politico agenda; some even seem left over from kinder, gentler times. Smile, if you wish, at the following mission, which appears to have been written by the sixth-grade cheerleading coach; the enthusiasm is refreshing. Hats off to whoever dares utter *self-esteem* these days. Kudos, too, to West Springfield, Massachusetts, where children's joy is a stated mission:

> The purpose of the West Springfield Public Schools is to educate all students, enabling them to experience the joy of reaching their full potential.

As schools eliminate playgrounds, recess, kindergarten blocks, and fingerpaints, as they chronicle the vomit on test days, is this statement mind-boggling, or what? These days, seeing *joy* and *schools* in the same sentence provokes a gasp of wonder. It seems especially significant that a Massachusetts school board, ruled as it is by onerous state standards, would choose to display such a statement. The sublimity of encountering *joy* almost wipes out the wretched jargon of *enabling* and the near-jargon of *full potential*.

Plenty of the mission statements reek of backroom cigar smoke and corporate-politico handshakes, but take heart: with *world-class* standards infecting so many education plans, we found only one school board intent on producing *world-class children*. Of course, *technological society* and *world of tomorrow* ooze their way into the rhetoric; they are all just euphemisms for the global economy, which is what this is all about. As many have noted, it's a mean economy, cruising the world for cheap labor. Note how many education plans promise to *deliver* the goods. Springfield, Massachusetts, actually claims to *deliver educational experiences*. We want to ask: via Fed Ex, U.S. Postal Service, or conveyor belt from a central warehouse? Kansas City promises to *produce* students who are competitive—as though educating children were like growing mushrooms. While St. Louis and DeKalb County offer a *guarantee*, Salt Lake City gives *ensurance*.

Does anybody believe that New Haven designs curricula and the school day to meet students' *social needs*? If true, this would make New Haven unique in the United States and maybe in the universe. New Haven's mission statement needs a footnote documenting the child abuse associated with preparing for what the superintendent termed the "die-on-your-sword exam."[3] Substitutes are hired while veteran teachers are pulled from their classes to do nothing but test prep on those bubble kids who might pass. The *Hartford Courant* reports, "Recess is a relic of the past." And here's how one mother describes her son's reaction to school:

> My son comes home tired, bored of the rigid academic day. Sometimes he cries at night from the deluge of homework—"I hate school, Mom,"—tears rolling down his red face and trembling hands. He's completely stressed out over enormous amounts of homework and test preparations. Quite honestly I do not blame him. How come one test holds so much weight?"[4]

How come, indeed.

> The New Haven [Connecticut] Public Schools will provide all students with learning opportunities designed to meet their academic and social needs. Curriculum content, technological assistance and instructional strategies will be integrated to raise student expectations, to ensure students' performance mastery, and to maximize student motivation.

Read with care the following mission statements from school districts across the country. Ask yourself why every word is there: what does it mean and what does it hide? Ask yourself who profits. Which statements seem to be emanating from a public relations echo chamber? As you read each mission, put yourself in the shoes of the five-year-olds, eight-year-olds, thirteen-year-olds, and eighteen-year-olds in that district. Does this sound like a happy place to be? A fit place for a child you love?

- *Albuquerque:* Every child graduates fully prepared and eager to become a world-class citizen.
- *Alexandria Township, New Jersey:* The Alexandria Township Board of Education is committed to the belief that the public schools of the district exist for the nurture and instruction of the children of the district.
- *Alexandria, Minnesota:* To achieve excellence as we prepare all students to be lifelong learners, communicators, decision-makers, and ethical, responsible citizens.
- *Alexandria, Virginia:* The fundamental goal of the Alexandria City School division is to enable each student to develop the skills that are necessary for success in school and preparation for life.
- *Ames, Iowa:* The mission of the Ames Community Schools is to ensure that all learners develop the knowledge, skills, attitudes, values, and personal esteem necessary to grow in and shape a changing society.
- *Anchorage:* Mission: To educate all students for success in life.
- *Baltimore:* The mission of the BCPSS [Baltimore City Public School System], in concert with students, families, and the broader community, is to prepare all students to be responsible citizens and afford them the opportunity to acquire the skills, knowledge, and abilities necessary to make informed decisions that lead to meaningful and productive lives. To this end, the Board believes that all children can learn and achieve, when given the proper resources and that high standards and expectations must be maintained through a system of accountability for all students, staff and schools. School readiness is critical to success, as is the engagement of parents and families, and business and community members. Each child should be entitled to a

high quality education in the least restrictive environment. Respect must be shown to all individuals and to the varied cultures and ethnic groups that make up the BCPSS community.

- *Charlotte-Mecklenburg, North Carolina:* The vision is to ensure that Charlotte-Mecklenburg Schools becomes [*sic*] the premier urban, integrated school system in the nation in which all students acquire the knowledge, skills and values necessary to live rich and full lives as productive and enlightened members of society.

- *Chicago:* The Chicago Public Schools will be the premier urban school district in the country by providing all our students and their families with high quality instruction, outstanding academic programs, and comprehensive student development supports to prepare them for the challenges of the world of tomorrow.

- *Concord, New Hampshire:* The mission of the Concord School District is to enable every student to acquire and demonstrate the skills, knowledge and attitudes essential to be a responsible world citizen committed to personal, family and community well-being.

- *DeKalb County, Georgia:* The mission of the DeKalb County School System, a major unifying force of our unique, diverse community, is to guarantee that each learner develops individual potential and becomes a contributing citizen through an educational system characterized by safe, nurturing environments; student-centered, creative learning; an active, collaborating community; and the management of all resources in an efficient, effective, and equitable manner. *"Every student will achieve."*

- *Detroit:* To develop a customer and data-driven, student centered learning environment in which students are motivated to become productive citizens and life-long learners, equipped with skills to meet the needs of their next customer, higher education or the world of work.

- *Fairbanks:* The mission of the Fairbanks North Star Borough School District is to create knowledgeable, self-sufficient, and compassionate citizens through an educational experience of unconditional respect for others and an uncompromising commitment to excellence.

- *Hartford, Wisconsin:* District Mission Statement: The SDH [School District of Hartford] is dedicated to the success of each student through the active participation of students, staff, family and community. Together, we will create an academically challenging environment and a desire for life-long learning.

- *Kansas City:* It is the Mission of the Kansas City Missouri School District to produce students with knowledge, skills, abilities and attitudes to become life-long learners, with the capacity for leadership and service. They will be productive and responsible citizens capable of successfully competing in a changing global society.

- *Los Angeles:* The teachers, administrators and staff of the Los Angeles Unified School District believe in the equal worth and dignity of all students and are committed to educate all students to their maximum potential.

- *Milwaukee:* The Milwaukee Public Schools will ensure that maximum educational opportunities are provided for all students to reach their highest potential so that:

  1. Students achieve their educational and employment goals, and

  2. Parents choose the Milwaukee Public Schools to educate their children.

- *Niobara (Wyoming) County School District #1:*

  High expectations

  Effective teaching

  Lifelong learning

  Positive self-esteem

- *Pembroke, New Hampshire:* The Pembroke School District is committed to preparing each student with the integrated knowledge, skills, and character necessary to achieve, contribute, and thrive throughout life by creating an environment distinguished by excellence and dedicated to the betterment of the community.

- *Pittsburgh:*

  Do What?   Provide world class educational opportunities for

  For Whom?   *All* students, one child at a time,

  How?   By providing outstanding teachers, programs and services which enable *All* students to be successful and contributing citizens.

- *Sacramento County:* The mission of the Sacramento County Office of Education, a customer-driven educational leader and agent for change in the county, region and state, is to support the preparation of students for a changing and global 21st century society, through a continuously improving system of partnerships and coordinated services for our diverse community.

- *St. Louis:* The St. Louis Public School District is a gateway to the 21st century. It guarantees all students a quality education. We will set the highest standards and demand the highest achievement, which will enable our students to become productive workers, citizens and contributors to our democratic and increasingly technological society.

- *Salt Lake City:* The Salt Lake City School District, as a catalyst for creating a new standard of educational excellence, will ensure high levels of student learning and performance in all schools and will prepare all students to pursue and celebrate lives of continuous learning and service in a diverse, global society.

- *San Diego:* The mission of San Diego City Schools is to improve student achievement by supporting teaching and learning in the classroom.

- *San Francisco:* The mission of the San Francisco Unified School District is to provide each student with an equal opportunity to succeed by promoting intellectual growth, creativity, self-discipline, cultural and linguistic sensitivity, democratic responsibility, economic competence, and physical and mental health so that each student can achieve his or her maximum potential.

- *Springfield, Missouri:* The mission of the Springfield Public Schools is to provide all students the opportunity to develop the knowledge, discipline, skills, and abilities necessary to reach their potential, adapt to continuing change and contribute positively to society.

- *Springfield, Oregon:* The Springfield Public Schools, in collaboration with parents and community, shall develop in all students the knowledge, understanding, skills and attitudes to empower them to become responsible, life-long learners and productive citizens in an ever-changing world. This will be accomplished in a climate that promotes high expectations, strives to meet individual needs, and values diversity.

- *Springfield, Massachusetts:* The mission of the Springfield Public Schools is to build a Culture of Achievement in all schools and classrooms that ensures the delivery of educational experiences in which all learners achieve success. A Culture of Achievement is a system-wide focus on achievement in which behaviors reflect belief that all learners can achieve. The system-wide goal is to maximize opportunities to learn so that all students can achieve the standards.

- *Springfield, New Jersey:* The Springfield Public School District is committted [*sic*] to providing high quality, efficient educational programs that are second to none. Every effort is made to ensure that the district's certificated and support personnel are among the best in their fields. The staff and Board of Education are dedicated to maintaining excellence in the delivery of child-centered educational programs. Very simply stated, in Springfield . . . **Schools are for kids!** (Emphasis in original.)

- *Springfield, Minnesota:* The mission of Springfield Public School, District 085, is to guide individuals to acquire knowledge, skills, and positive attitudes toward themselves and others. This should enable students to solve problems, think creatively, continue learning, and to develop maximum potential for leading productive lives.
- *Wake County, North Carolina:* The Wake County Public School System will educate each student to be a responsible and productive citizen who can effectively manage future challenges.

Some mission statements are surprising: Who would expect Alexandria, Virginia, in the hotbed of Standardista country, to deliver such a brief and modest statement? Look at San Diego's, where an adjective eraser must be on staff. And Anchorage's is briefer. On the other hand, who is surprised by Chicago's braggadocio? Looks like Charlotte-Mecklenburg has the same corporate-inspired competitive mission. Houston is a bit more understated, but it has put itself in the running for the same spot. Hawking numero uno as though school districts were just so many potato chips or cleansing agents.

Mission Statements Shift with the Times

1999   The mission of the Denver Public Schools, the center of learning for the community, is to guarantee that our children and youth acquire knowledge, skills, and values to become self-sufficient citizens by providing personalized learning experiences for all students in innovative partnership with all segments of the community.

2002   The Mission of the Denver Public Schools is to provide all students the opportunity to achieve the knowledge and skills necessary to become contributing citizens in our diverse society.

So the guarantee *and* personalized learning are gone. In their place is the "opportunity to achieve."

Opportunity is the weasel word of the global economy—brought to your neighborhood school by a corporate Standardista; he offers opportunity instead of money for building repairs. Then, in a hand-washing gesture, school boards declare that every kid has the opportunity to learn, but those who don't master algebra and other material business leaders have named high priority will be pushed out without a high school diploma. These push-outs are told, "You had the opportunity to learn; it's not our fault if you blew it." Denver is far from unique in putting *knowledge and skills necessary* at the center of its mission. With that mission, then Denver needs to "standardize learning materials within schools and improve consistency and articulation of programs" and to "monitor implementation of the board adopted grade specific curriculum that is aligned with district and state content standards." Furthermore, it will "[a]lign and integrate district Pay for Performance with state and district assessments."[5] When teachers' salaries depend on the performance of their students on an aligned and standardized curriculum, who will be eager to teach the nonstandard kids?

When functionaries start talking about *alignment*, parents and teachers need to watch their backs, their pockets, and, most of all, their children. Most children are out of alignment, and a policy of pushing round pegs into square holes causes destructive contortions of spirit and sanity.

When the CEOs Come Marching In

If the New York City Department of Education has a mission statement, it is well hidden. A query to the schools chancellor went unanswered. On July 29, 2002, Mayor Michael Bloomberg used his new powers to appoint Joel Klein as first chancellor under the new governance legislation, which gives the mayor control over New York's public school system. To make the appointment legal, state education commissioner and corporate party man Richard P. Mills quickly waived Klein's lack of professional education qualifications. Klein brings to the city's 1.1 million students his brief tenure as CEO of Bertelsmann, Inc., and his years of experience as assistant attorney general in charge of the Department of Justice's Antitrust Division, where he led the prosecution in the Microsoft case. These days, the corporate-politico-media alliance shuns experience in education as an asset; we are likely to witness similar shenanigans as mayors in a score of big cities scramble to get the same picking rights.

New York provides an opportunity to look at how the corporate-politico-infotainment crew operates. After five months on the job, Klein and the mayor announced the formation of Leadership Academy, a new training academy for principals. The media swooned in admiration as retired General Electric CEO Jack Welch Jr. was hailed as a major adviser to the academy, with hints that Welch would also offer his teaching skills. Breathless news accounts describe Welch as the executive who "turned around GE," not mentioning the human cost of his policies. People who lived in GE cities such as Schenectady, New York, and Pittsfield, Massachusetts, know firsthand how Welch earned the epithet Neutron Jack. Massive layoffs and union busting had the effect of a neutron bomb: the buildings were left standing—the people emptied out. As Schenectady and Pittsfield workers kept increasing productivity, Jack kept downsizing and outsourcing. GE stock soared as the cities deteriorated. In *Growing Up Fast*, Joanna Lipper chronicles the rise in teen pregnancies as Pittsfield's fortunes plummeted.[6] All sorts of social institutions have failed these teens, but most of all GE's perfidy looms large, and it seems worse than hypocritical for Neutron Jack to be held up as a role model for principals.

Forbes.com quoted Welch as saying of the new schools job, "This is a real chance to take a swing at something and make it sensational." Welch added, "We used to say in the corporation, 'any one of you jerk managers who's got a dull crowd hanging around with you don't [*sic*] deserve your job.' . . . We'll challenge principals in the same way."[7]

Yes, let's scrap any notion of schools as places to nurture children. Let's just challenge those principals who we know must be jerks. As to whether the *dull crowd* refers to teachers or students, just ask Jack.

Next, Klein hired Robert E. Knowling Jr., a corporate executive whose current press release bio doesn't mention that he was forced out at Covad, which went from boom to bust when he was at the helm, as first chief executive officer of the new Leadership Academy. Not long on the job, Knowling announced that he was astounded by "the perpetuation of incompetency" throughout the system.[8] He also declared to the *New York Times* that while just 15 percent of the workforce was "excellent," another 15 percent was "incapable."[9] He must have been reading Neutron Jack's autobiography. How could someone, in just four months on the job, without an intimate knowledge of schools in general and the New York City system in particular, pinpoint the abilities of twelve hundred people performing one of the most complex jobs in the world? Might someone ask what criteria Knowling used? So far, the media hasn't bothered.

Could there be a business formula afoot? Jack Welch, after all, was known for forcing top managers at General Electric to identify the bottom 10 percent of their staffs and make them leave.[10] Two things seem apparent: First, by his standards, Knowling is moving slowly in New York City. Second, principals had better get flak jackets. What also seems apparent is that Neutron Jack's playbook has been sent to other large-city districts. In early May 2003, Massachusetts governor Mitt Romney proposed giving principals of struggling public schools the power to eliminate up to 10 percent of their faculty and to create summer schools for other teachers. In the new corporate-managed schools, what's good for corporate America's bottom line is good for America's schoolchildren and their teachers.

Conspiracy theorists can ponder why news articles puffing the Leadership Academy are posted on the Small Schools website.[11] Probably there's no conspiracy; it's just a matter of keeping links to where the money is.

Under mayoral control, New York City lacks a school board. Here's the Leadership Academy Board of Directors:

- Peter A. Glaherty, director of McKinsey and Company, Inc., a management consulting firm advising the top management of leading companies and institutions.
- Joel I. Klein, chancellor of the New York City Department of Education.
- Robert E. Knowling Jr., chief executive officer.

- Diana Lam, deputy chancellor for teaching and learning (forced out March 8, 2004).
- Sy Sternberg, chairman and CEO of New York Life Insurance Company.
- Kathryn S. Wylde, president and CEO of Partnership for New York City, a network of business leaders "dedicated to enhancing the economy of the five boroughs." By June 2003, the Partnership had raised $15 million of the $30 million pledged to the academy. The $15 million came from the following Partner companies and Partners: AOL Time Warner; the Bank of New York; Bowne and Company, Inc.; the Hearst Corporation; J. P. Morgan Chase and Company; KeySpan; Mr. Kravis; News Corporation; New York Life Insurance Company; Russell L. Carson, general partner of Welsh, Carson, Anderson and Stowe; the Rudin Family; and Jerry I. Speyer of Tishman Speyer Properties.

And here's the Advisory Board:

- Anthony Alvarado, identified simply as the former chancellor of the New York City Board of Education and co–vice chairman. Alvarado was ousted from New York City and was also forced out of his position as chancellor of San Diego Schools. The Broad Foundation may be the link bringing Alvarado back to New York. The foundation financed Klein and Lam's Children First plan, which mirrors San Diego's Blueprint for Student Success, also funded by the Broad Foundation.
- Robert Arning, New York office managing partner of KPMG, LLP, a financial company operating "in the global business arena."
- Russell L. Carson, general partner of Welsh, Carson, Anderson, and Stowe, who bill themselves as the leading private equity investor in information services, health care, and communications.
- David Coulter, vice chairman of J. P. Morgan Chase and Company, which describes itself as a "global financial services firm with assets of $793 billion."
- Robert M. Johnson, chairman and CEO of Browne and Company, Inc., whose website subhead is "Empowering Your Information." One of its services is "Developing concepts and designs of brochures, conference materials and road-show presentations by experienced designers for print and production in almost any format."
- Richard Parsons, CEO of AOL Time Warner, co–vice chairman, whose mandate in April 2002 was to get AOL Time Warner's notoriously autonomous divisions working for the good of the whole company. It didn't quite work out that way.
- John F. Welch, former CEO of General Electric, chairman.

These are the people who are going to train principals on how to make their schools joyful, nurturing places. No, wait a minute: That's passé. Joy is not on the agenda these days; neither is nurture. This team will train principals on how to make their schools into efficient, competitive conveyor belts to the global economy. Ask yourself: would you let this crew baby-sit your kids?

Wanting to be in charge, Mayor Bloomberg persuaded the New York State Department of Education to waive the laws and disband the school board. Replacing it is the handpicked-by-the-mayor New York City Panel for Education Policy. In March 2004, to make sure a crucial vote on retaining third graders went his way, Bloomberg axed three wavering board members right before the vote. *New York Daily News* reporters noted, "It was a political hit that would make Tony Soprano blush." But Bloomberg explained, "This is what mayoral control is all about. Mayoral control means mayoral control, thank you very much. They are my representatives, and they are going to vote for things that I believe in."[12]

Casting a Broad Net of Influence

According to the Broad Foundation website, its plan is to "redefine the traditional roles, practices, and policies of school board members, superintendents, principals, and labor union leaders to better address contemporary challenges in education." Broad's deep pockets means it gets to define those challenges. Follow Broad money: A pattern emerges of business and foundation money moving in on local elections. Founder Eli Broad was influential in getting the Los Angeles superintendency for former Colorado governor Roy Romer, and it's no coincidence that the Broad Foundation gave its first urban ed prize to Houston—with Rod Paige at the helm. A tight circle of backslapping and influence peddling reigns.

Writing in the *San Diego Reader*, Matt Potter asked, "Why would two obscure East Coast liberal foundations unite with some of the most conservative and wealthiest of San Diego business interests in a secretive attempt to defeat incumbent board member Frances O'Neill Zimmerman?"[13] The answer is that Los Angeles billionaire Eli Broad's money reaches far and wide—from California school boards to East Coast foundations with liberal ties. In 1999, Broad teamed up with then–Los Angeles mayor Richard Riordan and Ron Burkle to get what they called a reform-minded school board elected. According to the *Los Angeles Daily News*, funds from the Coalition for Kids, created by Riordan and Broad, broke the union stranglehold over the Los Angeles Unified School District.[14] The *Los Angeles Times* agreed, also tabbing Riordan's manipulations as "reform."[15] A *Times* editorial praised Riordan and "the business-led Committee on Effective School Governance" for supporting school board reform candidates who would "hold greedy labor demands at bay

... and put improving student achievement ahead of teachers union wish lists." The alternative press put it differently. Writing in *LA Weekly*, Howard Blume noted, "Most of the money is from the pockets of the mayor himself and dozens of his closest rich friends and associates."[16] With big money being spent to dump three incumbents from their $24,000-per-year low-profile jobs, the operation is known as the most expensive school board campaign in the country's history. Incumbent George Kiriyama, a former teacher and school principal who was supported by the teachers union, raised $138,000 to fund his campaign. The Riordan-Broad Coalition for Kids handed Kiriyama's opponent $771,000. One incumbent called the Riordan-Broad enterprise a "naked power grab"; at a news conference, Rev. Robert Holt, chaplain for the Black American Political Association of California, told the mayor, "We object to your colonial mentality and your unmitigated gall in trying to select our leader."[17]

For those who think any big-business involvement is a conservative conspiracy, take a look at former California state senator Jack O'Connell's run for state superintendent of schools; he was backed by the California Teachers Association and the California Federation of Teachers, who together gave him more than $370,000. Eli Broad kicked in $100,000, and Reed Hastings, the president of the State Board of Education, gave $250,000.[18] Both Broad and Burkle are big contributors to the Democratic Party, spreading maximum donations to senators across the country. Hastings gave $350,000 to Governor Gray Davis' 2002 reelection bid. In summer 2003, Hastings was listed as one of Howard Dean's connections.

Not surprisingly, the Broad Foundation is enthusiastic about the way Chicago runs its schools. On August 21, 2001, the Broad Foundation and the American Productivity and Quality Center (APQC), which identifies itself as a nonprofit organization and "a recognized leader in benchmarking, knowledge management and best-practice information," announced that Chicago's school district had been chosen as a national model for leadership and principal development in our nation's public schools. The Broad Foundation's Benchmarking Project was putting up $600,000 to identify what works in public schools. "By mining the knowledge and experiences of successful school districts and then helping other districts use that knowledge and experience, this program aims to accelerate the gains in the bottom line—improved student achievement and school system performance," said Eli Broad.[19]

Mining the knowledge and experience. What a metaphor. What a reality. Dig right in.

According to Forbes 400, at $3.8 billion, Eli Broad places forty-fifth in U.S. wealth.[20] Number eighty-two in world's richest. You have to be quick on your feet to keep up with new Broad projects to reform education. On October 8, 2002, a press release from the U.S. Conference of Mayors and the Broad Foundation announced the intention of this new partnership to publish joint reports on "mayoral efforts to improve public schools, develop new ideas for federal education policymakers, and hold a mayors' education summit" in 2003.[21] Eli Broad addressed the conference, saying, "At The Broad Foundation, we recognize that leadership—bold new leadership—is critical if we are ever going to see the dramatic gains in student achievement that children across America deserve. Schools that fail to teach our children the skills necessary to participate and to succeed in our changing economy are infringing on each student's civil rights."[22]

There's that emphasis on schooling for the economy again, as though schools had any control over minimum wage, outsourcing jobs to Asia, policies of the World Bank, and so on. And by conflating high test scores with civil rights and co-opting those who raise alarms about the growing segregation of U.S. schools, *high standards for all* rhetoric hides the fact that minority and poor students are being ghettoized into dead-end, underfinanced, drill-and-kill, low-performing schools. Participants in conferences like this mayors conference carefully avoid talking about the crumbling neighborhoods surrounding troubled schools. Other participants in this so-called education summit included Sandra Feldman, president of the American Federation of Teachers; Michael Casserly, executive director of the Council of Great City Schools; and Lisa Graham Keegan, president of the Education Leaders Council; as well as other education experts, unnamed in press releases.[23]

Did you notice who's missing? The mayors are there. School boards aren't. The Broad website includes a heroes page. Headed by Rod Paige, it is a high-stakes testing crew par excellence. Take a look at <*www.broadfoundation. org/heroes/venture-net.shtml*>.

Here is a list of the participants at the 2002 Broad Foundation strategic planning retreat. Look at the list and notice that you can't label this group liberal or conservative: Standardistas cross party lines. In the foundation's words, "The Foundation solicited guidance on how best to scale-up current Foundation investments and develop new high-impact policy initiatives."[24] What fun: getting invited to figure out how to spend the foundation's $400 million. The participants: Arlene Ackerman, superintendent, San Francisco Unified School District; Richard C. Atkinson, president, University of California; Alan Bersin, superintendent, San Diego City Schools; Dominic Brewer, director, RAND Education; Dennis Chaconas, superintendent, Oakland Unified School District; Robert Chase, former president, National Education Association; Rudolph F. Crew, director, the Stupski Foundation; John Danielson, chief of staff, U.S. Department of Education; Chester Finn, president, Thomas B. Fordham Foundation; Patricia Harvey, superintendent, St. Paul Public Schools; Genethia Hudley Hayes, board member, Los Angeles Unified School District; David Hornbeck, founder, Good Schools Pennsylvania;

James Hunt, former governor, State of North Carolina; Nancy Ichinaga, member, California State Board of Education; Joel Klein, chancellor, New York City Department of Education; Wendy Kopp, president, Teach for America; Robin Kramer, senior fellow, California Community Foundation; Diana Lam, superintendent, Providence Public Schools; Arthur Levine, president, Columbia University Teachers College; Tom Luce, chairman, National Center for Educational Accountability; Joe Lucente, board president, California Network of Educational Charters; Don McAdams, executive director, Center for Reform of School Systems; Richard L. McCormick, president, University of Washington; Theodore Mitchell, president, Occidental College; Barry Munitz, president and chief executive officer, J. Paul Getty Trust; Mark Murray, president, Grand Valley State University; Joseph Olchefske, superintendent, Seattle Public Schools; Ron Ottinger, board member, San Diego City Schools; William Ouchi, professor, the Anderson School at University of California at Los Angeles; Roderick R. Paige, U.S. secretary of education; Tim Quinn, president, Michigan Leadership Institute; Richard Riordan, former mayor, City of Los Angeles; Nancy Daly-Riordan, children's rights activist; Waldemar "Bill" Rojas, former superintendent, Dallas Public Schools; Steven Sample, president, University of Southern California; Jay Schenirer, board member, Sacramento City Unified School District; Jon Schnur, CEO, New Leaders for New Schools; William Siart, president, ExED, LLC; Kim Smith, president, New Schools Venture Fund; Glen Tripp, president, Galileo Educational Services; Adam Urbanski, president, Rochester (New York) Teachers Association; Michael Usdan, senior adviser, Institute for Educational Leadership; Carolyn Webb de Macias, senior associate provost, University of Southern California; Randi Weingarten, president, United Federation of Teachers; Caprice Young, board president, Los Angeles Unified School District.

With throwaway lines about U.S. schoolchildren being "at the back of the pack of industrialized nations," the demands of globalization and free trade, and what "our 21st Century information economy requires," Broad hammers home the point that our "public education system is not providing our young people with the knowledge and skills necessary to become future knowledge workers." *Future knowledge workers.* It's a phrase that reeks of Business Roundtable hypocrisy. Why are so many college graduate *knowledge workers* out of work? "As we enter this new century, our nation's continued prosperity rests on a strongly educated, highly skilled workforce," Broad intoned in "Preparing Leaders for the New Economy" in *School Administrator*.[25] Fran Zimmerman, the school board member Broad wanted ousted from San Diego, told the *Los Angeles Times*, "He's dabbling in social policy with all his money, and affecting change with it, but it's not necessarily good change, and it's not really school reform."[26] She emphasized, "It's basically a business agenda for reshaping the public school system."

On April 6, 2003, Eli Broad put out a call for school boards to stop being part of the problem and become part of the solution. The Broad Foundation supports what it terms *leadership capacity-building initiatives,* promoting corporate-style school management in cities from Seattle to Atlanta. They include training for superintendents and board members, support for charter school development, and demonstration projects such as a merit pay plan in Denver.[27] In addition to the Broad Prize for Urban Education, there's the Broad Center for Superintendents, and the Broad Institute for School Boards.

On August 7, the Broad Foundation announced a first-of-its-kind residency program to recruit young business leaders for intensive management training and placement in urban school districts across the country. The program "seeks to attract talented young MBAs . . . and train them for managerial positions in the central operations of urban school districts." Broad will pay 75 percent of their $80,000 residency salary, with local districts picking up the rest. The plan is that "the residents will receive mentoring from district superintendents as well as hands-on experience in transforming a large public institution into a high-performing organization focused on raising student achievement."[28] Residents will be placed in senior-level positions in Chicago, Oakland, Philadelphia, New York City, and San Diego public school districts. Eli Broad said, "I am thrilled to see so many dedicated young leaders eager to use their leadership and management skills to remedy the inequities in urban education." Funny thing: Broad isn't shipping any Harvard MBAs to Houston, winner of the 2002 Broad prize for best urban district in the country.

In *Better Leaders for America's Schools: A Manifesto* (May 2003), the Broad Foundation and the Thomas B. Fordham Institute jointly proclaimed:

> It is no more essential for every education leader to be a teacher than for the CEO of Bristol-Meyers Squibb to be a chemist. In any organization, the similarities between technical and leadership roles and skills are incidental and the differences fundamental.[29]

Singled out by Broad and Fordham as exemplary in this model are

Joel Klein, Office of White House Council during the Clinton administration; superintendent of New York City

Roy Romer, chair of the Education Commission of the State; chair of the national Democratic Party; Colorado governor; superintendent of Los Angeles

John Freyer, major general U.S. Air Force; commandant of the National War College; interim president of the National Defense University; superintendent of Duval County, Jacksonville

Paul Vallas, policy adviser, Illinois state senate; Chicago city budget director; unsuccessful Democratic candidate for Illinois governor in 2002; superintendent of Chicago and Philadelphia

Alan Bersin, federal prosecutor; superintendent of San Diego

Paula Dawning, sales vice president of AT&T; superintendent of Benton Harbor, Michigan

On September 9, 2003, President Bush announced a partnership between the Broad Foundation and the U.S. Department of Education, "To improve our country's public education system."[30] They call it an unprecedented public-private collaboration. The third partner is Just for the Kids. They're combining "$4.7 million of federal funds with $50.9 million in private philanthropy to effectively lower the cost barriers associated with the data collection, analysis and reporting mandates of NCLB." Standard and Poor's is lending a hand. The deal is that the partners offer a website "that transforms disaggregated student achievement data into useful decision-making information." It will be free for two years. They call it private philanthropy. McGraw-Hill, owner of Standard and Poor's, Open Court, and Direct Instruction, as a leader in philanthropy for the good of children?

It is difficult to present all this information in a way that approaches comprehensibility. Keep your eye on Broad and you'll be watching a sophisticated, many-faceted plan for dismantling the local control of schools.

Worth an aside, perhaps, is another recipient of Broad largesse: the Broad Foundation supports coverage of leadership issues in *Education Week*. One can wonder if "America's online newspaper of record" would ever bite the hand that feeds it.

Changing Structures

As corporate interests have revved up their efforts to bring the structure of public school systems in line with the structures of the new economy, subverting the autonomy of school boards gets primary focus. The Danforth Foundation 1992 report *Facing the Challenge: The Report of the Twentieth Century Fund Task Force on School Governance* argued that the debate about the future of education in America would have limited impact "until the role of governance is addressed and the questions of how basic decisions are made is answered."[31] The report explained that school boards are obstacles to reform when they "interfere with the day-to-day tasks of administration of their districts that is properly the realm of the professional administrator."[32] The corporate party line is that so-called disinterested school boards need to focus on broad educational policy instead of what Danforth terms *constituent service*. On the other hand, Danforth observes, "boards recognize that they need leadership training as well as dialogue with the community to define areas of governance responsibility if they are better to meet constituents' expectations." The distinction between constituent *service* and *expectations* is instructive.

Writing in *Phi Delta Kappan*, J. P. Danzberger, one of the authors of the report, argued that the problem with school boards is that they are

> not structurally suited to govern effectively in an increasingly divisive society that is facing unprecedented social and economic challenges. The American public increasingly uses the public schools to fulfill immediate political demands (from creationism to Afro-centrism), at the same time that society faces the challenge of the need to improve schooling and increase educational achievement for all students.[33]

Danzberger worries that conflict "can be devastating for school systems attempting to effect long-range systemic reform." But to argue that debates over content are political and that school policy is *not* political suggests an alignment with propaganda rather than research. Or an inordinate passion for tidiness. As desert polemicist and rebel Edward Abbey observed, "The best cure for the ills of democracy is more democracy."[34] More democracy for schools—what a revolutionary notion.

The Assault on School Boards

Whether it's banning pentagrams in New Mexico, casting hexes in Louisiana, throwing a punch in Montana, offering bribes in Kentucky, declaring the need for slamming bratty students up against the wall to put the fear of God into them in Florida, or suing for the right to sprinkle voodoo powder outside the superintendent's office in New York City, stories of dysfunctional, ineffectual, and just plain loony school board members are the stuff of legend. But so what? We see the same vagaries in every human venture. In *Big City School Boards: Problems and Options*, a thirty-one-page report sponsored by the Annie E. Casey Foundation, Paul T. Hill and colleagues at the University of Washington's Center on Reinventing Public Education say the mission of urban school boards is muddled.[35] An appendix lists the various duties assigned to school boards in six states, and the list is indeed staggering. The paper presents possible solutions that are making the rounds: broaden the boards' constituency through mayoral appointment or districtwide elections; limit their powers and thereby get them out of day-to-day management and patronage. It's the third suggestion that is unique and the one that sparked an enthusiastic response from Chester Finn at the Thomas Fordham B. Foundation: eliminate a board's "exclusive authority to oversee schools in a particular geographical area." This plan calls for adding multiple boards or other competing entities. The idea is that competition breeds achievement—for school boards as well as for widget makers. Lead author Paul

Hill is a distinguished visiting fellow at the Hoover Institution and a member of the Koret Task Force on K–12 Education. He is also a nonresident senior fellow in the Brookings Institution's Economic Studies Program.

Why have school boards at all? asked *Washington Post* editorial page editor Fred Hiatt in an op-ed.[36] Hiatt's reasoning is we don't elect our city police chief or our county health commissioner, and nobody sees this as a denial of democracy. Why not let our elected mayors and city or county councils—the people who make the budgets—take similar responsibility for public schools? Hiatt quotes Michael Usdan, president of the Institute for Educational Leadership, who argues that today's separation of school boards from the rest of local government impedes the cooperation needed to deal with complex, diverse populations in cities and inner suburbs.

Guess Who's Coming to Dinner—and Breakfast and Lunch?

For a quick look at how business intrudes itself into the business of education—and those educationists who welcome the intrusion—take a look at the program for the Annual Conference of the National Association of State Boards of Education (Figure 5–1).

National Association of State Boards of Education Annual Conference Program

<table>
<tr><td colspan="2" align="center">2002 Annual Conference
October 10–12, 2002
Westin Horton Plaza Hotel
San Diego, California</td></tr>
<tr><td colspan="2">Thursday, Oct. 10
Preconference Activities</td></tr>
<tr><td>7:00 A.M.–1:00 P.M.</td><td>NASBE Foundation Golf Tournament
Torrey Pines Golf Course, La Jolla, CA</td></tr>
<tr><td>8:30 A.M.–5:00 P.M.</td><td>Healthy Schools Network</td></tr>
<tr><td>8:45 A.M.–4:45 P.M.</td><td>High School Institute
Restructuring High Schools:
    From Policy to Practice
    Sponsored by the Carnegie
    Corporation</td></tr>
<tr><td>2:00–3:45 P.M.</td><td>Boardsmanship Institute
"State Board Website Technologies"
Amivtav Thamba</td></tr>
</table>

> Thamba is with Crowe Chizek and Company, in partnership with IBM. In his report to the Indiana Education Roundtable, advocating comprehensive data collection on every student, Thamba said, "doing this costs less than not doing it."

Figure 5–1

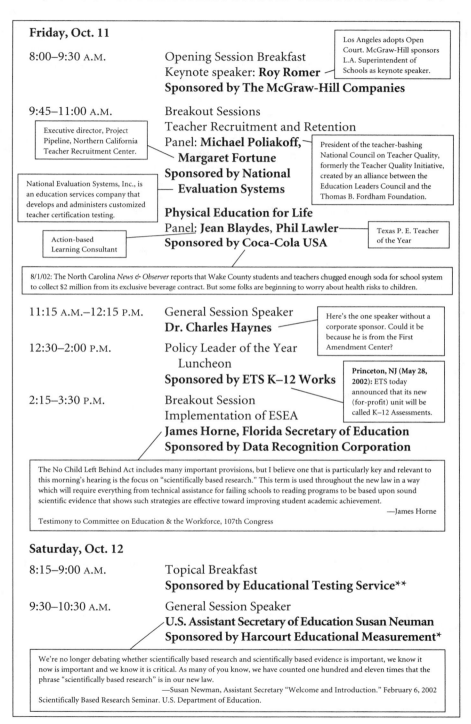

Friday, Oct. 11

8:00–9:30 A.M.

Opening Session Breakfast
Keynote speaker: **Roy Romer**
Sponsored by The McGraw-Hill Companies

Los Angeles adopts Open Court. McGraw-Hill sponsors L.A. Superintendent of Schools as keynote speaker.

9:45–11:00 A.M.

Breakout Sessions
Teacher Recruitment and Retention
Panel: **Michael Poliakoff,**
Margaret Fortune
Sponsored by National
Evaluation Systems

Executive director, Project Pipeline, Northern California Teacher Recruitment Center.

President of the teacher-bashing National Council on Teacher Quality, formerly the Teacher Quality Initiative, created by an alliance between the Education Leaders Council and the Thomas B. Fordham Foundation.

National Evaluation Systems, Inc., is an education services company that develops and administers customized teacher certification testing.

Physical Education for Life
Panel: **Jean Blaydes, Phil Lawler**
Sponsored by Coca-Cola USA

Action-based Learning Consultant

Texas P. E. Teacher of the Year

8/1/02: The North Carolina *News & Observer* reports that Wake County students and teachers chugged enough soda for school system to collect $2 million from its exclusive beverage contract. But some folks are beginning to worry about health risks to children.

11:15 A.M.–12:15 P.M.

General Session Speaker
Dr. Charles Haynes

Here's the one speaker without a corporate sponsor. Could it be because he is from the First Amendment Center?

12:30–2:00 P.M.

Policy Leader of the Year
Luncheon
Sponsored by ETS K–12 Works

Princeton, NJ (**May 28, 2002**): ETS today announced that its new (for-profit) unit will be called K–12 Assessments.

2:15–3:30 P.M.

Breakout Session
Implementation of ESEA
James Horne, Florida Secretary of Education
Sponsored by Data Recognition Corporation

The No Child Left Behind Act includes many important provisions, but I believe one that is particularly key and relevant to this morning's hearing is the focus on "scientifically based research." This term is used throughout the new law in a way which will require everything from technical assistance for failing schools to reading programs to be based upon sound scientific evidence that shows such strategies are effective toward improving student academic achievement.

—James Horne

Testimony to Committee on Education & the Workforce, 107th Congress

Saturday, Oct. 12

8:15–9:00 A.M.

Topical Breakfast
Sponsored by Educational Testing Service**

9:30–10:30 A.M.

General Session Speaker
U.S. Assistant Secretary of Education Susan Neuman
Sponsored by Harcourt Educational Measurement*

We're no longer debating whether scientifically based research and scientifically based evidence is important, we know it now is important and we know it is critical. As many of you know, we have counted one hundred and eleven times that the phrase "scientifically based research" is in our new law.

—Susan Newman, Assistant Secretary "Welcome and Introduction." February 6, 2002

Scientifically Based Research Seminar. U.S. Department of Education.

Figure 5–1. *Continued*

12:15–1:30	General Session Luncheon
New York State Regents Vice Chancellor, she produced the report "Perform or Perish."	**Adelaide Sanford** **Sponsored by Holy [*sic*], Rinehart & Winston and Harcourt School Publishers***
6:00–7:00 P.M.	President's Reception **Sponsored by Houghton Mifflin***
7:00–9:00 P.M.	President's Banquet **Sponsored by NCS/Pearson***

*When Congress increased the 2003–04 budget for the U.S. Department of Education by $11 billion, it set aside $400 million to help states develop and administer the tests mandated by the No Child Left Behind Act for children in grades 3 through 8. Among the likely benefactors of the extra funds are CTB McGraw-Hill, Harcourt Educational Measurement, and Riverside Publishing (a Houghton Mifflin company). According to an October 2001 report in Educational Marketer, CTB McGraw-Hill, Harcourt, and Riverside write 96 percent of the exams administered at the state level. The news has been filled with testing mishaps, but the drumroll for testing continues. An ad for NCS Pearson notes that it is the "nation's largest commercial processor of student assessments serving over 40 statewide K–12 testing programs." It does not mention the terrible mistakes, such as those in Minnesota that prevented seniors who'd passed the state test from graduating because NCS had flubbed the scoring.

**In a rather incredible statement on the Educational Testing Service website, ETS president and CEO Kurt M. Landgraf explains how, through testing, ETS is fighting terrorism.[37]

Figure 5–1.   *Continued*

Notes

1. *www.palmbeach.k12.fl.us/abp-04012003pdf.*

2. Ivins, Molly. 2003. "Corporate Greed at All-Time High." *The Oklahoma Observer*, 10 December.

3. See *www.susanohanian.org/atrocity_fetch.php?id=110.*

4. Gottlieb, Rachel, and Robert A. Frahm. 2002. "Mastery Test Grilling Heats Up." *Hartford Courant*, 19 September.

5. From *http://216.239.53.104/cobrand_univ?q=cache:UaFJ9MCcYsgJ:businessmanuals. dpsk12.org/allocationpdf/03sec-03.pdf+Mission&hl=en&ie=UTF-8.*

6. Lipper, Joanna. 2003. *Growing Up Fast*. New York: Picador.

7. From *www.forbes.com/free_forbes/2003/1006/106.html.*

8. Goodnough, Abby. 2003. "What a Fun Time to Be Working in the New York City Schools." *The New York Times*, 23 May.

9. Ibid.

10. Goodnough, Abby. 2003. "Executive Who Saved G.E. Is to Train School Principals." *The New York Times*, 14 January.

11. See *www.smallschoolsworkshop.org.*

12. Katz, Celeste, Joe Williams, and David Saltonstall. 2004. "Promote Vote Stacked." *New York Daily News*. 16 March. Accessed at *www.nydailynews.com/news/story/174062p-151646c. html*; Herszenhorn, David M. 2004. "Bloomberg Wins on School Tests After Firing Foes." *New York Times*. 16 March. Accessed at *www.nytimes.com/2004/03/16/nyregion/16SCHO.html.*

13. From *www.franzimmerman.com/Stories/SDRPotter102402.html*; also available at *www.substancenews.com/Dec02/letters4.htm*.

14. See *www.dailynews.com/Stories/0,1413,200~25405~1204294,00.html*.

15. "New Era at School Board." 1999. Editorial. *Los Angeles Times*, 15 April.

16. Blume, Howard. 1999. "The Best School Board Money Can Buy." *LA Weekly*, 9–16 April.

17. White, Kerry A. 1998. "Los Angeles Mayor Seeks to Unseat 4 on Board." *Education Week*, 30 September.

18. See *http://schoolsnotjails.com/print.php?sid=107*.

19. American Product and Quality Center. 2001. Press release. 21 August. Accessed at *http://old.apqc.org/about/press/dispPressRelease.cfm?ProductID=1431*.

20. From *www.forbes.com/free_forbes/2003/1006/106.html*.

21. From *http://216.239.51.104/search?q=cache:OhybRzPfuH0J:www.citycleveland.oh.us/mayor/press/2002/200210/021008usconfofmayors.pdf+%22+Eli+Broad%22+Chicago+schools&hl=en&ie=UTF-8*.

22. From *http://216.239.39.104/search?q=cache:OhybRzPfuH0J:www.city.cleveland.oh.us/mayor/press/2002/200210/021008usconfofmayors.pdf+%22mayors%27+education+summit%22+Eli+Broad&hl=en&ie=UTF-8*.

23. See *www.usmayors.org/uscm/news/press_releases/documents/edsummit_092303.pdf*.

24. See *www.broadfoundation.org/about/history-net.shtml*.

25. See *www.aasa.org/publications/sa/2001_03/broad.htm*.

26. Moore, Solomon, and Doug Smith. 2002. "Broad Denies Gift Was Improper." *Los Angeles Times*, 2 November.

27. Ibid.

28. From *www.broadfoundation.org/med-news/2003-0807.shtml*.

29. From *www.broadfoundation.org/med-pubs/BetterLeadersforAmericasSchools.pdf*.

30. Standard and Poor's School Evaluation Services. 2003. Press release. 9 September. Accessed at *www.ses.standardandpoors.com/broad_press_release_9__2003.html*.

31. Twentieth Century Fund Task Force. 1991: 1.

32. Ibid.

33. Danzberger, J. P. 1994. "Governing the Nation's Schools: A Case for Restructuring Local School Boards." *Phi Delta Kappan* 75 (5): 367–73.

34. Abbey, Edward. 1977. *The Journey Home: Some Words in Defence of the American West*. New York: Dutton, 230.

35. See *www.crpe.org/pubs/pdf/schoolBoard_Final.pdf*.

36. Hiatt, Fred. 2002. "What's So Sacred About a School Board?" *The Washington Post*, 6 May.

37. See *www.ets.org/aboutets/issues13.html*.

6

Houston

Where School Business Is a Corporate Affair

The Houston Independent School District superintendent and our HISD board of trustees, all good people, failed to speak up when they knew for years the district's figures for dropout rates were a lie. . . . I hope HISD will soon come clean, face reality and have the courage to publicly address the real issues facing our community instead of claiming on a daily basis that they are the best urban district in the nation.

—Robert Kimball, Houston assistant principal and
whistle-blower, 2003

Ten years as a trustee on the Houston school board convinced Donald McAdams that the "core issue in urban school reform is governance." More specifically, "school reformers must design systems of governance that get politics out of schools." Pay attention what to McAdams means by *politics*: in his universe, public involvement is political and something to be gotten around. Not surprisingly, McAdams argues for appointed or elected-at-large school boards; privatized noneducation functions; expanded charter schools; and voucher programs. McAdams declares that the board must institute every possible reform to "insulate the education of children from direct democratic control."[1] Thus, once again, *reform* travels an ugly road.

Up Close in Houston

McAdams joined the Houston board in 1989, elected at the same time as Rod Paige. We'll get to that, but first a little history is in order.

A detailed look at school board maneuvers in Houston provides insight into what's at stake when school boards operate according to a corporate business model instead of representing multiple (and often rival) goals of schooling. Corporate wheeling and dealing in school matters is certainly not unique to

Texas; the state is just more flamboyant about it. Even without Rod Paige as education czar, there's plenty to be learned from Houston.

The wave of Texas reform started in 1983, when Governor Mark White, a Democrat, needed to make good on his campaign promise to raise teacher pay. The economy had tanked and some legislators balked. Then *Nation at Risk* hit the streets. White named a panel to study teacher raises, choosing billionaire H. Ross Perot, who got rich off government money, to head the Select Committee on Public Education (SCOPE). The flamboyant Perot identified the Texas education problem as a management issue. And then, in his inimitable way, Perot announced, "We've got to drop a bomb on them. We've got to nuke them. That's the way you change these organizations."[2] As Eli Broad and Bill Gates would do two decades later, Perot used his own money and zeal to stamp his vision on education reform, though Perot's style was more colorful and headline-grabbing. Not one reader in ten thousand knows who Eli Broad is; everybody knew Perot. After all, this was the can-do Electronic Data Systems (EDS) chief who sent his own commando team of company volunteers and Green Berets to rescue kidnapped employees in Iran. In education matters, like Broad, Perot didn't bother talking with educators, dealing instead with political and corporate power brokers. One is reminded of the old saw about Boston aristocrats: "The Lodges spoke only to Cabots and Cabots spoke only to God." Perot spoke only to business and business spoke only to Mammon. Writing a history of the reform moment, *U.S. News and World Report* writer Thomas Toch offered a largely admiring portrait of Perot:

> Nonstop for over a month, Perot worked his rhetorical magic before The Texas and Southwest Cattle Raisers Association, the Mid-Continent Oil and Gas Association, the Texas Association of Businesses, the Texas Association of Taxpayers, and other pillars of the state's economy. Audiences doubled over in laughter at his homely but telling portraits of life in Texas schools. They sat in silence through his lectern-pounding homilies on education and the state's economic well-being. Time and again they greeted his calls to action with standing ovations.[3]

In *Contradictions of School Reform*, Rice University Center for Learning professor Linda McNeil offers a more telling portrait, documenting how politicians led by Perot wreaked havoc on teacher professionalism in Texas. McNeil chooses Houston as the locus of reforms gone wrong: the fifth largest public school system in the U.S.; 150 languages spoken by the children in public schools; the seedbed of some of the most extreme forms of standardization in education. McNeil documents how Perot, instead of destroying the bureaucracy, actually increased it. Like other corporate movers on a mission, Perot had no curiosity about how schools actually work—how teachers teach, how students learn. He was a man with a plan—and a steamroller of ego, connections, and personal fortune. Through sharp observation and telling anecdote, McNeil shows the effects: business-controlled management accountability systems in Houston compacted the curriculum into test prep and subverted the skills of the best teachers while actually providing shelter for the weak ones.

Instituting a Top Command Structure

From standards and curriculum to school board elections, when anybody who cares about public education sees the word *alignment*, she should duck for cover. Autocrats look for alignment because they're sure they know better; autocrats are determined to subvert democratic processes, and they do it in the name of standards. At the state level, Perot disregarded elected state school board officials as political hacks. Not surprisingly, he wanted a state board appointed by the governor, so that the top command structure would have management alignment and be immune to local politics. Perot called it *local politics*; others would say *democracy*. Perot had contempt for local school boards, superintendents, and principals and was determined to get teachers in line by instituting merit pay. To this end he paid for a consulting firm that had no experience with schools to design a corporate-style merit pay system.

> That model, slightly modified, became the Career Ladder. . . . The Career Ladder plan, according to those close to the reform process, was constructed in isolation from any expertise on children's development, teacher practice, or the curriculum in any subject or grade level.[4]

This is the way the No Child Left Behind Reading First plan was set up. Expertise on children's development, or, most especially, experience working with children, is shunned. One of the Reading First experts choosing reading methodology and materials for the nation's children is a certified public accountant. Many have degrees in psychology. Coming from the Florida, Texas, Oregon axis, they have intertwined interests in commercial reading materials that impose a deficit model of learning on the nation's children. It also sounds like Broad's corporate model: construct and disseminate a model of leadership isolated from teachers and children. Remember the Broad Foundation and Thomas B. Fordham proclamation in *Better Leaders for America's Schools: A Manifesto*: the CEO of Squibb doesn't need to be a chemist. Management is the thing. Kid savvy isn't mentioned.

McNeil observes that when the state school system was nuked under Perot's plan, the bombs did not fall on the targeted state education agency or middle-level managers; instead, teachers and students suffered the collateral damage from Perot's reform nukes. These reforms included "reinforcement of systems for prescribing curriculum and for testing students. Together, they had the effects of de-skilling teachers' work, trivializing and reducing the content of the curriculum, and distancing children from the substance of school-ing."[5] Worst of all, these reforms institutionalized de-skilling in a two-tiered approach. Schools judged as high-performing are exempt from the skill drill-and-kill that passes for curriculum in low-performing schools. Thus, poor and minority students who excel in school enter college at an increased disadvantage with middle-class kids whose high school courses were not infused with a test-prep curriculum. And poor and minority students who enter the workforce after high school find themselves shortchanged by a test-prep curricula that supplanted vocational courses. Either way, middle-class kids get an education; the poor and minorities get a skill gap.

Good Cop/Bad Cop

In 1989, with five of the nine school board members, called trustees, up for re-election, the campaign for systemic reform in Houston intensified. The five candidates backed by Houston's business leaders won all five of the contested seats. Two of the newly elected trustees were Rod Paige and Don McAdams. That same year, the Texas Business and Education Coalition (TBEC) and the Texans for Education (TFE) were established to "provide a mechanism through which business leaders [could] . . . influence the direction of state education policy and stimulate local school-improvement activities."[6] TBEC, the good cop, cultivated a neutral image as a policy think tank. With the agenda wrapped in a cloak of so-called objectivity, state legislators could introduce TBEC policy and program suggestions without the appearance of undue influence.

> From the beginning, TBEC members believed it was important that the organization not lobby because there were programs the organization wanted to implement, policy issues which it wanted to objectively analyze, and the TBEC contribution stream was targeted for these purposes.[7]

At the same time, the second organization, TFE, the bad cop, was set up to keep legislators lined up behind TBEC policy initiatives. TBEC and TFE were intertwined, with TFE as the lobbying arm of TBEC. Until 1989, TBEC and TFE had no formal ties with the national Business Roundtable. Then, the BRT assigned Tenneco, a national energy company headquartered in Texas, the responsibility of coming up with a plan to improve education in Texas. The centerpiece of this plan was for the Business Roundtable to fund TFE's lobbying effort. Where lobbying had once been a matter of reacting and responding to each issue as it came up, now it would be an unremitting drumbeat of message. The BRT called this highly structured campaign a *constructive dialogue* between business professionals and educators, a dialogue allowing both parties to "successfully advocate and support reforms that would otherwise have become mired in infighting and controversy."[8]

In other words, the BRT pumped money into Texas to help systemic reform avoid controversy. What they call *controversy* others call democratic process.

This bad-cop enforcement of good-cop planning resulted in the adoption of the Business Roundtable agenda in Texas. Note that when TBEC and TFE line up their state policy accomplishments, we can see how closely they fit the BRT's nine-point agenda.

1991—Texas legislature required school districts to develop site-based decision making.

1993—Texas legislature established annual testing.

1995—Texas legislature rewrote the entire Texas Education Code, which included authorization at both the state and the local level to establish charter schools.

1997—Texas legislature enacted a reading program and new student learning standards.

Houston school board trustee Donald McAdams has written about the profound effect this state legislation had on the Houston board;[9] his account, not surprisingly, has been corroborated by TBEC executive director John Stevens as "fair representation of what has happened in Houston."[10]

In 1989, the newly reconstituted Houston board developed a mission statement called Beliefs and Visions. The core principles were decentralization, accountability, and a "common core of academic subjects for all students . . . so that [graduates] could enter college or the workforce fully prepared to be successful and not need remediation."[11] When the superintendent, who didn't like the mission statement, decided to implement the principles of Beliefs and Visions in only 10 percent of the schools, the new board members engineered her termination. As McAdams told a Heartland Institute interviewer years later, "The superintendent didn't like it and we ended up appointing a new one to try to drive the district into a reform mode."[12]

In 1991, after promising to implement systemic reform, Dade County, Florida, associate superintendent Frank Petruzielo became Houston superintendent. Both the Latino and African American board members objected to Petruzielo, but using divide-and-conquer tactics, white board members were able to cut a backroom deal with the Latinos. Two years later, a Texas Education Agency (TEA) accreditation evaluation of the Houston Independent School District (HISD) termed Petruzielo "visionary" and "a staunch advocate for urban education, site-based decision-making, and quality education in an urban setting."[13]

TBEC successfully lobbied the state legislature to use the Texas Assessment of Academic Skills as a means to sanction individual school districts whose performance was unacceptable. Believing that the formulas created by the legislature were too complex, McAdams worked with his school board allies to create a *matrix* of performance that would use the TAAS scores, be tied to teacher performance, and yet be simple enough so that it "could be explained to a parent in sixty seconds." Not surprisingly, the Houston Federation of Teachers (HFT) lobbied against such a formula, and in 1993–94 the board failed to link performance with assessment. McAdams reveals at least his own point of view (and remember, he was one of the *reform* HISD trustees) toward teachers and their evaluation when he writes that the HFT "found plenty of reasons to oppose a plan that put teachers in the cross hairs."[14]

In 1992, the Greater Houston Partnership, Houston's business elite, created an advisory group, the Houston Business Advisory Council, to push decentralization issues. After protracted meetings, the business elite decided they were going to move the process along, with or without Petruzielo.[15] Petruzielo had come into conflict with CEOs by asking for more taxes than they wanted to pay. McAdams notes the way things worked in Houston was for business leaders to advise the superintendent and the superintendent to take their recommendations to the board. "Historically, business leaders determined how much tax they would pay, and they had kept HISD's tax rate low."[16]

Houston Gets a New Superintendent

After a hammering from the business community, Petruzielo decided to leave, and Houston was looking for a new superintendent. Without conducting a nationwide search,[17] the school board took the controversial step of hiring one of its own—Rod Paige. Not only was Paige one of the self-proclaimed reform school board members, who were mostly Democrats,[18] but he also had the advantage of being African American. McAdams contends that because higher academic standards, greater employee accountability, and outsourcing "can be perceived as threats to minority self-esteem, minority jobs, and established centers of minority power . . . only minority leaders can reform America's urban districts."[19] Thus, by bringing in Paige, the business community could play the reverse race card to undermine black opposition to systemic reform. The appointment was not without dissent. A *Houston Post* editorial used the adjectives *appalling, arrogant,* and *bizarre* to describe the board's action. The large Latino community was outraged at having no role in selecting the new superintendent, and the Hispanic Education Committee sued the board for failure to follow the Texas Open Meetings Act. A TEA assessment report ordered by State Commissioner Lionel Meno charged that Paige had violated Texas Education Code by soliciting the position of superintendent while serving on the board. Leaders of Houston's African American communities began to mobilize, with a group of black ministers calling for Meno's resignation and the abolishment of the TEA. Longtime Harris County district attorney Johnny Holmes, who gained infamy for enforcing sodomy laws and making Harris County the most productive death-row pipeline in the Western world,[20] announced that in reviewing TEA findings, he found no wrongdoing. Maybe he should read McAdams' own account, which is part of a course at Brown University.[21] The reform members of the board certainly engaged in secret conversations that excluded Latino board members. In any case, Democratic governor Ann Richards stepped in, pressured Meno, and the TEA confirmed an alternative credential for Paige, who held a doctorate in physical education, with a dissertation on the response time of football linemen.

The race card helped Superintendent Paige implement systemic reform, just as it helps Secretary of Education Paige make stump speeches for No Child Left Behind. Repeated accusations about *low expectations*, coupled with the promotion of test-driven instruction and curricula as *the* solution, make dissent difficult.

As mentioned previously, while still an HISD trustee, Paige had discussed decentralization with the Greater Houston Partnership, which established the Houston Business Advisory Council, which sponsored the Hook Committee, chaired by Harold Hook, chair and CEO of American General. All parties were looking for ways to move the budget process from the central office out to school sites. As superintendent, Paige went whole hog for Hook's Model-Netics, a system of management phrases and symbols.[22] Everybody learns the same phrases, which are unintelligible to the uninitiated. For example, *the Northbound train* means "get with the program or else." *The Cruel Sea* means "layoffs."

After the failure of a school bond vote, the district tried again, and the overlapping agendas of the reformers on the school board, the Coalition for Educational Excellence (CEE), the Houston Partnership, the TFE, and the TBEC came together. The Greater Houston Partnership agreed to provide $400,000 in contributions to fund a campaign to pass a reduced school bond measure to repair crumbling buildings—in return for the board's promise to pursue policies of site-based decision making, accountability, public school choice, outsourcing, merit pay, reduction of administration costs, and establishment of a continuous maintenance program. Local Republican clubs indicated they would support the bond measure only if the school board could promise to privatize all noneducational support services, offer vouchers to all students, and abolish the limit of twenty-two children in K–4 classes. The bond failed and the stage was set for Paige to make a move.

On October 16, 1997, Paige began a series of media events that unveiled A New Beginning for HISD, which rested upon four pillars: accountability, best efforts, choice, and decentralization. McAdams reports that despite mounting opposition to these initiatives by the NAACP, employee groups, organized labor, and others, Paige's arm-twisting prevailed. McAdams credits enormous staff work behind the scenes with persuading HISD to begin "to embrace the principles of competition." Here are the reforms of 1996–97:

- reduction of board meetings from two to one a month
- superintendent's personnel decisions completely independent of the board
- contract with Community Education Partners to teach 450 "at risk" students
- neighborhood schools admissions selectively open to non-neighborhood students
- increase in number of charter schools
- implementation of phonics-based reading program
- curriculum alignment among standards, instruction, and testing
- testing grades 1–11 with the Stanford 9 test
- elimination of continuing contracts, hearings, and appeals for new teachers
- teacher appraisal linked to student achievement and discipline
- complaints supervised by HISD's chief of staff for business services
- outsourcing contracts for installing management systems (Main Event Management Corp.); building repairs (Brown and Root); facilities management (ServiceMaster Management Services Co.); food service supervision (Aramark); and revising human resources management (IBM) [23]

McAdams insists that this package is responsible for the increase in Houston students' TAAS scores since 1994.[24] Screaming headlines in the *Houston Chronicle* and the *New York Times*, among others, revealed different reasons for a rise in scores, including eliminating probable low scorers. Language is important here, and *push-out* is the accurate term: the deliberate and systematic derailing of targeted students with the unspoken purpose of improving test score averages. Often students aren't excluded but are held in ninth grade until they give up and quit.

Using McAdams' calculations, from 1994 to 1998, the number of schools labeled *low-acceptable* decreased from eighty-one to zero; from 1990 to 1997, the dropout rate declined from 10.4 percent to 2.8 percent, and the number of violent crimes in school fell 38 percent. And all with the lowest effective tax rate among large urban school districts and a per-pupil spending rate lower in 1999 than in 1992. John Stevens, executive director of TBEC, insists that along with the "significant and constructive force" of the business community,

"Superintendent Rod Paige must be given an enormous amount of credit . . . his leadership has been the single most important factor in the success of [HISD]."[25]

But the miracle numbers don't stand up to scrutiny. In *The Texas Miracle in Education*, Walt Haney pointed out that the actual graduation rate of blacks and Latinos was under 50 percent.[26] In the summer of 2003, Robert Kimball, a Houston assistant principal, spilled the beans on push-outs. Twelve of the city's poorest schools had reported dropout rates of fewer than 1 percent, with some schools reporting zero dropouts. Later the public learned that to achieve a measured decrease in violence in the schools, authorities stopped counting things like rape. Here's the lead in a front-page *New York Times* expose:

> It was one of the most unforgettable of schoolhouse crimes: a disabled 17-year-old student was shoved into a boys' bathroom in her wheelchair by a classmate at Yates High School here, dragged to the floor and raped. Her attacker was sentenced to 20 years in prison.[27]

The Houston Independent School District didn't count this rape in its required report on campus crimes. The *New York Times* provided chapter and verse of many other unreported crimes. Terry R. Abbott, Houston's spokesman, explained to the *Times* that "the district reports only offenses for which students face school disciplinary procedures. Since the rapist was jailed after his arrest, the authorities never bothered to expel him, and so the crime went unmentioned in the district's reports." And so on and so on.

In 1997, on the advice of the business community, the board hired a press secretary for Superintendent Paige. Accomplished spin doctor Terry Abbott was paid $102,800 plus car fare of $7,200 per year, a salary two times that of HISD's highest-paid teacher. Writing in the *African-American*, Roy Douglas Malonson noted, "It didn't take long before it became perfectly clear . . . that Abbott was hired mainly to help Dr. Paige become Pres. George W. Bush's Secretary of Education."[28] Certainly Paige was slickly packaged—to the Harold McGraw Award committee, to the American Association of School Administrators AASA award committee, to the Broad Foundation, and to the U.S. Congress. No other superintendent in the country had such packaging. As Philip Martin wrote in 2001, "Paige's biggest asset is not what he has done for Houston schools but his PR ability."[29] And it worked:

1999—Harold W. McGraw Jr. Prize in Education

2000—American Association of School Administrators, National Superintendent of the Year

2001—to HISD, first annual Broad Prize for Urban Education

Software entrepreneur Steve Kirsch talked to someone on the McGraw award committee, who reported on Paige's great PR department. When most of the committee members ignored negative information about Houston, one committee member quit.[30] And then, in 2003, the chickens came home to roost—even for the mass media. The *Houston Press* and *African-American*—alternative press weeklies—had been telling the story all along, but suddenly the mainstream media began playing catch-up.

Nobody Is Safe from School Reform

The outsourcing of the food service in Houston deserves a note: it reflects a nationwide trend and it provides a glimpse of how broadly the reform brush sweeps. And how many people get hurt. Between 1987 and 1995, the number of school systems nationwide contracting out food service doubled. Somebody should figure out if this corresponds to the obesity epidemic. Intent on restructuring district operations, Paige appointed panels to look at all school operations, and he resolved to privatize noneducational functions. Paige insisted that reformers should see public education not simply as a service for children, but as an investment in a healthy economy and a lure to business.[31] So Paige asked McAdams to launch a trial balloon before the board. Predictably, some board trustees worried about relatively good-paying (union) minority jobs. As Robert Jefferson, pastor of the Cullen Missionary Baptist Church, told the *Houston Chronicle*, "I'm totally, totally unequivocally against it. It is going to hurt black folk and Hispanic folk. Privatization is tagged 'lose jobs' for members in our churches and in our community."[32] In the same article, Carol Galloway, another board trustee, pointed out that affected employees were parents of schoolchildren and their employment at a living wage was a "vital component to the education of our young people."

The *Houston Chronicle* published an editorial favoring the plan, asserting, "HISD is not a jobs program. Its mission is to educate children as well and efficiently as possible." The NAACP, representatives of labor unions, and religious groups held a press conference denouncing privatization, outsourcing, and the contracting out of services. Houston mayor Bob Lanier spoke out against it as well. In July 1997, the board contracted with Aramark Corporation to manage HISD's food service operation.

The *African-American* offered a critical view, asking how the mainstream press allowed Paige (1) to get away with going back on his promise of not ever privatizing HISD's food service and (2) not to rebut HISD board president Laurie Bricker's claim that food services had lost money the year before Aramark took over, when, in truth, the district made a profit of $1.8 million. Furthermore, in 2002, Orell Fitzsimmons, who represents the Service Employees International Union, said, "Aramark cost HISD $4.5 million over the past two school years." *African-American* publisher Roy Douglas Malonson doesn't mince words: "History will reflect that Paige lied."[33]

By the summer of 2003, the mainstream press began to report that someone in Houston has been lying about a number of things, including what had happened to thousands of high school students.

In February 2001, Paige made his first public address as U.S. secretary of education to a receptive audience of business and high-tech leaders at the Silicon Valley Education Summit at the Westin Hotel in Santa Clara, California. Designed to address the private sector's role in improving education, the meeting was sponsored by the ultraconservative Pacific Institute of San Francisco. In commenting on "a Cabinet that looks like corporate America," political commentator Molly Ivins noted that while Paige was Houston superintendent, "Food service went to Aramark Inc., payroll to Peoplesoft and accounting to SAP. Last year, he cut an exclusive marketing deal with Coca-Cola to put machines in the school hallways. He also brought in Primed Corp's Channel One, the (so-called) 'educational channel' that spends two out of every 10 minutes of broadcast time selling M&M/Mars, Pepsico, Reebok and Nintendo."[34] As Don McAdams noted, Houston had a board that believed in competition.

The United Electrical, Radio and Machine Workers of America (UE), an independent union not affiliated with the AFL-CIO, proud of its democratic structure and progressive policies, observes that Bush's appointment of Rod Paige, who as Houston administrator "appeared in advertisements for corporations promoting the privatization of the Houston schools support services," is part of the business plan to make destruction of our public school system one of the federal government's top priorities.[35]

Looking Behind and Beyond the Numbers

The reality behind the corporatized numerical definitions of success cited by McAdams and Stevens is poignantly described in Linda McNeil's research. Looking for "organizational models of schooling that provided structural support for authentic, engaged teaching and learning," McNeil began her research in Houston's magnet schools. The focus of McNeil's research dramatically shifted, however, as she observed the effects of a deformed notion of accountability and high-stakes testing on how teachers teach and students learn. At first, McNeil was observing students enthusiastically engaged in a "rich and complex" curriculum in schools specifically established as high-quality model schools. But,

> [a]s the controls were imposed, and regulations increasingly standardized, the quality of teaching and learning at even these exemplary schools began to suffer. . . . The practice of teaching under these reforms [TAAS, etc.] shifted away from intellectual activity toward dispensing packaged fragments

of information sent from an upper level of the bureaucracy. And the role of students as contributors to classroom discourse, as thinkers, as people who brought their personal stories and life experiences into the classroom, was silenced or severely circumscribed by the need for the class to "cover" a generic curriculum at a pace established by the district and the state for all the schools.[36]

McNeil concluded that not only does standardization de-skill teachers and dumb down students, but it "restratifies education by race and class."[37] McNeil notes that this happened within the context of the long-standing and intractable correlation of test scores with socioeconomic status.[38] Under the pressures of high-stakes testing, McNeil has observed the development of two curricula in the Houston school system. Affluent schools continue to teach an academically challenging college-preparatory curriculum in the upper grades and a hands-on, exploratory, and thought-provoking curriculum in the lower grades. But in schools dominated by poor and minority students, kids get a test-prep curriculum that offers "strategies to simplify their thinking" and "practice weeding out 'distractors' " among multiple-choice options.[39] McNeil's detailed descriptions of what actually goes on in classrooms reveal that an increase in test scores signifies an increase in thoughtless, meaningless, test-taking skills.

Just to bring the connections full circle, Donald McAdams, who joined the Houston Board of Education at the same time as Rod Paige, the man the Dallas *Morning News* calls "the district's pre-eminent evangelist," now leads the Broad Institute for School Boards. And in October 2002, the Broad Foundation named Houston the best urban school district in the nation.

Notes

1. McAdams, Donald R. 2000. *Fighting to Save Our Urban Schools . . . and Winning! Lessons from Houston.* New York: Teachers College Press, 222–226.

2. McNeil, Linda. 2000. *Contradictions of School Reform: Educational Costs of Standardized Testing.* New York: Routledge, 153.

3. Toch, Thomas. 1991. *In the Name of Excellence.* New York: Oxford, 84.

4. McNeil. 2000, 182.

5. Ibid., 189.

6. From *www.tbec.org/history.*

7. Ibid.

8. Ibid.

9. McAdams. 2000.

10. Personal communication with K. Emery. 2000.

11. Avoiding "remediation" in college is a major objective of the Education Trust.

12. Clowes, George A. 2002. "School Board Members: The Forgotten Reformers." The Heartland Institute, 10 April.

13. Texas Education Agency, Department of Accountability. 1993. *District Report for Performance-Based Accreditation, Houston Independent School District.* 28 July.

14. McAdams, Donald R. 1999. "Lessons from Houston." In *Brookings Papers on Education Policy,* ed. Diane Ravitch, 137. Washington, DC: Brookings Institution Press.

15. Ibid., 138.

16. Ibid., 134.

17. McAdams had expressed annoyance at how long it had taken to find Petruzielo, complaining that the Texas Open Records and Open Meetings Act made it "difficult to attract the best candidates." So this time, they just skipped the process. From McAdams, 1999, 132.

18. McAdams says Paige, dean of the school of education at Texas Southern University and a longtime Republican activist, was "the scholar of the group." Other reform board members were Cathy Mincberg, a former HISD biology teacher, an Ed.D., and active Democrat (her husband was chair of the Harris County Democratic Party); Ron Franklin, another Democrat, and a trial attorney; and Paula Arnold, former social worker and real estate broker, and an "active Democrat." McAdams, a former university professor and college president, was a management consultant and a Republican. From McAdams, 1999, 139.

19. McAdams. 2000, 255.

20. Tolson, Mike. 2001. "A Deadly Distinction." *Houston Chronicle,* 5 February. Accessed at *www.chron.com/cs/CDA/story.hts/special/penalty/813783.*

21. Starr, John Bryan. 2003. "Political Levers for the Corporate Community in Houston." ED164/PS182. Education Department/Political Science Department, Brown University. Fall.

22. See *www.maineventmanagement.com/model-netics_what.html.*

23. McAdams. 2000, 232–41.

24. Not including special education students. McAdams. 2000, 253.

25. Personal communication with K. Emery. 2000.

26. Haney, Walt. 2000. *The Education Miracle in Texas.* New Orleans: AERA. Accessed at *http://epaa.asu.edu/epaa/v8n41/refs.htm.* "The Myth of the Texas Miracle in Education." Education Policy Analysis Archives. 19 August. Accessed at *http://epaa.asu. edu/epaa/v8n41.*

27. Dillon, Sam. 2003. "School Violence Data Under a Cloud in Houston." *New York Times,* 7 November. Accessed at *www.nytimes.com/2003/11/07/education/07HOUS.html? tntemail1.*

28. From *www.aframnews.com/archives/2002-08.htm.*

29. Martin, Philip. 2001. "Political Capital." *African-American,* 10 January.

30. See *www.skirsch.com/politics/rodpaige/rod_paige_page.htm.*

31. Coyle, Pamela. 1998. "Houston Schools Chief Shares Success Story." *The Times-Picayune,* 1 August.

32. Marley, Melanie. 1994. "HISD to Ponder Privatizing Services, Critics Say Minorities Will Take Big Job Hit." *Houston Chronicle,* 24 July.

33. Malonson, Roy Douglas. 2002. "Dr. Paige Created Aramark Food Service Monster." *African-American News and Issues,* 3–9 July. Accessed at *www.aframnews.com/archives/2002-07-03/lead1.htm.*

34. Ivins, Molly. 2001."A Cabinet That Looks Like Corporate America." *Boulder Daily Camera*, 9 February.

35. From *www.ranknfile-ue.org/polact_isu_pe.html*.

36. McNeil. 2000, 5.

37. Ibid., xxvii.

38. Close reading of the history of the development of standardized testing will reveal that such a correlation is not by chance. Furthermore, one reason for the development of standardized testing was that administrators did not want to rely on the judgment and expertise of teachers in evaluating students, even though those very judgments were used to measure the validity of the first IQ tests. See Thorndike, R. M., and D. F. Lohman, 1990, *A Century of Ability Testing*, Chicago: Riverside.

39. McNeil. 2000, 245–56.

7

No Matter Who's Talking About Education Reform, Look for the Footprints of the Business Roundtable

No matter how paranoid you are, what they are actually doing is worse than you can possibly imagine.

—RALPH J. GLEASON

In 1989 and again in 1995, the national Business Roundtable put its special brand on education reform, hammering home an agenda that defined reform thusly: state content and performance standards; a state-mandated test; rewards and sanctions based on test scores; school site councils composed of administrators, teachers, and parents; professional development focused on using test scores to drive instructional decisions; and phonics instruction in prekindergarten. Not only did the BRT flood the media with this agenda, but since 1989, a network of public and private organizations promoting this beast called systemic reform has developed; it is a network characterized by incestuous partnerships, overlapping alliances, and common funding sources. It is difficult for teachers, education researchers, and even parents to avoid operating in one or more of these organizations, and the temptation to succumb to the rhetoric is ever present. After all, most people don't want to bite the hand that feeds them—any more than they want to stand up against reform. Instead, many education groups scramble to claim reform as their own. But as we discover that the essence of reform is not politics, not even philosophy—but money and power—the word quickly loses its sheen. In order to understand school reform, one need remember only two words: Standardistas lie.

New American Schools (NAS) is a case in point. The BRT worked with the U.S. Department of Education and numerous foundations to create the New American Schools Development Corporation as part of President Bush the elder's America 2000 program. Initial announcements indicated that private sources would come up with $200 million for break-the-mold schools that would raise standardized test scores. The goal was *dramatic* test score gains. After seven years, the operation closed down, and its successor organization, New American Schools, was created to continue to proffer reform models for schools. Not surprisingly, the original NAS board of directors was a who's who of corporate America.[1]

In the first round of grant giving, proposal readers were instructed to concentrate on criterion 1: the likelihood that the design would enable students to meet the national education goals and to attain world-class standards.[2] It was soon clear that neither the proposal writers nor the readers knew just what *world-class standards* meant, but that didn't stop the award of grants to well-known promoters: James Comer, Howard Gardner, Theodore Sizer, Robert Slavin, Robert Glaser, Lauren Resnick, Mark Tucker, William Bennett, Chester E. Finn Jr., and Denis P. Doyle.

President Clinton continued federal support of NAS, signing the Comprehensive School Reform Program (CSR) in 1997 (formerly the Comprehensive School Reform Demonstration, or CSRD). On January 8, 2002, when President Bush II signed the reauthorization of the Elementary and Secondary Education Act (ESEA), the No Child Left Behind Act, CSR became part of Title I—with the same requirements of proven methods based on scientifically based research, aligned components, professional development for teachers and staff, measurable goals and benchmarks for student achievement, the support of school staff, meaningful parent and community involvement, high-quality external technical support and assistance from an external partner, plans for evaluation, identification of resources to support and sustain the reform effort, and significant improvement in academic achievement of students.

Sea Changes: Meeting the Challenges of Schoolwide Reform gives us a glimmer of how this educationese translates to the classroom.[3] Northwest Regional Educational Laboratory, one of the external partners, leads off an article titled "Stepping Up the Rigor: Finding Answers Within Themselves" with a boxed quote from a teacher:

> Success for All is quite prescriptive. I can tire of it and that's just the way it goes. But if students are learning to read, that's what I want. I want whatever is going to help them the most.

This is meant to be confirmation and even celebration of turning a school over to Comprehensive School Reform Demonstration (CSRD). The teacher quoted is one of the reform leaders. The article doesn't explain why his students, the acknowledged strongest readers in the school, needed a scripted curriculum that tells teachers "how to say things and when to say them." The heart of the article explains that

> [t]he CSRD program encourages schools to consider adopting well-researched reform models with solid evidence of success in turning low-performing schools around. These external reform models generally reorganize the entire school, often providing a new structure, materials, and extensive training and staff development.

Clearly, while many ivory towerists stew over labeling programs "conservative" or "liberal," the corporate syndicate is devouring everything in sight.

Co-Opting Teachers Unions

The leadership of both national teacher unions, the National Education Association and the American Federation of Teachers, has expressed support for state standards and school deregulation, often called site-based management. Funny thing: one of the Business Roundtable's Nine Essential Components of systemic reform, school autonomy, is part of the larger design by which teachers are expected to work with administrators and parents in site councils to figure out the means by which to raise student test scores.

Recasting an old question about monkeys who are given a typewriter and plenty of time eventually producing *Hamlet*, one can wonder how long it would take six monkeys left in a room of typewriters to type out this definition: *School autonomy means raising scores on standardized tests.* Launching a technologically updated approach to an old theme, researchers at Plymouth University in England gave six monkeys at the Paignton Zoo a computer for a month.[4] Elmo, Gum, Heather, Holly, Mistletoe, and Rowan, Sulawesi crested macaques, made a mess but failed to come up with a single word. One monkey smashed the computer with a stone. Others urinated and defecated on the keyboard. In thirty days they produced five pages of text—mostly the letter *s*. That's a start: the first letter in *school autonomy, state mandates, systemic reform,* and *standards.*

By agreeing to support this definition of autonomy, the national union leadership indulged in its own monkey business, implicitly accepting the BRT agenda and relinquishing any rights to a leadership role in deciding what the goals of education should be. Of course the capitulation of the central office doesn't mean that plenty of the unions' rank and file don't continue to object to systemic reform. But their effectiveness is impoverished by their inability to speak, as does the Business Roundtable, with one cohesive message. This message is fractured by the fact that national leaders don't listen to the concerns of the locals.

Under the pressure of a constant media barrage—editorials carping about teachers meddling in policy combined with editorials accusing teachers of caring only about money—NEA and AFT agreed to a division of labor: teachers are given the autonomy to make sure students meet goals established by outside forces. In the language of systemic reform, this is called site-based decision management or site-based decision making (SBDM). The NEA adopted SBDM as a bargaining goal in 1991. At the local level some hoped that this autonomy, peculiar though it is, would finally allow teachers to have some say in what they taught. But this claim to autonomy, although sounding professionally high-minded, was, of course, a chimera. In agreeing to SBDM, the NEA leadership put its members in the position of accepting responsibility for increasing student achievement while relinquishing the very power that might help them do it. In 1997, NEA president Bob Chase encouraged teachers gathered at the annual convention to support the BRT agenda—rigid standardization, deregulation, and parental support of expert teachers.

> The fact is that while NEA does not control curriculum, set funding levels, or hire and fire, we cannot go on denying responsibility for school quality. . . . The fact is that *no group knows more about the solutions that will work in our schools than America's teachers.*[5] We know what our schools need: higher academic standards; stricter discipline; an end to social promotions; less bureaucracy; more resources where they count, in the classroom; schools that are richly connected to parents and to the communities that surround them.[6] (Emphasis added.)

Chase did not explain *how* teachers were to implement those solutions. Clearly this was a case of the word being enough. Forget the deed.

The history of SBDM in Montgomery County, Maryland, one of the largest NEA local chapters, suggests that in promoting the BRT agenda, the NEA not only pushes a type of teacher professionalism that alienates parents but puts itself out of touch with the rank and file. In 1998, in step with the demands of the national leadership, Montgomery County NEA (MCEA) successfully negotiated site-based decision-making councils called Quality Management Councils, or QMCs, into the contract. That name is no accident, making explicit the connection between systemic reform and economic reform. Schools didn't rush to sign up: during the first year, only 10 of the 187 schools in the district set up QMCs. And the expectation that QMCs would lead to rich relationships between schools and parents proved hollow. Neither the local PTA nor the parents in the local NAACP chose to participate.[7]

The BRT publication *A Business Leader's Guide to Setting Academic Standards* gives readers a look at the symbiotic relationship between the BRT and the AFT.[8] In citing the contributions the AFT has made to ensure that state standards are high, the BRT simultaneously makes the case for its version of high standards and confers status upon the AFT.

Examples of Ineffectual, Unclear or Poorly Written Standards:
The following selections of standards are cited by the American Federation of Teachers as examples of what to avoid. The AFT criticizes these standards for being confusing, not academic enough and overly focused on skills at the expense of knowledge. . . . Many of the standards below met objections from members of the public and business community and were rewritten as a result.

"Students will demonstrate the ability to examine problems and proposed solutions *from multiple perspectives*" (Missouri's Standards, Draft, 1995).

"[A high school graduate] understands and describes ways that a *specified culture shapes patterns* of interaction of individuals and groups" (Minnesota's High School Standards, Draft, 1994).

"While performing individual and group tasks, students organize and intellectually process symbols, pictures, objects and information in a way which *permits the mind to generate the reality* of what is being represented" (Florida's Blueprint 2000, 1992).

". . . A student will demonstrate the ability to think critically, *creatively and reflectively* in making decisions and solving problems" (Oregon's Certificate of Initial Mastery, 1991).

"All students demonstrate *care-giving skills* and evaluate, in all settings, appropriate child care practices necessary to nurture children based on child development theory" (Pennsylvania's Student Learning Outcomes, Draft, 1991).

The emphasis is added in these samples to highlight a pattern of what the AFT deems unacceptable. The first four examples encourage divergent thinking and a diversity of viewpoint and, of course, aren't conducive to standardized testing. The fifth is clearly not academic enough.

In 1998, at the AFT convention, union president Sandra Feldman used BRT rhetoric to define the agenda: "we must do everything *within our power* to make turning around low-performing schools—improving all schools—the top agenda of every community in this nation!"[9] (emphasis added). Feldman assured her audience that in spite of the lack of support for teachers, "education reform is working! Academic standards and requirements are up, student attendance is up, dropout rates are down, and our students are achieving at much higher levels." Implicitly acknowledging the small box within which teachers are allowed to move, Feldman's agenda is not for teachers to claim the right to collective bargaining over textbook selection, standard setting, or school design, but for teachers to demand that they be involved in the hiring process through "peer review and intervention programs." Feldman says this would result in the "professionalizing [of] dismissal proceedings."

By abandoning the fight over the goals of education and allowing themselves to be confined to arguing for a peculiarly narrow definition of increased professionalism, Feldman and Chase earn halfhearted kudos from such public influence makers as the *New York Times* editorialists, who expressed satisfaction that the AFT

> is rushing to cast itself as an agent of change [i.e., promoting the goals of the high-stakes testing agenda] instead of an advocate of the status quo. A new report from the teachers' union embraces stronger teacher training and breaks with a longstanding union tradition by calling for more rigorous tests for prospective teachers. The report is encouraging, but it will take more than rhetoric for the A.F.T. and its sister union, the National Education Association, to be seen as reformers.[10]

New York Times editors identify the major items in the AFT's report with approval, items that are completely consistent with the BRT's professional development goals identified in the Nine Essential Components. And there's more. The editors continue:

> The unions can take an open-minded approach to special incentives and new assignment strategies, and can crackdown on local unions that resist vitally needed reforms.

That the editors feel a need to call for a "crackdown on local unions" indicates that teachers have reason not to be happy with the official position taken by national union leadership on high-stakes testing reform.

Co-Opting Parents

Business leaders have identified parent opposition as one reason for the initial failure of the standards movement, and systemic reformers have carefully planned strategies to enlist parent support of high-stakes testing. The obvious ploy is to convince parents that schools aren't educating the kids. Writing in an October 1999 op-ed, California governor Gray Davis complained about a survey result showing parents to be "generally satisfied with the quality of their children's education."[11] Davis argued that "tests scores show otherwise. Parents must throw off their complacency." Nationwide, this has become a repeated refrain: Don't trust teacher judgment. Mandate a test that more than half the kids fail, and that proves that you need more tests. And, of course, more test prep. In an op-ed, Maureen Steinbruner, president of the Center for National Policy, where Sandra Feldman serves on the board of directors, acknowledged the existence of parental opposition while framing systemic reform (by "politicians and experts") positively, as an attempt to "challenge children"—one variation on the "high standards for all" theme.[12]

> [There is] a great 'disconnect' today between politicians and experts, on the one hand, and citizens, on the other, over how American schools are doing. . . . Business and government leaders want school systems that challenge children. The public, in contrast, sees kids as overly challenged without enough support, either at home or in school. Arguments over what government should do make voters frustrated and annoyed.

The Center for National Policy, labeled liberal by ABC News, is perhaps seen differently by others. The U.S. Embassy in Seoul, Republic of Korea, lists think tanks and research centers on its website. In the category of "Social Process," the Center for National Policy is listed next to the Cato Institute, the Capital Research Center, the Hudson Institute, the Manhattan Institute, and the Reason Foundation, among others. In this company, maybe CNP does begin to look liberal, but its publication on schooling, *Passing the Test: The National Interest in Good Schools for All*, from which Steinbruner draws her op-ed, brings together the not-so-strange bedfellows politics and big business. It was published in cooperation with the College Board; Senator Edward Kennedy wrote the foreword; and Milton Goldberg, executive vice president of the National Alliance of Business, "dedicated to building an internationally competitive workforce through excellence in education and workforce development," wrote Chapter 1. In 1983, Goldberg was executive director of the National Commission on Excellence in Education, which issued *A Nation at Risk*, and he quotes heavily from it in his chapter. With big business, politics, and education, six degrees of separation is not acceptable: they prefer to get in bed together.

Nonetheless, despite all the dire pronouncements, parents still think schools are pretty good. In *Tinkering Toward Utopia*, David Tyack and Larry Cuban point to the Gallup-PDK polls showing that nonparents rate schools considerably lower than do parents and that "familiarity with local schools seems to breed not contempt but respect."[13] Particularly significant, a 1992 Gallup-PDK poll revealed that the public trusts local institutions much more than state or national ones: 57 percent of those polled want school boards to have more control of education than the national or state government.[14] To counter community concerns over the loss of influence over the goals of education, George W. Bush and the Republican Party used the BRT rhetoric of local control of schools during the 2000 election campaign. But as the No Child

Left Behind legislation steamrolls into districts with its labels of failure, the public is finding out how hollow this rhetoric was.

Parents Fight Back

In Massachusetts, parents have organized to transform their concern over the loss of control of educational policy into active opposition. Opposition to the Massachusetts Comprehensive Assessment System (MCAS), a state-mandated, high-stakes test, has provoked the creation of MassParents and the Massachusetts Coalition for Authentic Reform in Education (CARE), both associated with the Assessment Reform Network listserv (ARN) and FairTest. FairTest, the parent group, "is funded by generous grants from the Boston Foundation, The Ford Foundation, the Joyce Foundation, the Spencer Trust, and many individual contributors."[15] The funding allows FairTest to employ an executive director, an education director, a university admissions analyst, three organizers for ARN and CARE, and professional website managers. This is a critical point, as the testing-resistance landscape is littered with the broken URLs of grassroots groups that tried to sustain themselves on the enthusiasm and hard work of volunteers. Periodically, the possible constraints imposed by corporate funders have become the topic of fierce debate on the ARN email discussion list, but the fact of the matter is that FairTest couldn't survive without outside funding. Independent resisters speculate on what a think tank not dependent on such funding would look like, but in the meantime they keep struggling with only their idealism to keep them warm. Idealism and notes from desperate parents, asking them to save the kids from brutal regulations in Texas, Florida, New York, Massachusetts, and elsewhere.

FairTest focuses on academic research concerns rather than populist activism, though it offers extensive technical assistance to those requesting it. In 2003, three of FairTest's seven projects focus on college entrance topics; other projects include creating a new framework for assessment, attacking the false notions that test scores equal merit, monitoring the highly profitable testing industry, and exposing flawed employment tests such as the National Teacher's Exam. Parents, both home-schoolers and public schoolers, join teachers, professors, and researchers on the ARN listserv.

Using a webpage and an email discussion list, CARE coordinates opposition to the MCAS but, like FairTest, pulls back from condemning all standardized testing. CARE tends to emphasize the legislative route, advocating that resisters lobby their legislators to amend the legislation that created MCAS. Coalition members spearhead petition drives and hand out brochures on street corners and at school committee meetings; some have tried to reach the public by volunteering their PowerPoint presentations as programs for service organizations.

Resistance Fizzles

CARE's community activism has provoked numerous school boards, called committees, to pass resolutions similar to the one passed in July 2000 by the Berkshire Regional School District:

1. WHEREAS an MCAS program as currently devised will increase high school dropout rates, discourage some middle and high school students who perform at marginal levels, and unnecessarily frustrate some younger children, especially those with special needs, who are unable to succeed in the challenging MCAS test, and

2. Whereas there is evidence that states that have implemented education reform without high-stakes [testing that links passage to graduation] are having better results in providing academic performance than states that have voted high-stakes testing,

3. Now, THEREFORE BE IT RESOLVED, that the Central Berkshire Regional School Committee opposes the use of a passing grade on the 10th grade Language Arts and Mathematics MCAS tests as a requirement for graduation from high school, and

4. In ACCORDANCE WITH THE EDUCATION REFORM ACT, REQUIRING A VARIETY OF ASSESSMENTS OF STUDENT PERFORMANCE, now BE IT FURTHER RESOLVED, that the Great and General Court of the Commonwealth of Massachusetts, the Massachusetts Association of School Committees, and the Massachusetts Association of School Superintendents, urge the Board of Education to not link MCAS test results with the granting of high school diplomas and the aforementioned groups lobby for legislation that will prohibit the use of MCAS test results for this purpose. [16] (Emphasis in original.)

School committees in Newburyport, Cambridge, Falmouth, Easthampton, Northampton, Hampshire Regional, and Berkshire Hills all voted to give their own diplomas. Despite the resolutions, when push came to shove, school committees folded under threats from the state, and the resolutions proved to be worthless in protecting kids.

In late April 2003, the Massachusetts Department of Education threatened to yank the licenses of superintendents whose school committees voted to give diplomas to students who passed all local requirements but failed the MCAS. Education Commissioner David Driscoll widened the threat to include principals. "We're clearly not going to sit back and just allow them to do this after we've so carefully established standards," Driscoll told the *Boston Globe*.[17] Then the state began talking about withholding funds. The legality here is that the Department of Education can't fire local personnel—but it can take their licenses, and their money. In Springfield, the mayor wanted to defy the state. "I think a message would be sent here, across the Commonwealth, that Springfield cares about its students, cares about a quality education, and is not going to rely on a high-risk test that leaves students behind."[18] The reporter noted that the mayor was "surrounded by area clergy and officials from the local teachers union." Northampton School Committee member Stephanie Pick told a *Boston Herald* reporter, "It's a fear-based vote."[19] The paper revealed its allegiance to Standardistas with its choice of headline: "Rogue Schools Get Lesson in MCAS Laws." Presumably, *rogue* was chosen carefully: One can wonder just what is deceitful, unprincipled, or scoundrel-like about a school community wanting to protect its children. A school committee, after all, is entrusted with the well-being of students; it should strive to protect those students who have completed thirteen years of successful studies.

What was needed was a strong grassroots movement of the public, declaring its support of school committees and school officials. What was needed was for teachers to refuse to give the tests. *En masse.* Neither happened. And the counterbarrage from the media was fierce. When, in late October 2002, the Massachusetts Association of School Committees came out solidly for the districts' right to award diplomas to students who failed the MCAS, a *Worcester Telegram & Gazette* editorial called them "Spineless," insisting that "diploma-granting authority rests with the state."[20] The *Boston Herald* seemed to temper its editorial somewhat by settling on the descriptor "Wrong" as its characterization of the vote. But then it pulled out all the corporate Standardista stops. In answering association executive director Glenn Koocherk's assertion that school committees "best understand the needs of the community," the *Herald* editorial asserted, "For legal purposes the community is the state as a whole; for intellectual purposes the community is the whole wide world." Then the editorialist made this astounding assertion:

> No town or city is in a position to say what the needs of the Community are for MINIMUM INTELLECTUAL COMPETENCE.[21] (Emphasis in original.)

The editorialist conceded that school committees have autonomy over things like attendance; the rest they should leave to the Business Roundtable cronies. Sam Smith, editor of the *Progressive Review*, observes, "It is at moments when the status quo is thoroughly shaken that the media most faithfully performs its duty as stenographer to the powerful."

In the end, school committees decided to do what CARE and FairTest do: rely on the courts to settle the high-stakes testing issue. When, in August 2002, the parents of six students who had failed the MCAS brought a class action suit charging that the test punishes kids for historical inequities in the education system, Mass Insight hired lawyers to help the Department of Education fight the suit.

Mass Insight

Mass Insight Education and Research Institute, whose name itself is carefully chosen to impress and intimidate, bills itself as a nonprofit independent corporation, working in public outreach to achieve its goals, which are Massachusetts' sustained economic growth and global competitiveness. Putting the global economy on the backs of kids. The Massachusetts Department of Education funds Mass Insight under a public service information grant to provide such things as community updates. Here's a sample of a community update:

Did You Know . . .

- **Massachusetts' English and Math Curriculum Frameworks have been recognized as models for the nation**. National groups that compare state curricula say that ours are among the very best. Massachusetts also gets high marks for the strong links between the state curriculum frameworks and the MCAS tests.

- **Students are responding to higher standards by taking more advanced courses**. In 1993, just 22% of Massachusetts' eighth-graders took algebra. By 2001, that figure was 37%. The same is true for high school students; the percentage taking trig/pre-calculus climbed from 36% in 1993 to 51% in 2001. What's more: the Council of Chief State School Officers reports that the percentage of African-American and Hispanic students taking high-level math courses has risen faster in our state than in any other.

In addition to the state, Mass Insight has other partners; its Education Leadership Group brings together a rogues' gallery of corporate America. These partners have helped MassINC.[22] orchestrate the most expensive public relations campaign ever mounted in Massachusetts on behalf of any educational initiative. It produced videos, brochures, personal contacts, and newsletters by the thousands to promote acceptance of the MCAS, not to mention strong editorials in the *Boston Globe* and the *Boston Herald*.

In October 2001, the state kicked off a $700,000 advertising campaign to promote MCAS, with ads set to run through November. It had spent $500,000 the previous April on a similar round of ads. "This specifically targets parents, and in particular parents of the Class of 2003 who are the most anxiety-ridden right now," said Heidi B. Perlman, spokeswoman for the Massachusetts Department of Education."[23] In his May 2003 testimony at the State House, Representative Frank Smizik offered this rebuke: "During this fiscal year, at a time of unprecedented fiscal problems, the state signed a $300,000 contract with Mass Insight to promote the MCAS and to hold forums where all of the speakers are pro-MCAS."

Why Not Refuse?

One can't help but wonder what some of the independent grassroots groups might do with even a fraction of that kind of money. Mass Refusal, to name one, proposed an innovative strategy rejected by CARE and ignored by the teachers union. Sponsored by New Democracy, a Boston-based grassroots group calling for democratic revolution, Mass Refusal urges, "We cannot rely solely on our legislators or political figures to solve the problem of MCAS. We have to rely on our own individual and collective strength." The group calls on all teachers and teacher union locals to refuse to administer the MCAS. It calls on parents to support teachers in this move and to refuse to allow their children to take the MCAS. It calls on high schoolers to refuse to take the MCAS. Such a strategy, instead of depending on "the other" to change the world, calls on people to do it themselves. In the words of a Mass Refusal flier, "We call on all parents and parent organizations to support teachers' refusal to administer the MCAS."[24]

- We call on all people to copy and distribute this *Call for MassRefusal* as widely as possible.
- We call on all people to ask that any organization of which they are members—teacher unions, PTOs, school councils, trade unions, faith-based groups, civil rights, civic, and professional organizations, political groups, etc.—endorse this *Call for MassRefusal* and publicize their endorsement.

The flier concludes, "We have a right and duty to protect our children from these destructive tests. Only by standing together and refusing to participate will we end MCAS." The idea here is teachers and parents working together: Don't ask a handful of teachers to martyr themselves, but if 60 or 70 percent of teachers in a building agree not to give the test, then the union should shut down the test in that building. If this happened in a few schools, it would be a second revolutionary shot heard round the world. Tests would fall like dominoes across the country. But someone has to start this mass refusal.

Lacking the resources to get the message out and failing to capture more than scattered support from the teachers union leadership or from such organizations as FairTest and CARE, the Mass Refusal plan didn't happen. Nonetheless, there are parents and teachers across the country who think test refusal is an idea whose time will come. If any grassroots group that truly believes in people power ever gets a smidgeon of a fraction of the moneys the Massachusetts Department of Education or the Massachusetts teachers union has spent on TV ads, then big business had better watch out.

Texas Activism

Dennis Shirley has chronicled a different route for the development of community organizing. In 1992, after a twenty-year history of community organizing in Texas, the Industrial Areas Foundation (IAF), founded by pioneering Chicago activist Saul Alinsky, teamed up with, of all outfits, the Texas Education Agency, to create twenty-one Alliance Schools. Although the IAF began its work in Texas in an attempt to help communities take back control over their lives from huge corporations, the mass media, and benevolent government, it seems to have ended up promoting the educational reform agenda sponsored by these very institutions. For example, at one Alliance School, Hueco Elementary, on the outskirts of El Paso, 95 percent of the students qualify for free or reduced-price lunch and more than half are limited English proficient. Alliance funding encourages teachers to make home visits and train parents to support learning at home. Hueco parents are also encouraged to become involved in their children's education through the Success for All program. The school's Success for All facilitator provides training "for parents interested in becoming Success for All volunteer tutors for children."[25] One can only wonder how training parents to deliver such a highly regimented program as the controversial Success for All could be construed as helping parents take control of their lives.[26]

Saul Alinsky must be rolling in his grave. In an interview shortly before he died in 1972, Alinsky said that people need to "go out and fight those fascist trends and build a mass constituency that will support progressive causes."[27] Certainly, Texas parents should be organizing to protest their children being put in a scripted curriculum, not parroting such a robotic program in their homes. Instead of building the constituency Alinsky describes, this parent training borders on the grotesque, seemingly intent on training parents to be good participants in the party line of the state department of education and its corporate handlers.

Such co-option is, of course, a testament to the effectiveness of the systemic reformers' structural design—with the removal of goal-setting functions from local control, organizers feel unable to help parents address the issue of curriculum content and teaching methods. In 1986, Morningside Elementary School in Fort Worth, Texas, became the pilot for the Alliance Schools, funded by the state, local business leaders, and foundations.[28] An organizing staff identified and trained local leaders through church education committees, home visits, and training sessions.

The visitations and training sessions gradually changed Morningside from a school with no ties to the community to a fulcrum of parental involvement. Many parents had never understood the actual course of study for their children in the school or how their children were assessed. ACT [Allied Communities of Tarrant] leaders prepared training sessions to teach the parents about the structure of the school and to advise them about ways they could reinforce activities at home. At this stage, abstract debates about the legitimacy of the curriculum or the problems of Texas' standardized tests were avoided; the focus was on helping parents to understand the given realities of the school and how they could assist their children within that framework.[29]

The given realities: there's a whole lot of politics and disenfranchisement in that neat little phrase. As long as local organizers stayed clear of addressing *the legitimacy of the curriculum or the problems of Texas' standardized tests*, they could expect corporate foundations to continue to support them. In 1990, the Rockefeller Foundation agreed to fund the training of organizers to spread the success of Morningside.

Shirley describes how parents were sidetracked from debating the goals of education. Specifically, in 1994, parent opposition to tracking in El Paso, Texas, was channeled by corporate-funded IAF community organizers into a renewed commitment to the traditional curriculum.

The parents of children at Alamo Elementary School knew that for many years, through some slow, opaque, and seemingly inexorable process, their children always ended up tracked to the lowest level when they arrived in middle school and high school. The parents refused to believe that that tracking was a reflection of students' natural abilities rather than the culture of their schools, but they were reticent to pin responsibility on their children's teachers and principal. Working with El Paso Interreligious Sponsoring Organization [EPISO] organizers and leaders, Alamo parents decided to address the problem of academic standards by looking neither to the "Essential Elements" mandated by the TEA nor to the curriculum experts of the El Paso Independent School District. They decided that they wanted to play a major role in setting the curriculum standards for the school themselves. In a series of house meetings, parents discussed what they wanted their children to know at the end of each grade level. [School staff and IAF organizers participated in but did not lead the discussions.] The parents would need time and a supportive environment to develop their leadership and to establish those curricular goals which most deeply emanated from their own thoughts and experiences.

What kinds of curricular themes did the parents identify? Parents wanted their children to be literate and skilled in arithmetic, science, and social studies. "As the conversations evolved, there was an almost perfect overlapping between the parents' curriculum and that which traditionally was taught at Alamo"[30].

Reading between the lines, we see that IAF organizers loaded the deck with Business Roundtable lingo that is worse than a fraud, selling people false dreams and thereby disarming them from fighting the system. It's the BRT flimflam: systemic reform is needed, not to reform economic injustice but to reform school curriculum. Kati Haycock, director of Education Trust, is front and center on the BRT chorus line: "It's a new century. It's time to set aside our Industrial Age Curriculum and agree on a common core curriculum for the Information Age." Haycock wants business to provide a rock-solid list of the skills needed for these new Information Age jobs. Never mind the forecasts showing hundreds of thousands of Information Age jobs being shipped overseas. In a perverse twist on W. P. Kinsella's vision in *Shoeless Joe* (later popularized in the movie *Field of Dreams*), "Build it and he will come," Education Trust insists that if students take high-skilled subjects like algebra and calculus, then the jobs will come.[31]

Even a cursory examination of any job statistics—not to mention media accounts of college graduates delivering pizza—and of the U.S. Department of Labor job projections over the next ten years reveals what a dubious and deceptive proposition this is. By setting the realities of education essentially off limits, the IAF organizers followed the pattern set by the Business Roundtable across the nation: for parents of children on free and reduced lunch, content and instruction is a given. By presenting the goals of education as *ugly realities*, IAF organizers prevented parents from considering education as a process by which they and their children could learn how to change those realities. Carol Holst, a Texas parent who, in the face of an oppressive curriculum, decided that homeschooling was the only option for her son, says, "Parents need to know that the people who are shipping their jobs to the Philippines are the same ones making their kids vomit on these tests."

In his introduction to *Valley Interfaith and School Reform: Organizing for Power in South Texas*, Shirley makes it clear that he accepts the canard that American children make a poor showing in international comparisons. Significantly, he calls those developing "a massive battery of high-stakes standardized tests" *reformers*.[32]

When the IAF organized school-parent involvement at the Palmer Elementary School in rural Hidalgo County, arrangements were made so teachers could make home visits, talking with parents about their perceptions of the school, urging parents to volunteer in the school. "Parents are also informed about Texas' standardized test, the Texas Assessment of Academic Skills (TAAS), and are advised that whatever one's beliefs about standardized tests, failure to learn to do well on them can result in their children being tracked to a lower level in secondary school or failing to graduate from high school altogether."[33] What kind of activism is it that trains parents to take high-stakes testing as a given? Is protest only for suburban soccer moms?

The parent room at the school is filled with books, computers, and "drill activities that parents can use to reinforce classroom activities at home." Parents are encouraged to advocate for sewage treatment and for construction of new classrooms; curriculum and testing are presented as givens. No resistance possible. And even Shirley measures the success of the IAF Alliance Schools by TAAS results. For example, when discussing a different elementary school in the alliance, Shirley concludes, "If Sam Houston's teachers want to raise those scores, they may need to pay less attention to cultural influences and instead focus more specifically on linguistic capabilities or test-taking skills."[34] There is no hint that drill-and-kill test prep robs children of an education—and culture.

That IAF organizers allowed themselves to be a part of such entanglement, given their commitment to helping communities articulate "curricular goals which most deeply emanate from their own thoughts and experiences," is disheartening. Even the Annie E. Casey Foundation website states that "[t]he Alliance Schools Project is grounded in the belief that schools should engage parents to the point where they take responsibility for—and action that results in—changing their schools to meet their children's needs."[35] Changing their schools. Meeting children's needs. One could wish the organizers had chosen to draw on the teachings of Paulo Freire, whose work with poor and working-class communities in South America resulted in very different educational goals and practices, rather than the ugly realities dictated by the power elite.[36] We can hope it's not too late for Texans to start reading the work of Saul Alinsky.

Co-Opting Education Researchers and Teachers

Many education researchers face the dilemma that their research depends on corporate and federal funding, and as a result they end up as technocrats trying to find ways to implement some form of the BRT's Essential Components of a Successful School Systems. The California-based Bay Area Schools Reform Collaborative (BASRC) is a case in point of how the BRT agenda influences the goals of many research organizations. The BRT's essential components of high standards, its rigorous and measurable assessment aligned with those standards, its focus on every student and on parent involvement, teacher development, and technology are fundamental both to the BASRC research and development priorities and to its definition of Core Reform Issues. This is not surprising,

given that the Hewlett and Annenberg Foundations, who are, not coinciden-
tally, among the most generous sources of funds for national systemic reform,
are BASRC's principal funders.

In turn, BASRC disperses research and development funds in six areas
that are "of critical importance to finding better methods and more effective
responses to the new challenges that face our schools":[37] school-to-career approaches, technology, professional development, teacher practice, equitable
outcomes[38] on standardized tests, and support for school reform leaders.
BASRC also has established a club to which individual schools can apply
"through a rigorous portfolio process." To qualify as a BASRC member, one
must already "show concrete evidence of effort" in the areas of quality teaching,
high standards, partnerships with key stakeholders (local business leaders),
systems to manage the change process, and development of a sense of professional community and internalized accountability among teachers.[39]

The benefits of being accepted as a BASRC member include access to facilitators and the potential for funding. North Campus Continuation High in
San Pablo, California, for one, received a Hewlett-Annenberg Leadership
grant by establishing a partnership with the local chamber of commerce to develop a performance-assessment matrix reflecting the skill requirements of
local businesses. Washington Science Elementary School, a magnet school in
Richmond, California, received $380,000 over four years for building a com-
munity culture committed to increasing test scores on the Iowa Test of Basic
Skills.

Fremont High School in Sunnyvale, California, is BASRC's showcase
Leadership School.[40] Its economic and ethnic diversity (sixty different languages) make it the "picture of what California—and the rest of the country—
will look like in the next century." Its success in implementing high standards
has attracted the attention of such scholars as Linda Darling-Hammond and
made it a must-see for international educators. According to BASRC, the reason for Fremont's success is that it "looks at student data to diagnose what is
and isn't working"—a fundamental requirement in BRT's theory of educational reform. When looking at the data, the Freemont staff discovered low test
scores in math, science, and English, so it rearranged the daily schedule to give
students more time for instruction in those subjects. But not wanting to rely on
test scores only, Fremont High also has programs to "increase student input on
campus." Lip service is paid to student—and teacher—input because "research
shows that democratically run schools increase student achievement."[41] Sounds
good, and yet one must question how democratic school decision making can
be when the goals of education are decided by an interlocking network consist-
ing of BRT members, state governors, and foundation support for Institute for
Educational Leadership studies and programs.[42]

One Teacher Faces Skills for the Global Economy

Although Gabriel Proo's experience at Belle Air Elementary School (2000–01) is only one teacher's testimony, it provides dramatic evidence that BASRC's emphasis on data-driven reform has made test scores a blunt instrument by which teachers are de-skilled and students humiliated.[43] Before becoming a teacher, Gabriel had been a paralegal for seven years and a purchasing agent for five years. He has a B.A. in Spanish, a multicultural credential from San Francisco State University, and a master's in Spanish literature. He came to Belle Air with six years of teaching experience.

Every Belle Air teacher was expected to attend a three-day retreat in June and a two-day retreat in August with the purpose of creating a site plan to improve the school's test scores. When Gabriel arrived at Asilomar State Park near Monterey for the June retreat, he learned that he was one of approximately sixty teachers attending—all part of a BASRC cluster of six schools. The gung-ho enthusiasm of the BASRC-trained facilitators who ran the three-day retreat was intense. Their sales pitch for using test scores as the basis of a cycle of inquiry resembled a marketing workshop, with the cycle of inquiry becoming the cyclone of inquiry, with constant repetition: *diagnosis and cure, diagnosis and cure.* A point of interest: one year later, Gabriel could not remember the five or six steps of the cycle.

For three days, teachers were drilled on how to analyze test data. Belle Air scores were distributed and teachers were asked, "What do you see?" Teachers dutifully pointed out "gaps in performance," for example, a precipitous drop from third grade to fourth grade. There was no discussion of test-score validity, reliability, or accuracy; no mention of the Joint Committee on Testing's Code of Practice. There was no discussion as to why scores should be reported as a range and not a single number; no discussion of the American Psychological Association position that important decisions about students should never be made on the basis of test scores alone. Teachers were told that where there was a gap or disparity in test scores, the cure should be applied. *Diagnosis and cure. Diagnosis and cure.*

The cure required teaching only math and English during the first four hours of school. Teachers were handed two scripted curricula to follow during those four hours—Open Court and Math Steps. A sample lesson on addition and subtraction with regrouping has these teacher instructions: *Say, Ask, Say, Say, Ask, Say, Ask, Ask, Ask, Say, Ask, Say, Say, Ask, Say.*[44] Skills for the global economy.

Teacher manuals were distributed to help teachers implement the curriculum of interrogation. Teachers were told explicitly not to bring in any other subjects to help teach the reading and computation skills outlined in the given curricula. As Gabriel followed the curriculum plans of Open Court and Math Steps and administered the required blizzard of practice tests, students became first indifferent and then hostile, with discipline problems escalating. The rigidly prescribed curriculum left no time to give students the individual attention they needed. Gabriel was not provided with scaffolding materials in simplified English or Spanish to help students understand what was being asked of them. He was told that English-only instruction was vital because the tests are in English. At one point Gabriel was sent to a three-day workshop on how to teach learning disabled students, but he couldn't use those techniques because they "went against the BASRC program . . . in BASRC, there are no LD students."

When Gabriel had questions about the teacher manuals, his requests for explanation were ignored, so he did the only thing possible: he started to lie about what he was doing in the classroom. It seems more than ironic that BASRC's claims of fostering democratic decision making became manifested only in a teacher's lies.

The BASRC site plan mandated testing students three times a year (in addition to the SAT-9 testing required by the state): five tests per student in the fall, five more in the winter, and five again in the spring. Several of the five-test battery that BASRC provided (only one copy of each so the teacher had to make copies for every student) had to be administered individually. This meant that while Gabriel was giving a test to one child, other children were supposed to work on test-prep materials, which they hated. Worse, many students didn't speak English well enough to understand what the test was asking of them, so Gabriel had to watch them sit in silent humiliation. When students persistently failed to come to school on testing day, Gabriel was supposed to track them down for make-up sessions.

The administrative load of all the testing swamped any idea of teaching as an art, a passion, or even a reasonable occupation. Teaching was now, in Gabriel's words, "just grading papers and tests." Out of frustration, Gabriel began to invent test scores for those students he failed to track down. Call it more democratic decision making.

At the end of the year, the school's test scores did go up, but not enough to garner any cash incentive awards dangled by the state. Teachers were resentful, feeling they had worked just as hard as schools that did get the extra cash. At the end of the year Gabriel left teaching, not willing to participate any longer in systemic reform.

Gabriel's experiences echo Linda McNeil's research.[45] McNeil argues that low-performing schools are targeted with test-prep materials, resulting in the de-skilling and dumbing down of at-risk students. Targeted students no longer have access to a rich and varied curriculum. Teachers, also de-skilled and dumbed down, aren't able to change the curriculum to fit individual interests and needs of students. Where a library was once deemed central to a school, with a tightly controlled curriculum, it disappears.

Which Comes First, the Money or the Plan?

California Tomorrow (CT) promotes workshops similar to the training retreat Gabriel attended. CT is a nonprofit organization partnered with the Institute for Educational Leadership. In 1994, California Tomorrow submitted to the California state legislature an executive summary of its research based upon several demonstration sites. The summary included twelve conclusions and sixty-one recommendations. Following are two recommendations CT urged the state legislature to act upon.

Recommendation #4—Create and fund a major five-year professional development campaign with the goal of supporting mainstream teachers and administrators to develop the expertise needed to teach in a diverse society. These skills include: knowledge of second language acquisition processes and supports for students through the process; familiarity with a wide range of materials about different cultures and historical periods to enable teachers to build inclusive curricula; approaches to creating a climate supportive of diversity; exposure to the major cultures and national backgrounds of the student population of California; and strategies for working in partnership with other children and family agencies.[46]

Recommendation #7—Invest in the development of a data-driven accountability system that builds upon existing data and management information systems and holds schools accountable for both high-level standards and equitable student achievement and participation. The accountability system must promote self-examination of sub-aggregated data at the school site level, and include three basic components: incentives for schools to improve their performance, technical assistance and professional development for schools engaged in good faith efforts but not sufficiently improving, and reasonable sanctions for those schools which ultimately fail to improve over prolonged periods of time.[47]

There is no acknowledgment of the potential conflict between recommendations 4 and 7. Nor is there any indication of an understanding that the emphasis on "data-driven accountability" often reduces issues of diversity and equity (issues typically raised at the community level) to test-score results (issues raised at the corporate level).

So which comes first, the chicken or the egg? Do researchers and regional labs earn corporate funding because they exhibit affinity with the goals of systemic reform and have a plan for achieving these goals? Or do they adopt these goals after receiving the funding? In some cases, reorientation is fairly obvious. For example, one researcher who had a position of leadership in California Tomorrow had been a proponent of such community concerns as bilingual education, student empowerment, and the ways in which the public school system forces non-Anglo students to abandon their home cultures. But after receiving a five-year Mellon grant, her research turned to promoting the BRT agenda: "finding ways to use data and inquiry for accountability purposes, developing standards and exit criteria for ESL classes and increasing access to academic classes," as well as finding new models of professional development that would support data-driven decision making. She became involved in finding ways to help immigrant children learn English in order to master academic content so as to qualify for college.[48] This, by itself, is a laudable goal. But if BRT is able to control what academic content is taught, then other goals—empowerment, divergent thinking, problem-identifying skills, caretaking skill, even preserving bicultural identities—cannot be pursued in the school system or even supported by it.

One can wonder if Dennis Shirley's research might also have been influenced by the overarching goals of his funders—the Mellon and Ford Foundations. Early on, Shirley states that his research is motivated by the need to

> learn about forms of community self-mobilization and political action that not only confront the despair which haunts our urban schools, but also address Kozol's question about the presence of the ghetto itself.[49]

Jonathan Kozol believes that teachers should not just teach in the ghetto but teach the ghetto—asking, with their students, why the ghetto exists. The rest of Shirley's book never returns to Kozol's question but focuses instead on the ways in which community organizers need to learn how to better "enhance academic achievement," that is, increase scores on the statewide mandated standardized test. Shirley doesn't question whether the tests themselves contribute to the presence of the ghetto. He buries in a footnote his observation that

> many convincing studies have been conducted by educators who warn about the reductionist nature of standardized test scores. Regrettably, some of the newer and more promising forms of assessment, which focus on exhibitions, demonstrations, and performances have not been in place for enough time to measure their efficacy in promoting higher order thinking skills.[50]

The focus of Shirley's research is on the means by which the differing cultures of school and home in poor, urban school districts can be fused so students can better develop the cognitive skills they need to get the better jobs in the so-called new economy. Shirley notes that after four years of community organizing in support of the Texas state exam, the principal of a Fort Worth elementary school, in 1990, confessed that a key part of her strategy to improve test scores focused on recitation and memorization—skills that are valuable components of cognitive development but that need to be balanced with higher order thinking skills involving creative expression, synthesis, and evaluation to enhance children's many sided development.[51]

Shirley points out that teaching to the test only worsened in 1994, when the new TAAS was made public and schools began to build their curricula around the test. And yet, in spite of these and other problems, Shirley feels compelled to use the test scores as the means to evaluate his ethnographic and historical independent variables.

> One cannot know to what degree community-based organizations and the Alliance Schools network operate as independent variables in the data [TAAS scores from 1990 to 1996] . . . there are many limitations on the test scores. Nonetheless, they do provide one resource for attempting to gauge academic progress. Recognizing the above qualifications, one may explore the TAAS results to ascertain if they provide clues about the development of the Alliance Schools.[52]

Clearly, Shirley is conflicted. His research reinforces the legitimacy of tests by using them as his measurement device. Yet, at the same time, he understands not only the limited validity of tests but also their destructive consequences.

Systemic Reform: Rhetoric—and Cold Cash— Trump Reality

The rhetoric of union leaders, the concerns of parents, the implementation workshops of regional laboratories, and education researchers have all lined up behind systemic reform. High-stakes testing, enforced by content standards and written by state committees, provides the framework within which people seem to feel they must work. Otherwise, they risk being accused of not wanting every student to be successful, not believing that all students can achieve. Very few people are asking, Successful at doing what? and Achieving for whom? We've seen that the number of high-paying jobs is shrinking. If schools produce more skilled people, they will also increase the number of losers failing to grab the golden ring as more and more jobs are shipped overseas. Systemic reformers don't entertain any questions about the economic reality but instead stifle such questions by painting their critics into a corner—as people who don't believe in that clever phrase *high standards for all*. Teachers are persuaded to support systemic reform both because they want to believe the rhetoric and because golden promises are dangled—cash incentives, increases in job status.

But underneath the folderol and flimflam, teachers are living lives of quiet desperation—hapless participants in the transformation of public schools. Parents are persuaded to support systemic reform because of the relentless corporate-politico drumbeat, recycled in the media as news, that unreformed schools have a long history of failure and that these schools fail because lazy and/or incompetent teachers don't have high expectations of their students and/or lack the skills to do the job. Researchers support systemic reform because, otherwise, they can't even get a job, never mind find funding for their research. Once again, the very few in this country have managed to give marching—and teaching and research—orders to the many. And they call it systemic reform.

The Ten Commandments of Securing Funding for Systemic Reform

And the funders spake:

    I. We are the State and its business partners, which have brought students out of the wilderness of student-centered classrooms and into the kingdom of test prep. Thou shalt have no other guidance before thee, and then it will follow as night follows day that No Researcher Is Left Behind.

    II. Thou shalt not make unto thyself any graven images, not any likeness of anything that contradicts the Standards and their tests. For the State is a jealous god, visiting the iniquity of the fathers upon the children unto the third and fourth generation of them who don't obey.

    III. Thou shalt not take the name of systemic reform, thy god, in vain. For the State nor the Business Roundtable will not hold him guiltless that takes its name in vain.

    IV. Remember the Standards and keep them holy. The State blessed the tests and hallowed them. Thy adequate yearly progress scores shall comfort thee.

    V. Honor thy Standards, that thy days as systemic reformers may be long upon the land of test preparation, which the State gives you.

    VI. Thou shalt not kill Standardistas.

    VII. Thou shalt not have intercourse with any other than thy lawful Business Roundtable Nine Essential Components and Open Court.

    VIII. Thou shalt direct teachers not to steal time away from the Standards and preparation for the State's tests for frivolous matters such as art, music, and recess.

    IX. Thou shalt not bear false witness against the Standardistas or the systemic reformers who bring grants to you.

X. Thou shalt not covet daydreams of bygone times. Nor shalt thou covet independence, individuality, nor anything that went before.

Blessed are those who follow the Standardista drumroll, for theirs is the kingdom of government contracts.

Notes

1. Thomas Kean, former governor of New Jersey, chair of the board of directors; W. Frank Blount, president of the Communications Products Group of AT&T, president of NASDC; Louis V. Gerstner Jr., chair of RJR Nabisco; James K. Baker, chair of Arvin Industries; Frank Shrontz, chair of Boeing Co.; Walter H. Annenberg, philanthropist; Norman R. Augustine, chief executive of Martin Marietta Corp.; Gerald L. Balilies, former governor of Virginia; John L. Clendenin, chair and chief executive of BellSouth; James R. Jones, chair and chief executive of the American Stock Exchange; Lee R. Raymond, president of Exxon Corp.; Paul Tagliabue, commissioner of the National Football League; Earl Graves, publisher of *Black Enterprise* magazine; Joan Ganz Cooney, executive committee chair, Children's Television Workshop; Kay Whitmore, chair, chief executive, and president of Eastman Kodak; James J. Renier, chair and chief executive of Honeywell; John Ong, chair of B. F. Goodrich; and Stanley A. Weiss, chair of Business Executives for National Security and the BENS Education Fund.

2. Sherry, Mark. 1992. "Searching for New American Schools." *Education Week*, 6 May.

3. Northwest Regional Educational Laboratory. 1999. "Stepping Up the Rigor, Part 3." *Northwest Education Magazine*, fall. Accessed at *www.nwrel.org/nwedu/fall99/article6c.html*.

4. Bernbaum, Brian. 2003. "Monkey Theory Proven Wrong." CBS News, 9 May. Accessed at *www.arn.org/docs2/news/monkeysandtypewriters051103.htm*.

5. Phrases like this one—*no group knows more*—are likely to alienate parents by calling upon the legacy of professionalism. Chase, in the face of a concerted assault on *real* teacher autonomy through the imposition of state standards and tests, is attempting to assert teacher expertise as a means to carve out some space in which teachers can retain some respect or prestige. But in seeking status from state officials and editorialists instead of from parents, Chase threatens to alienate the only constituency that would support real decision-making authority for teachers—parents. Many parents who come to school to speak to teachers about their children want to have a dialogue with the teachers. They don't want to be patronized with an attitude that the teacher rather than the parent knows what is best for the child. As long as teachers couch their opposition to systemic reform in a professional paradigm (we know better than parents or state policy makers), they will be vulnerable to divide-and-conquer tactics by the BRT network.

6. Chase, Bob. 1999. "The New NEA: Reinventing Teacher Unions." In *Transforming Teacher Unions: Fighting for Better Schools and Social Justice*, ed. B. Peterson and M. Charney, 107–10. Milwaukee: Rethinking Schools.

7. Simon, Mark. 1999. "Resisting Resistance to Change." In *Transforming Teacher Unions: Fighting for Better Schools and Social Justice*, ed. B. Peterson and M. Charney, 66–67. Milwaukee: Rethinking Schools.

8. Business Roundtable. 1996. *A Business Leader's Guide to Setting Academic Standards*. Accessed at *www.Brtable.org/pdf/225.pdf*.

9. Feldman, Sandra. 1999. "Whither Public Education." In *Transforming Teacher Unions: Fighting for Better Schools and Social Justice*, ed. B. Peterson and M. Charney, 111–14. Milwaukee: Rethinking Schools.

10. Editorial. 2000. *New York Times*, 24 April.

11. Davis, Gray. 1999. "Schools on the Road Back." *San Francisco Chronicle*, 4 October.

12. Steinbruner, Maureen. 1999. "Parents, Leadership Disagree over How to Fix Nation's Schools, San Francisco Schools." *San Francisco Chronicle*, 29 September.

13. Tyack, David, and Larry Cuban. 1995. *Tinkering Toward Utopia: A Century of Public School Reform*. Cambridge: Harvard University Press.

14. Ibid., 32–33.

15. From *www.fairtest.org/Who%20We%20Are.html*.

16. From the CARE listserv, 24 July 2000.

17. Kurtz, Michele. 2003. "Pressured Communities Threaten to Defy State on MCAS Students Failing Test." *The Boston Globe*, 6 March.

18. Ibid.

19. Lazar, Kay. 2003. "Rogue Schools Get Lesson in MCAS Laws." *The Boston Herald*, 1 June.

20. "Spineless: School Boards Beat Shameful Retreat on Standards." 2002. Editorial. *Worcester Telegram & Gazette*, 3 November.

21. "Committees Wrong on MCAS." 2002. Editorial. *The Boston Herald*, 2 November.

22. The Massachusetts Institute for a New Commonwealth "works to ensure that every citizen has the tools to succeed in today's dynamic, technology-driven economy." It sees its mission as "[e]nsuring that the state's pre-K and K–12 Education Reform effort stays on track." See *www.massinc.org/mission/initiatives.html*.

23. McElhenny, John. 2001. "State to Launch Pro-MCAS Ads." *South Coast Today*, 10 October. Accessed at *www.s-t.com/daily/10-01/10-10-01/a13sr126.htm*.

24. From *www.massrefusal.org*.

25. Funkhouser, Janie E., and Miriam R. Gonzales. 1997. *Family Involvement in Children's Education: Successful Local Approaches: An Idea Book*. Washington, DC: U.S. Department of Education. Accessed at *www.ed.gov/pubs/FamInvolve/title.html*.

26. See, for example, Stanley Pogrow's *Phi Delta Kappan* article: Pogrow, Stanley. 2000. "The Unsubstantiated 'Success' of Success for All: Implications for Policy, Practice, and the Soul of Our Profession." *Phi Delta Kappan* 81 (8): 596–600.

27. From *www.progress.org/2003/alinsky14.htm*.

28. Shirley, Dennis. 1997. *Community Organizing for Urban School Reform*. Austin: University of Texas, 100.

29. Ibid., 109.

30. Ibid., 211.

31. Education Trust. 2003. "A New Core Curriculum for All: Aiming High for Other People's Children." *Thinking K–16*, winter. Accessed at *www2.edtrust.org/NR/rdonlyres/26923A64-4266-444B-99ED-2A6D5F14061F/0/k16_winter2003.pdf*.

32. Shirley, Dennis. 2002. *Valley Interfaith and School Reform: Organizing for Power in South Texas*. Austin: University of Texas, xiii.

33. Ibid., 31.

34. Ibid., 82.

35. From *www.acef.org/publications/success/family.htm*.

36. Freire, Paulo. 1970. *Pedagogy of the Oppressed*. Trans. Myra Bergman Ramos. New York: Seabury Press.

37. Bay Area School Reform Collaborative. 1999. *Initiatives*. BASRC. Accessed at *fwl.org/basrc/initiatives.html*.

38. When Linda McNeil (2000; see Chapter 6) studied the impact of the high-stakes testing agenda in Houston, Texas, she found that in the pursuit of "equitable outcomes" (attempts to raise the test scores of poor and minority students to the levels of middle-class whites and Asian Americans), school administrators were forcing teachers to abandon "rich and authentic" curricula for a "dumbed-down, test-prep" course of study. Too often, the euphemisms of "equitable access," "equitable outcomes," "equity and excellence," and "high standards for all" mask an insidious development—the reinstatement of the principle "separate but equal," that is, the growing resegregation of our nation's schools.

39. Bay Area School Reform Collaborative. 1999. *What's Working*. BASRC. Accessed at *fwl.org/basrc/whats_working/index.html*.

40. Ibid.

41. Ibid.

42. IEL corpoate funders include ARCO Foundation; J. P. Morgan Chase & Co.; Lockheed Martin Corp.; MetLife Foundation; the Procter & Gamble Fund; and United Parcel Service. Its foundation funders include Atlantic Philanthropies; Broad Foundation; Carnegie Corp. of New York; Annie E. Casey Foundation; Chicago Community Foundation; Wallace-Reader's Digest Fund; Ford Foundation; Bill and Melinda Gates Foundation; E. M. Kauffman Foundation; W. K. Kellogg Foundation; KnowledgeWorks Foundation; Charles Stewart Mott Foundation; David and Lucile Packard Foundation; the Pew Charitable Trusts; Polk Brothers Foundation; and Sylvan Learning Foundation, Inc. Listed as others are Temple University; George Washington University; University of Minnesota; U.S. Department of Labor; U.S. Department of Justice; U.S. Department of Education; National Association of State Directors of Special Education; National Center for Public Policy and Higher Education; and Council of Chief State School Officers.

43. Emery interviewed Gabriel on 15 October 2001.

44. See *www.eduplace.com/math/mathsteps/2/c/2.addsub.ideas1.html*.

45. McNeil, Linda. 2000. *Contradictions of School Reform: Educational Costs of Standardized Testing*. Sacramento, CA: Routledge.

46. Connor, K., and M. Melendez. 1994. *Education Reform Briefing Book. Volume I, First Edition. Education Reform in Review and Emerging Education Issues in California*. Sacramento: California State Legislature, Senate Office of Research.

47. Ibid.

48. University of California at Santa Barbara. 1998. "Laurie Olsen." Accessed at *imrinet. ucsb.edu/confs/olsen_bio.htm*.

49. Shirley. 1997, 4.

50. Ibid., 310.

51. Ibid., 114.

52. Ibid., 215–16. The innovations included intensive summer courses to prepare students for college-preparatory courses in their high school (Tenneco Corporation offered $1,000-per-year college scholarships for every Davis High School student who could maintain a 2.5 grade point average and attend two monthlong summer institutes at the University of Houston, for which they were paid $150 a session); block scheduling (ninety-minute classes, fifteen-minute intersessions; an hour for lunch); alignment of feeder schools with high school curriculum; and thirty thousand hours of professional development "in new forms of instruc-

tion and curriculum development"—"hands-on mathematics, collaborative approaches to reading, student self-discipline and self-governance" paid for by Tenneco and its corporate allies. Tenneco's scholarship program was cited by the BRT as one of several "Exemplary Corporate Policies and Practices to Improve Education."

8

As Goes California, So Goes the Nation

It used to be said that you had to know what was happening in America because it gave us a glimpse of our future. Today the rest of America, and after that Europe, had better heed what happens in California, for it already reveals the type of civilization that is in store for all of us.

—ALISTAIR COOKE, 1968

In 1989, a year after the California Business Roundtable (CBR) published *Restructuring California Education: A Design for Public Education in the Twenty-First Century*,[1] the national Business Roundtable devoted its entire annual meeting to carving out an education agenda, and it adopted the basic principles of the California report. In the fall of 1989, this Business Roundtable agenda was then circulated to the nation's governors as America 2000, which Clinton later renamed Goals 2000. Think of this history the next time you hear pontification about the *scientific evidence* behind the No Child Left Behind rules and regulations. What hogwash: The Reading First provisions of NCLB is as about as scientific as the astrology chart in your newspaper.

The CBR's 295-page blueprint and the Minnesota plan were rough drafts for what became national systemic reform for the next fifteen years. Adopting principles of QM that would characterize both state and national agendas in the ensuing years,[2] the CBR report incorporated concerns over dropouts and test-score disparities into a new theory of educational reform. *Restructuring* or *bottom-up* reform meant that the state legislature would control the goals of education while school sites would be accountable for the strategies for meeting those goals.

The State (that is, the legislature, the State Board of Education, and the State Department of Education) would be concerned with performance, not with the education process. It would set the goals for education; develop means for measuring how well schools meet these goals; disseminate information

141

about their performance; take a proactive role in stimulating research, development, and training; and provide an adequate level of financing. The state would work with teachers to set standards for the teaching profession and assure quality control. The state would also intervene in failing schools, and help schools to develop and become outstanding or not permit them to continue.[3]

As we will see, *not permitting them to continue* becomes known as *restructuring*, which becomes known as *staff vacating*.

Restructuring Education

The CBR report argued that the growth of an "educationally disadvantaged economic underclass" was proof that previous reforms had been inadequate. Funny, isn't it, that doctors, whose path to professionalism is so admired by the CBR, aren't blamed for the appalling problems of the health-disadvantaged economic underclass? Nor are lawyers blamed for the appallingly high incarceration rate of the disadvantaged economic underclass. But just pile the blame on teachers who work with this same economic underclass.

The report posited two solutions: increase funding for reforms already on the books or restructure the system. Citing the first solution as too expensive, the report adopted the second.

The report's first recommendation will astonish thousands of teachers: The CBR advocated *developmentally appropriate* schooling for all students from the ages of four to six, recommending that formal academic coursework shouldn't begin until age seven. That sounds almost quaint. These days, power brokers are testing preschoolers on academic content and, emblematic of what's happening to five-year-olds across the country, the Gadsden, Alabama, city schools have eliminated kindergarten nap time so the children will have more time to prepare for new mandated standardized tests. Wynell Williams, elementary education director for the Gadsden school system, said, "If the state is holding us accountable, this is the way we have to do it. Kindergarten is not like it used to be."[4]

Kindergarten teachers and parents, listen up: Kindergarten is not like it used to be because you're giving your children over to the Business Roundtable. You could try saying, "No!"

The CBR recommends that children from ages seven to sixteen (up to grade 10), should all learn the same *core competencies*, eliminating separate junior and senior high programs. Whether students' plans after high school are work or college, the CBR decrees they all need the same *knowledge, concepts, and skills*. State committees would develop these competencies and "would specify only what students should learn, not how they should learn it." Under this plan, secondary students are allowed one free elective per semester. The state dictates the rest of the schedule. High school ends at tenth grade, with students taking exit tests to qualify for a post-10 option. Those who pass can "choose specialized educational programs such as college prep, vocational or technical education, fine or performing arts, and other areas that would [be developed] to meet the needs of the twenty-first century." Freed from having to be comprehensive, grades 7–10 schools would be able to

> reorganize and focus on providing the curriculum, programs, and instructional services they do best. Some high schools might decide not to offer courses for the eleventh and twelfth grade so that they could direct their energies to excellence in the earlier grades in the common high school. The advantages of the post-10 option [are that students] would no longer be tracked but instead would be able to choose specialized schooling that fits their needs.

This setup allows high achievers to advance more rapidly and thereby save schools money, since there's no need to offer "advance material that might distort the curriculum for others."[5] This idea has gotten plenty of mileage. Remember Marc Tucker's infamous eighteen-page "Dear Hillary" letter?

The authors of the 1988 CBR report expressed confidence that the plan would work in California because they had seen it work so well in Minnesota in 1984 and 1985. Surprise, surprise, the Minnesota plan was written by the same Berkeley-based Berman and Weiler Associates as the California report. The Minnesota plan promoted a passive, technology-based learning model, changing Minnesota schools from a K–12 to a K–10 structure. All students would complete school in tenth grade, with the top 20 percent or so being invited back for special college-prep programs. Here is a point of information often ignored, or carefully buried: Minnesota had the highest school completion rate in the country, with a high percentage going on to college. So don't you wonder, with their schools doing so well, why did business leaders want them to end school in tenth grade? Ask the people at Education Trust. They're the ones touting this formula these days.

Master Teachers and Others

> The Minnesota plan included a Master Teacher program: A typical Teacher Team would consist of a Lead Teacher, three Teachers, three Teaching Assistants, and one Adjunct Teacher. The "pay raise" would consist essentially of a "one-time 20% Lead Teacher salary increase."[6]

Ken Nelson, a Democrat and member of the Minnesota House of Representatives, was chief author of Minnesota's education reform bills, at the time working closely with the Education Commission of the States, the National

Governors' Association, the National Alliance of Business, and the Business Roundtable.[7] In 1994, Congress appointed him executive director of the National Education Goals Panel.

A decade and a half later, when you read of business leaders intoning that teachers don't get paid enough and qualified teachers should receive pay of upward of $100,000, the key word here is *qualified*. What they have in mind is a tiered teacher structure. This might be why the No Child Left Behind bill requires both that paraprofessionals have two-year college degrees and classrooms be filled with a scripted reading curriculum. A $100,000 lead teacher can be put in charge of a zillion paraprofessionals who are trained to read the script to the children.[8]

In Roswell, New Mexico, with an associate's degree, the job of paraprofessional pays $9 an hour. Here's what Lucy Haab, longtime kindergarten teacher in California, says her aide offers to children:

> She works with small groups, she mixes paints, she helps with art and cooking activities, she reads to the children or is read to by the children, she answers questions, she helps prepare the room environment so the children can work as independently as possible. When I had a child in a wheel chair, whenever we did creative dance, the aide picked up the child in her arms and they both became falling snowflakes, whirling leaves, or whatever else we were being at the time.

Quite an image, that: helping a child become a falling snowflake. Does anybody on the planet think that the No Child Left Behind spinmeisters and their corporate pals might grasp this concept? Noted educator Yetta Goodman points out that in Arizona, paraprofessionals are important support personnel for teachers, administrators, and especially kids. "Some of these folks never graduated from high school but have become a crucial part of the culture of the school." It's not the degree, stupid; it's the heart, the training, the commitment, and the ties to the community. But the feds are moving ahead with the plan to jack up the requirements. So far, the staff-restructuring plan isn't on the table, but, ask yourself, how can they sell to parents the idea of a paraprofessional delivering reading instruction to their children—unless that para has a college degree and is supervised by a superteacher earning $100,000? Since 80 to 90 percent of a school district's budget is teacher salaries, this is another scheme to reduce labor costs, destroying the power of the unions and downsizing the professional teacher ranks.

In *We Can Change the World*, Dave Stratman points out that school site management, another feature of the Minnesota plan, was designed

> to fragment communities by making each school an island unto itself, narrowing people's perspectives and undermining their ability to work together

for system-wide change; it breaks the connections among parents, teachers, and students with people at other schools, while it encourages competition among special interests within each school.[9]

Stratman emphasizes the importance of teachers understanding what's behind these business partnership reform plans:

> Teachers have goals not just as wage-earners; they also have goals as teachers—concerns about education—and as members of the larger society. The [Minnesota] union did not attempt to extend the morality of a collective vision or the power of collective action to these other crucial areas of its members' lives.[10]

One way for teachers to break out of their isolation is to understand the meaning of the assault on public education and to lead a struggle for democracy and against corporate power. Particularly in the face of No Child Left Behind, this is a mission we need now more than ever.

Deregulation with a Twist

Deregulation, CBR-style, meant phasing out state laws and regulations setting state graduation, course, and seat-time requirements. Good-bye Carnegie units, hello school-to-work. According to the CBR, "new tests and other measures [would] assure that quality education is provided for all students without destroying the local autonomy essential to effective education."[11] The CBR posited performance-based assessment as the key element for holding teachers accountable while at the same time giving them the freedom they needed to be successful.[12] This was a state-designated freedom with test results allowing state functionaries to define which strategies were successful. Later, under No Child Left Behind, we see that when the feds decree which methodologies are successful, teachers are free to choose Open Court or Success for All.

Under the CBR definition, the state held the trump card: Classify every school in California as either "Class I (high or adequately performing), Class II (inadequately performing), or Class III (chronically low-performing or failing)."[13] Districts must develop improvement plans for Class II and III schools.

> These plans might involve reallocating district resources to increase the inputs for failing schools, replacing school principals or teachers, or contracting out for educational services in those schools.

Parents would have the right to transfer students out of Class III schools, with the district guaranteeing the availability of alternative sites for anybody who asked. If no alternative site existed, parents (representing a minimum of thirty students) would be able to start their own school.[14] Insisting that only a "carrot and stick approach assures action," the CBR report envisioned private schools playing a key role in helping districts provide these alternative sites. The carrots were technical assistance, possible extra funding, and the suspension "of certain due process and collective bargaining constraints in order to facilitate improvement plans." The stick was parent choice.

Is all of this beginning to sound familiar? For California, No Child Left Behind is deja voodoo.

The California Business Roundtable was maneuvering for a kind of *deregulation* known variously as lean management, total quality control, total quality management, or site-based decision making. Such a reorganization would, on paper, anyway, eliminate the number of bureaucrats needed to ensure compliance with CBR-defined education goals. According to the plan, parent/teacher/student self-regulation would replace bureaucratic red tape and ineptitude. The CBR report argues that in the past, teachers didn't choose effective instructional strategies because they assumed that only 15 or 20 percent of students are A students. Instead, teachers should expect 85 percent of students to master enough material to receive As. The report asserts that if teachers expect all children to learn what A students can learn, then the teachers will want to adopt *mastery learning*[15] techniques.

The report recommended that the state should provide each school with a discretionary budget that it could spend as it wished—just so long as all spending was "related to the development and delivery of the instructional program."[16] Each school would have a Parent-Community Governing Body and a School Coordinating Council made up of teachers. The former would have budgetary authority; the latter would be an "extension of the School Site Council operating under the [already existing] School Improvement Program." The School Coordinating Council would serve as an advisory board to the principal, thereby providing teachers with an "opportunity to become actively involved in long-range planning, hiring prospective colleagues, development of school philosophy, setting staff development priorities, and managing school resources."[17]

This is what teacher autonomy looks like to a businessman? A Southern California teacher of a combined fourth- and fifth-grade class who has been given just twenty-four hours in which to correct and enter data sheets for thirty twenty-three-page tests—just six days after she had to correct thirty five-paragraph themes and turn in that data—might have difficulty finding the time to hire prospective colleagues and manage school resources, not to mention develop a school philosophy, set staff development priorities, and engage in long-range planning. And still find a little time to teach. Also, given that the state remains firmly in control of setting the goals of public education, one can only presume that what the CBR authors mean by *school philosophy* is confined to textbook selection, teaching methods, and figuring out when the bells should ring.

Again, all these nuts and bolts of a decade-and-a-half-old plan provide a window on what's happening in our schools right this minute. NCLB is not a Republican blitzkrieg; it's the result of years of careful corporate planning.

Pay heed to the niche staked out for alternative schools. Historically, the degree to which corporate moguls have announced a crisis in the basic public school system has matched the degree to which they have provided support for alternatives. During the Progressive Era (c. 1890–1940) and in the sixties (c. 1960–1975), corporate funding swelled the ranks of alternative schools, which was pulled when many of the alternative schools stopped toeing the party line. In the sixties, policy elites proposed to make hierarchal school systems less crisis-ridden by giving them more choices. TQM supported by magnet and small schools became the trumpeted solution. Today, the Bill and Melinda Gates Foundation has contributed millions of dollars with the expectation that a Small Schools national network will offer solutions to the public school system. One problem is that the Small Schools movement tends to make each school an island, breaking the connections with the people at other schools and further fracturing the system. The competition for grant moneys is fierce, encouraging special interests rather than the common good.

Christopher Reeve offers illumination on this point. As he searches for relief from his spinal cord injury, Reeve's frustration with the widespread careerism in the scientific community offers a point to consider about Small Schools and other education innovations. Reeve says, "Professors with tenure submit a grant application to get a little bit of money to try to have a little bit more success, which would then get them another grant and then another few years to achieve another little bit of success, but not to launch a major preemptive strike to get rid of the whole problem."[18] So, too, with Small Schools: it's hard for the rest of us to celebrate an island of excellence that doesn't care about the mainland. And to the rest of us, it seems that Small Schools people spend a whole lot of energy getting grants to protect their islands.

What would happen if Gates spent his gazillion millions organizing for a return of schools to the community? What if he used his moneyed clout to fight NCLB? To establish a countermovement to the Broad Foundation?

Just asking.

Principles of Reform

Figure 8–1 compares the six recommendations of the 1988 CBR report with the 1989 BRT principles of reform. The comparison reveals a high level of congruence between the two plans, offering more than a hint that the California

Comparison of CBR and BRT Reform Agendas

CBR 1988 Six Recommendations	BRT 1989 Principles of Reform (summer)
• Establish accountability based on performance and choice (rewards and penalties for schools based on exit and end-of-course tests of "higher-order individual skills in core subject matter")	• Outcome-based education
	• Strong and complex assessments of student progress
	• Rewards and penalties for schools
• Establish school autonomy, and empower parents, teachers, and principals	• Greater school-based decision making
• Strengthen the teaching profession	• Emphasis on staff development
• Expand and focus schooling (add pre-K and 85 percent of students should achieve at A-level work on the same core curricula)	• Establishment of prekindergarten programs
	• High expectations for all children
• Modernize instruction (technology, cooperative and mastery learning)	• Greater use of technology in schools
	• Provision of social health services
• Capitalize on diversity	

Figure 8–1

Business Roundtable was at the forefront of the development of the BRT's high-stakes testing agenda.[19]

In the fall of 1989, President Bush Sr. and the nation's governors, led by Arkansas governor Bill Clinton, held a national education summit. Their report, *America 2000*, was later renamed *Goals 2000* under President Clinton's tenure. The corporate-politico cabal massaged educational policy as a function for maintaining the disproportionate use of the world's resources.[20] Policy makers left the summit with the task of developing a game plan for their states—and for identifying "those elements which would increase the success in any *forthcoming national efforts*"[21] (emphasis added).

By the time Congress passed President Clinton's Goals 2000: Educate America Act in March 1994, the infrastructure was already in place. Take a look at *Reinventing Education: Entrepreneurship in America's Public Schools*, by Louis Gerstner Jr. (with Roger Semerad, Denis Doyle, and William Johnston), chairman and CEO of IBM. The fact that it was published within a month of the passage of Goals 2000 is no coincidence. One of the noteworthy features of Goals 2000 is that Gerstner and his cronies got to name the problem as well as define the solution: claiming the need for choice, competition, and technology in the schools; defining students as human capital and the teaching-learning compact as a "protected monopoly" offering "goods and services"; describing the relationship between teachers and the communities they serve as that of "buyers and sellers." Gerstner and company talk about measuring school productivity "with unequivocal yardsticks."[22] They speak of the need for national tests and "absolute standards," insisting that schools must compare themselves with each other the way "Xerox, for example, compares itself to L. L. Bean for inventory control."[23] Now that's a fine notion: *teaching as inventory control.*

Gerstner and his crew address the big questions of education: "How much do students learn each month. . . ? How great are these learning gains per dollar spent?"[24] They define the business of teaching as "the distribution of information."[25] Functionaries writing state standards quickly warmed to this metaphor. At their April 1997 meeting, members of the California Academic Standards Commission of the State Board of Education, whose job it was to approve academic standards in the various disciplines, showed a similar fondness for teaching as the delivery of skills: "A fifth-grade teacher would have a firm grasp on what skills and knowledge had been conveyed in grades K–4, and would deliver kids to the next grade ready to continue with the next set of expectations." How many minutes does a fledgling teacher have to be in a real classroom before she realizes that students don't pass by her desk like goods on a conveyor belt? You can teach and teach and teach. You can even teach the California seventh-grade history standards.[26] But all your teaching doesn't mean those pesky students are going to learn—and deliver their skills intact to next year's teacher.[27]

Union Involvement

Bill Hauck, current head of the California Business Roundtable, bemoans the power of the California Teachers Association (CTA) and other public employee unions for slowing down CBR education reform.[28] In a phone interview, Hauck explained that the lack of union opposition in both Texas and North Carolina allowed the implementation of BRT goals earlier than in California. In his complaint about the power of the CTA, Hauk reveals that he thinks teachers have no place at the table during discussions of education policy. Historically, business and political leaders have allowed unions to survive only if they played the game, agreeing to wait at the door, confining their organizational efforts to promoting wages and working conditions.[29] Most decidedly, unions are supposed to keep quiet about substantive issues such as what it means to educate students for a democracy.

The Legislative Timetable

Eight years—from 1991 to 1999—produced a series of education bills transforming the education agenda of the BRT and its allies into legislation. The California Assessment of Academic Achievement Act (AB 265) was passed in 1995, authorizing the development of a new state test, the California Assessment of Applied Academic Skills (CAAAS), a test aligned with state standards. The law also called for a commission to oversee the development of content and performance standards in all major subjects for 1–12 schools.[30] By November 1997, the first subject-based committees had been appointed to begin writing content standards.[31] The science standards were the last of the content standards unanimously approved by the Academic Standards Commission in July 1998. An article in the *Sacramento Business Journal* indicated that business interests were well served by the commission, while the scientific community deplored the contents of the science standards.[32]

> Rigorous new science standards for the California students will probably be adopted. That's either good news or terrible news, depending on whom you talk to. Representatives of business groups that have followed the issue say they welcome higher standards for California students and think these standards will make California graduates competitive in a global economy.
>
> But more than two dozen members of the national scientific community have spoken out against the standards. Their official letters of protest to the state board of education complain that the standards are so overstuffed with specific facts that there's no room left for hands-on investigation. Scientists predict that only a small fraction of students will be able to meet these standards and that teachers and students will have to resort to rote memorization rather than achieve true understanding of scientific concepts.[33]

In 1997, the state superintendent of education, Delaine Eastin, convened the Rewards and Interventions Advisory Committee and charged its members, in accordance with SB 1570 (1966) to develop a plan for a system of "incentives for the improvement of pupil academic achievement."[34] According to the committee's[35] argument in *Steering by Results*, attaching *rewards and interventions* to test-score performance

> would lead to improved instruction because teachers would focus on what was important; . . . would motivate students and parents to put more effort in school work; . . . would encourage greater parental involvement in children's

education; . . . [and] would enable the state and districts to target resources more effectively to give special assistance to those schools in trouble.[36]

The report made seven recommendations:

- Develop a school performance index based exclusively on the new state test.
- Establish a rewards program for successful schools, with the rewards being cash for teachers.
- Set up interventions for low-performing schools, including funds and a coach, and establish an interventions program to assist low-performing schools. If interventions don't work in two years, state takeover and school closing are two options.
- Motivate students with rewards and interventions.
- Provide adequate funding to implement the rewards-and-interventions program.
- Establish an advisory group to deal with policy and technical issues.
- Conduct comprehensive, ongoing, external evaluations of rewards and sanctions.

In 1997, California got its annual state test, the SAT-9, a commercial, off-the-shelf, norm-referenced, multiple-choice test. Obviously, the state needed the test scores to plug into its performance index in order to impose the rewards-and-interventions piece of school reform:

> This is the test that provides the score that makes the index that gives the rewards in the school reform that the CBR built.

In spring 1998, the SAT-9 was administered to all California schools. In 1999, the legislature passed SB X1, the Public School Accountability Act (PSAA), which linked high stakes to standardized testing.

> PSAA called for the creation of three basic components: 1) an index to rank the performance of schools, 2) an assistance and intervention program for schools that fall below expectations, and 3) a rewards program for schools that exceed them. . . . For the first time in the state's history, public schools are operating under a high-stakes testing and accountability system that defines a sequence of events and consequences for schools that continue to fall below expectations. The hope is that such a system will force schools to focus on improving academic results—thereby raising the performance of all students.37

The first component ranks schools from 1 to 10 according to a complicated formula. The number ranking is called the Academic Performance Index (API).

WestEd, hired by the Department of Education to perform an external evaluation,[38] noted the implications that the Public School Accountability Act and the SAT-9 would have on everyday life in the classroom.

> Until other indicators of academic performance are deemed valid and reliable, the SAT-9 is the sole indicator currently being used in an index that will help to rank schools' performance and determine their eligibility for an intervention and rewards program.
>
> Unclear is whether attaching high stakes to such a test may drive teachers to "drill and practice"[39] techniques on a narrow subset of skills or eventually lead to a stronger focus on standards-based skill development.[40]

Opposition to High-Stakes Standardized Testing

In their commissioned study, WestEd evaluators discovered a number of problems relating to the implementation of California's standards, accountability, and assessment system. First, district and school personnel viewed the SAT-9 as inherently flawed.[41] Second, there was an "overall concern that rankings and subsequent sanctions may exacerbate already-difficult conditions for the lowest performing schools."[42] Third, "the information [teachers] receive about new policies appears contradictory to the purpose of existing reforms."[43] Nevertheless, using the logic of *Steering by Results*, the evaluators concluded in fall 1999 that

> for the most part, California should "stay the course"[44] with developing the existing components of its accountability infrastructure: standards, assessment, and a system of interventions, rewards, and sanctions. However, no approach is perfect from the start. Modifications may be necessary to rectify unintended consequences and ensure the system is meeting its primary objective [of improving student performance].[45]

The criticism that WestEd noted in its report was a national phenomenon. By 2001, disparagement had become so widespread that the Business Roundtable started to talk about *a testing backlash*. Eager to defend its education agenda, in spring 2001, the Business Roundtable published *Assessing and Addressing the "Testing Backlash": Practical Advice and Current Public Opinion Research for Business Coalitions and Standards Advocates*. Using polls by its crony, Public Agenda (see Chapter 4), the BRT argues that public opinion still supports the standards movement. The growing opposition to the effects of the new reforms is merely "warning signs of discontent" that can be countered by "getting the policy right, and communicating more broadly about how to make the system work." The BRT's strategies for doing this (see Chapter 3) are remarkably similar to the ones that WestEd recommended to the California

State Board of Education in November 1999. WestEd's overarching recommendation for political leaders and educators is *to align what already exists* before implementing any further pieces of the high-stakes agenda.

The state now claims that the CAT-6 is aligned with state standards and is a standards-based test. Ostensibly, this answers the criticism that the SAT-9 was norm-referenced and not standards-based. But the CAT-6 is also a commercial off-the-shelf standardized test defended by test makers for its ability to get the same results as the SAT-9. Sounds like a classic bait and switch.

Both WestEd and the Business Roundtable advise controlling people's opinions by controlling the information from which they form opinions. WestEd argues that part of the alignment problem lies not only in the need to clarify the chain of command but in making sure that each link in the chain fully understands what its responsibilities are. One way to do this is "to ramp up [the state government's] use of the World Wide Web in communicating accountability policy to all stakeholders within the system."[46] The Business Roundtable advises, "communicate more broadly about how to make the system work."[47]

WestEd evaluators recorded the following comments showing teacher backlash:

[In the newly adopted district standards] there's an obvious philosophy behind it that it should be hands-on. . . . My biggest complaint with the hands-on is that [students are] not tested that way. It's like they [the district] want us to use hands-on materials, but then they test us in a much more traditional way. . . . I don't get a consistent message. No one fully explains to you how you're supposed to prepare kids for tests.

I think the standardized test that we have to take gets in the way. Because it forces me to teach to the test, instead of teaching to what the standards are.

The SAT-9 tests a lot of stuff that they haven't even learned. . . . The seventh graders had to take this test, the STAR test. . . . While they were taking it, I could just see the frustration on their faces, and I was like, what's going on? So I grabbed a copy of the test. I started looking at it; I was like, oh my gosh, they're so frustrated because this is the stuff I'm teaching my eighth graders right now, but my seventh graders haven't even seen this material yet.

Some kids [e.g., English language learners, special education students] shouldn't have to take the standardized test, and if they still have to, and those scores are counted into my scores, into my teaching, and I'm held accountable for that, then I kind of have a problem with that.

The kids I have . . . are good kids; they came in with good scores, they'll go out with decent scores; they probably could have done that no matter whether I did a good job or not. On the other hand, you can get kids that are ill-prepared, and you know, how much you can help them improve—I don't know that anybody knows, is that 5 percentage points? Is that 25 percentage points? I guess we're all wondering, what's going to be the measure of achievement? So that's all a little iffy when the test is the thing.[48]

Instead of concluding from such comments that there may be multiple, legitimate goals of education and that forcing a uniform curriculum upon diverse communities undermines the very democratic processes for which this country is supposed to stand, both WestEd and the BRT's *Advice* conclude that teacher resistance equals teacher ignorance.[49] Both argue that better teacher training, both preservice and inservice, will help teachers better understand and thus effectively implement standards reforms.

In its 1999 report, WestEd recommends that districts "ensure that professional development programs are aimed at building teacher knowledge and skills related to content standards" and that the state university teacher preparation programs should "specifically address issues related to accountability." Furthermore, "the governor and the legislature should fund capacity-building opportunities for teachers and administrators to learn about analyzing data to improve student achievement and school performance."[50] BRT's *Advice* encourages standards advocates to "make more of a concerted effort to reach out to classroom teachers. Explain these changes [standards-based reforms], tell them that many teachers think there are benefits, and show them how other schools are using standards and tests to improve student learning."[51]

For standards advocates, this isn't about changing any goals of systemic reform; it's about massaging the message through focus group research.

> Public opinion research contains valuable ideas about what messages on education and standards make the most sense to the public.
>
> Stress that the effort is about better schools and higher levels of learning—not standards, tests, accountability or education reform.[52] Parents and educators want to know that better schools are needed because we have to be fair to all students, not because schools are failing. Your communications efforts should emphasize:
>
> - the importance of raising expectations for all students;
> - the fairness that comes from higher expectations (too many are not getting the education they deserve);
> - the ability of testing to diagnose strengths and weaknesses of students (helping them learn and teachers teach);
> - the value of test scores for comparing schools and identifying necessary improvements—and as part of the decision to promote and graduate students.[53]

The similarities between the WestEd recommendations and those of the BRT's *Advice* are no coincidence. Although WestEd evaluators could not help noting the limitations of such top-down reform,[54] all of their recommendations were created within such a paradigm, representing another example of how the BRT network has successfully co-opted educational researchers. The state government had charged the researchers with finding out what the state needed to do to implement systemic reform—reform driven by the Business Roundtable. Remember, Edward Rust, chair of the BRT's Education Task Force, wasn't shy about being a bully when he declared that schools "don't change because they see the light; they change because they feel the heat."

WestEd's evaluation pointed to where the heat needed to be applied. In December 1998, Larry McCarthy, president of the California Taxpayers' Association in Sacramento, stoked the furnace:

> Now, in an unprecedented way, thousands of California companies, through their associations—the California Business Roundtable, the California Chamber of Commerce, the California Manufacturers Association, the California Taxpayers' Association, Technology Network, and the American Electronics Association—are joining forces to speak with a united voice on education policy.
>
> They have formed California Business for Education Excellence (CBEE). With key corporate support from Hewlett-Packard, IBM, Boeing and the business-labor California Council for Environmental and Economic Balance, it is bringing the voice of business to the education policy debate.
>
> The intent is to influence the development of methods that encourage new education standards, assess how they work, and assure accountability to the standards. The new organization will work as a partner with the education community, the new Gray Davis administration.[55]

Delivering the Goods

In 1999, the Legislative Analyst's Office published a report written by policy wonk Paul Warren that would guide the legislature's "planning process for kindergarten through high school." In the report, titled *K–12 Master Plan: Starting the Process*, Warren recommended that a master plan should focus on defining the "separate responsibilities for most decisions as a way of creating clear lines of accountability"—in other words, "clarify state and local responsibilities." Citing a 1998 National Education Goals Panel report,[56] Warren argued that

> state strategies adopted in Texas and North Carolina reinforce our assessment of appropriate state roles. The [1998 NEGP] evaluation concludes that critical elements of the states' strategies have resulted in sustained long-term

increases in student achievement. These elements include: state content standards accompanied by a student assessment system; a state accountability system that has consequences; deregulated state fiscal and program policies; state data systems to encourage continuous local improvement; [and] a long-term state commitment to these strategies.[57]

The report emphasizes two factors that appeared to make the difference in North Carolina and Texas. Both states viewed the state role in school improvement as a "long-term endeavor requiring stability and continual refinement of state policies. The other factor was the sustained commitment to the reform strategy by political and business leaders".[58]

One thing is worth observing here: policy wonks don't devise policy; they deliver the requested goods. Following is an exchange from Warren's deposition in the the the class action lawsuit Eliezer Williams et al. State of California; Delaine Eastin, Department of Public Instruction, State Department of Education, State Board of Education.[59] This lawsuit asks the governor to set minimum standards of school quality. Mark D. Rosenbaum, Esq., for the ACLU Foundation of Southern California, is asking the questions. Paul Warren, the deputy superintendent of accountability in the California Department of Education, is answering them.

Q: Do you consider yourself an expert in the area of accountability?
A: No.
Q: Do you know the names of any individuals whom you regard as having specialized knowledge in the area of accountability?
A: No.

In spring 2000, Bill Hauck confirmed the intention of California Business for Education Excellence to support a "long-term state commitment" to the BRT agenda. In an interview with the magazine of the California School Boards Association, Hauck explained that the first priority is to keep the SAT-9 in place so that five years of data can be collected. He conceded that it may not be "the best test in the world [but] if it is testing whether we are achieving the standards that the [state] board adopted, then we have what we need." When asked to comment about the recent joint legislative committee's development of a master plan for K–16 public education, Hauck explained that he told the committee members to "pick specific objectives rather than to try to cover every issue under the sun." If the master plan includes "thousands of other issues" apart from "those things that are critical to teaching young people more effectively" then the plan will be doomed.[60] These comments can be interpreted as ignorant, evasive, or euphemistic. Given the history of CBR's role in California educational reform, and specifically Hauck's role, one can surmise with some certitude that Hauck was being euphemistic, referring to state-mandated tests, content standards, rewards, and sanctions as *those things* or *specific objectives*.

More Effective Tools of Control

With content standards, assessment (SAT-9, CAT-6, and the California High School Exit Exam), and accountability (Academic Performance Index and Immediate Intervention/Underperforming Schools Program [API and II/USP]) now in place, California's business and political leaders are turning their attention to transforming the state and district bureaucracies into more effective tools of control. As part of this process, Paul Warren recommends that "the state should review the 'health' of local school boards" by asking the question "does at-large representation result in broader representation than 'regional' [district/ward] representation?"[61] For *broader representation*, read state view rather than the local community views, which, in this scheme, are labeled *narrow*. Simply put, the state should ensure that school board members are committed to implementing and enforcing the state educational policy over which parents and students have little to no influence.

Not surprisingly, Warren's report also recommends that teacher credential programs be centralized into a single agency supervised by the California Department of Education (with the state superintendent of public instruction no longer being an elective office but one appointed by the governor). Again, Warren justifies this consolidation by appealing to the "broader perspective of the state board of education and the state department of education over educational issues."[62] A more centralized state agency could assign clear and specific roles to each institution responsible for teacher training, holding each agency "accountable for desired results."[63] Then, every teacher trained in a state credential program would be conditioned to ignore the daily reactions of students; it wouldn't occur to her to question whether the demanded results were desirable.

Professors working in colleges of education in the California state university system report being required to turn in their syllabi so checkers can make sure that the federally mandated scientific reading topics are adequately represented. What is scientific reading? Whatever the feds say it is. The feds' motto is pay out 7 percent of the local education budget but carry a big enough stick to get attention. No one can deny that they get a huge bang for their buck with that 7 percent—teachers from pre-K through graduate school marching to their orders.

We've heard a lot from the Business Roundtable partisans, from the research institutions, and from policy wonks. Let's give the last word on education policy to a Southern California teacher who is in charge of a classroom of thirty children. Here's Kelley's schedule:

> Newly implemented for this school year: quarterly testing (even though we run on trimesters) in addition to yearly testing. Quarterly tests come straight from the "summative assessment" portion of the newly adopted language arts series and the recently adopted math series. As well as a writing test. None of these scores is to be used for classroom grades or reporting. They are to be sent to the district office, who won't say what they are doing with them. I asked.
>
> The district doesn't send the tests until the day before the testing window. They send packets of tests and directions for giving it, with a deadline (5 days) for turning in scores. All absences must be made up within that window. No answer key, no instructions about how the scores are to be reported; just the info that we score our own. The day before the deadline they give us the answer key and answer sheets to be filled out and sent to the district. This means that I have one day to correct 30 23-page packets, enter the scores for each section on two different sheets for each student, and get them turned in. The schedule looks like this:
>
> Oct. 27th–31st: Writing test. Five paragraph essays. All scored and turned in by Friday.
>
> Nov. 3rd–7th: Language Arts test. 23 pages worth per kid. All to be scored by me and turned in by Friday.
>
> November 10th–14th: A 3-day week, due to Veteran's day. The end of the trimester; whatever classroom assessments need to be finished up for the reporting period will be done this week.
>
> The weekend of November 15th–16th: I get 30 report cards ready for the 30 conferences I'll be doing the week of the 17th–21st.
>
> November 17th–21st: 30 conferences before and after school. Meanwhile, we are doing the required district math test. To be scored and turned in by Friday. They won't tell me how long it will take to give or score. They don't expect to pass it out until the day we give it.
>
> Three weeks' worth of tests. They aren't paying me any extra to grade 30 essays or 23-page exams in one or two days in addition to our regular classwork. They aren't saying what they'll do with all of those numbers. Did I mention that the test is based on the new language arts series, which they ran out of before they got to me? We haven't seen it the entire first trimester. It's "on order."
>
> But boy, oh boy, we're enthusiastic testers. Whether or not we've got the budget for it; it can just be one of those "duties as necessary" mentioned in a teacher's contract.[64]

Kelley refers to her schedule and the regulations that dictate it as "weigh the cow some more." This is an allusion to "No Cow Left Behind," an op-ed written by Underhill, Vermont, principal Kenneth Remsen.[65] Remsen writes that since testing seems to be a cornerstone to improving performance, maybe the situation of Vermont's falling milk prices could be rectified by having the federal government mandate testing of cows. All cows. Every year.

> I'm sure there are plenty of statistics to show what good milk producing performance looks like and the characteristics of cows who achieve this level of performance. It should, therefore, be easy to figure out the characteristics necessary to meet this standard. . . . If improvements do not occur over a couple of years, the state will take over your farm or even force you to sell. . . .
>
> It is important to remember that every cow can meet the standard. There should be no exceptions and no excuses. . . .
>
> Some farmers may be upset that I proclaim to know what is best for these cows but I certainly consider myself capable of making these recommendations. I grew up next to a farm and I drink milk.

Notes

1. Berman, Paul. 1988. *Restructuring California Education: A Design for Public Education in the Twenty-First Century*. Research/Technical ED 302618. Berkeley: California Business Roundtable. Berman was a partner in the Berkeley-based nonprofit research group Berman and Weiler, contracted to produce the report.

2. Bill Hauck, president of the CBR, insists that the CBR is independent of the BRT, yet he did admit that the impetus to adopt educational reform as an issue came from Sam Ginn (Air Touch, Pacific Bell), who was a member of both the CBR and the BRT in 1988 (personal interview, 18 March 2002).

3. Berman. 1988, 14–15.

4. Associated Press. 2003. "Schools Drop Naptime for Testing Preparation." *Atlanta Journal-Constitution*, 3 October.

5. This would be, then, a new form of tracking, which is another indication as to why such systemic reform rhetoric as "high standards for all," "equity and excellence," "excellence for all," and "leave no child behind" is disingenuous at best.

6. Stratman, David G. n.d. *We Can Change the World*. Boston: New Democracy, 71.

7. See *www.negp.gov/page1–15.htm*.

8. If you think this is paranoia run rampant, take a look at the math requirements for a paraprofessional seeking an A.A. degree—everything from linear, quadratic, other polynomial, exponential/logarithmic, power/radical, and rational functions to extracting solvable quantitative problems that are embedded in a situation that is not inherently quantitative. See *http://susanohanian.org/show_nclb_stories.html?id=38*.

9. Stratman. n.d., 71–72.

10. Ibid.

11. Berman. 1988, 71.

12. In 1988, business leaders were still attracted to performance assessment because of its promise to encourage the development of "problem-solving" skills. This was later abandoned in favor of off-the-shelf, commercialized standardized tests. One reason for this change might have been that since performance assessments could not "sort" as well as multiple-choice exams could, they could not distinguish between an 85 percentile and an 86 percentile. When Kentucky adopted performance and portfolio assessment as part of its state's systemic reform, many criticized these forms of assessment as being "unreliable." See W. James. Popham (2001) *The Truth About Testing: An Educator's Call to Action*, Alexandria, VA: Association for Supervision and Curriculum Development, Chapters 3 and 4, for an explanation as to why sorting and reliability are important to test givers.

13. Berman. 1988, 91.

14. Berman. 1988, 91–93.

15. The report defines "master learning" in the following "simplified terms": (1) "teachers identify in advance the level of learning that they expect all students to achieve"; (2) teachers "divide the curriculum into small units [e.g., two weeks] and provide instruction geared to students learning the unit"; (3) "after each period of instruction, students are tested to see how much they have learned"; (4) students keep learning until "they have mastered the material," while those who have mastered it before the others become "peer instructors" or are given material to master "beyond the expected mastery level"; (5) "the class continues as a group to the next curriculum unit after all students have reached the mastery level." From Berman, 1988, 141–42.

16. Ibid., 117.

17. Ibid., 129.

18. Groopman, Jerome. 2003. "The Reeve Effect." *The New Yorker.* 10 November.

19. Bill Hauck, the president of CBR, indicated as much when he complained that other states took the lead in school reform only because they didn't have strong unions to oppose passage and implementation of systemic reform (personal interview, 12 March 2002).

20. In 1948, George Kennan, in a State Department memo discussing the future shape of the Cold War, wrote: "We have about 50% of the world's wealth, but only 6.3 percent of its population. . . . In this situation, we cannot fail to be the object of envy and resentment. Our real task in the coming period is to devise a pattern of relationships which will permit us to maintain this position of disparity without positive detriment to our national security" (quoted by Lewis Lapham in "Notebook," *Harper's*, March 2002, 9). See also LaFeber, Walter. (1991), *Russia and The Cold War*, New York: McGraw-Hill, for a description of the Cold War as a "pattern of relationships" that has successfully "maintain[ed] this position of disparity."

21. Conner, K., and M. Melendez. 1994. *Education Reform Briefing Book. Volume II, First Edition. Excerpts from Selected California Education Studies and Reports, 1983–Present.* (Information Analyses [070], Research/Technical [143] ED 373438). Sacramento: California State Legislature, Senate Office of Research, 130.

22. Gerstner, Louis V. Jr., et al. 2000. *Reinventing Education: Entrepreneurship in America's Public Schools.* New York: Dutton, 69.

23. Ibid., 70.

24. Ibid., 69.

25. Ibid., 155.

26. It's hard to choose a favorite: seventh graders analyzing the geographic, political,

economic, religious, and social structures of Islamic civilizations in the Middle Ages, of China in the Middle Ages, of the sub-Saharan civilizations, of Japan in the Middle Ages, of Europe in the Middle Ages, and of Mesoamerican and Andean civilizations; or the theological, political, and economic ideas of the major figures of the Reformation (e.g., Erasmus, Martin Luther, John Calvin, William Tyndale). These are just two of eleven standards to be covered by California seventh graders.

27. Ohanian, Susan. 2000. "Goals 2000: What's in a Name?" *Phi Delta Kappan*, January. Accessed at *www.pdkintl.org/kappan/koha0001.htm*.

28. Telephone interview with K. Emery, 18 March 2002.

29. One only need compare the history of the Knights of Labor with that of the American Federation of Labor to see which unions survive and which do not and why. Interestingly enough, such a history never made it into the California history and social science standards.

30. The California Academic Standards Commission was made up of two members appointed by the legislature, eleven members appointed by Governor Pete Wilson, six appointed by the state superintendent of public instruction, Delaine Eastin, and Eastin herself.

31. Guth, G. D. Joltzman, S. Schneider, L. Carlos, J. Smith, G. Hayward, and N. Calvo. 1999. "Evaluation of California's Standards-Based Accountability System." Evaluation final. Menlo Park and Davis, CA: WestEd Management Analysis and Planning, 7.

32. Marquand, Barbara. 1998. "As Approval Nears, Science Standards Still Draw Flak." *Sacramento Business Journal*, 12 October. Accessed as *http://sacramento.bizjournals.com/sacramento/stories/1998/10/12/focus2.html*.

33. Ohanian, Susan. 1999. *One Size Fits Few: The Folly of Educational Standards*. Portsmouth, NH: Heinemann. In a chapter titled "Californication," Susan Ohanian provides an irreverent look at this standards-making process, distilling the standards committee meeting minutes.

34. Rewards and Interventions Advisory Committee. 1998. *Steering by Results: A High-Stakes Rewards and Interventions Program for California Schools and Students*. Sacramento: California Department of Education.

35. The committee was cochaired by Sam Araki, former president of Lockheed Martin Missiles and Space, and Charles McCully, former superintendent of Fresno Unified School District. The largest group among the thirty-five members of the committee were twelve representatives of major corporations (e.g., National Semiconductor, Chevron, Hewlett-Packard). The second largest group comprised eight school district administrators of various levels. Other members included one person representing each of the two teacher unions (California Federation of Teachers, California Teachers Association), a representative from the California PTA, one from the Education Commission of the States, one from the National Center of Education and the Economy, one school board representative, and the director of Policy Analysis for California Education.

36. Rewards and Interventions Advisory Committee. 1998, 4.

37. Gutth et al. 1999, 11.

38. WestEd is a nonprofit "research, development and service agency." In 1995, two federally established Regional Educational Laboratories, Far West and Southwest, joined together to form WestEd. With its headquarters in San Francisco, WestEd provides "services" throughout the United States by its four hundred–person staff and fifteen regional offices. Among the members of the 2002 board of directors were the superintendent of the San Francisco Unified School District, the current state superintendent, a former president of Pacific Telesis Foundation, and

the program manager from Silicon Graphics. In 1997, WestEd prepared a report on the role of technology in education with IBM for a state education symposium. In 1998, WestEd published a report supporting state intervention as a method to improve academic performance. WestEd houses federally funded Comprehensive Centers to help schools accomplish "system-wide reform" and oversees BASRC (see Chapter 7). It is partnered with Education for the Future, whose *Initiative* was developed upon the recommendations of the California Business Roundtable.

Peter Farruggio, an Oakland, California, bilingual teacher, teacher educator, organizer, and Ph.D. graduate student in the fall of 1996, described being invited to an all-day Equity Committee meeting at WestEd. Farruggio described the meeting thusly: "Ray Bachetti of the H-P Foundation was the obvious biggest shot of the big shots present. Other foundation honchos and 'professional minority' types [were there as well as] a handful of real educators from poor schools with more than just a few years of experience. I guess I fit in this latter group, and we were there to 'make it real.' Anyway, I remember the general discussion being about how we all felt about things, and if we were sensitive to the issues of poor minorities in poor schools. . . . So when it came my turn I told about how I had organized the Mexican and Black parents in my neighborhood in Oakland to protest the bad principal we had been stuck with, and the horrible year round schedule, and the fact that downtown had been ripping off our categorical budget and not allowing us to exercise our legal rights to choose how to spend our funds, etc. And I described the parents' strike and picket line we had and how we marched into a few school board meetings demanding action, and how we used to meet clandestinely in local churches because our school board 'rep' was in cahoots with the official bureaucracy and was trying to threaten both parents and teachers. You know, a little slice of life from the urban ed jungle. Well, there was a polite chill around the table of 20 or so people. Real uncomfortable, like I had farted in church. And there was a look of horror on Mr. Bachetti's face, like King Kong was coming through the huge conference door. So I realized that this was too much 'equity' for this crowd." Personal email, 12 March 2002.

39. Linda McNeil's description of the effects of high-stakes testing on teaching and learning makes "drill and de-skill" more accurate than WestEd's "drill and practice." See McNeil, 2000. *Contradictions of School Reform*, Chapter 6.

40. Guth, G., Joltzman, D., Schneider, S., Carlos, L., Smith, J., Hayward, G., & Calvo, N. 1999. "Evaluation of California's Standards-Based Accountability System," Evaluation final, Menlo Park and Davis, CA: WestEd Management Analysis and Planning, 9.

41. McNeil, 2000, 61.

42. Ibid., 98.

43. Ibid., 164.

44. "Stay the course" was the same expression used by Louis Gerstner at the 1999 governor's education summit that he convened in Palisades, New York. Gerstner, CEO of IBM, explained, "We understand the pain [that is being inflicted by high-stakes testing]. And we're going to have to deal with it. But we're not going to deal with it by backing off" (Steinberg, Jacques. 1999. "Academic Standards Eased as a Fear of Failure Spreads." *New York Times*, 3 December). The use of quotation marks by the WestEd authors indicates that, among the people they associate with, it is a common expression.

45. Guth, G., Joltzman, D., Schneider, S., Carlos, L., Smith, J., Hayward, G., & Calvo, N. 1999. "Evaluation of California's Standards-Based Accountability System," Evaluation final, Menlo Park and Davis, CA: WestEd Management Analysis and Planning, 165.

46. Business Roundtable. 2001. *Assessing and Addressing the "Testing Backlash": Practi-*

cal Advice and Current Public Opinion Research for Business Coalitions and Standards Advocates. Business Roundtable, 25. Accessed at *www.Brtable.org/pdf/525.pdf.*

47. Ibid.

48. Guth et al. 1999, 64–77.

49. Deborah Meier, founder and principal of Central Park East Secondary School in Harlem, argues that "there are multiple, legitimate definitions of 'a good education' and 'well-educated' and it is desirable to acknowledge that plurality" (16). She explains that the new standards movement "will not help to develop young minds, contribute to a robust democratic life, or aid the most vulnerable of our fellow citizens. By shifting the locus of authority to outside bodies, it undermines the capacity of schools to instruct by example in the qualities of mind that schools in a democracy should be fostering in kids—responsibility for one's own ideas, tolerance for the ideas of others, and a capacity to negotiate differences. Standardization instead turns teachers and parents into the local instruments of externally imposed expert judgment. It thus decreases the chances that young people will grow up in the midst of adults who are making hard decisions and exercising mature judgment in the face of disagreements. And it squeezes out those schools and educators that seek to show alternate possibilities or explore other paths. The standardization movement is not based on a simple mistake. It rests on deep assumptions about the goals of education and the proper exercise of authority in the making of decisions—assumptions we ought to reject in favor of a different vision of a healthy democratic society" (4–5). Meier, Deborah, et al. 2000. *Will Standards Save Public Education?* Boston: Beacon.

50. Guth et al. 1999, 162.

51. Business Roundtable. 2001, 20.

52. This is a particularly egregious example of manipulation. While everyone can agree that we want "better schools" and "higher levels of learning," disagreement emerges immediately when one begins to define what these vague terms mean.

53. Business Roundtable. 2001, 21.

54. "Study findings, however, suggest that communication about accountability becomes increasingly diluted (or even worse, becomes increasingly muddied) from the pinnacle of the system (the state) to the foundation of the system (the classroom). In addition, very few districts appear to have a consistent local vision of accountability. In many cases, districts' notions of accountability had not filtered much beyond district staff. Principals often had different notions of what accountability required, and teachers either had no awareness or a different concept of the accountability process" (Guth et al. 1999, 164).

55. McCarthy, L. 1998. "Business Cranks Up Volume on Public Education." *San Francisco Business Times*, December. Accessed at *www.bCentral.com.*

56. Grissmer, David, and Ann Flanagan. 1998. *Exploring Rapid Achievement Gains in North Carolina and Texas.* Washington: DC: NEGP, November.

57. Warren, Paul. 1999. *K–12 Master Plan: Starting the Process.* Report-Evaluative ED 438590. Sacramento: California State Legislative Analyst's Office, 3–4.

58. Ibid., 20.

59. Warren, Paul. 2001. No. 312236. 23 May, 51–53. Accessed at *www.mofo.com/decent schools/depositions/warren-p1.pdf.*

60. Selections from the California Schools magazine interview with Hauck can be found by going to *www.csba.org>>Q&Awith Bill Hauck.*

61. Warren. 2001, 25.

62. The State Board of Education is appointed by the governor. As of December 31, 2003, the seven-member board consisted of three businessmen, a business consultant, a teacher union representative, a retired elementary school principal, and a student who had been an intern at the Brookings Institution (see *www.cde.ca.gov/board/bio.htm*). One member, Donald G. Fisher, founder and chair of Gap, has been particularly virulent in his attacks on public schools. He offered $25 million to the state's school systems if they turn themselves over to Edison Schools, the nation's largest private manager of public classrooms (see *www.motherjones.com/ news/special_reports/mojo_400/184_fisher.html*).

63. Warren. 2001, 44.

64. Personal communication with the authors. May 2003.

65. Remsen, Kenneth. 2003. "No Cow Left Behind." *Burlington Free Press*, 25 July.

9

San Francisco

Vacating Justice

The enemy is anybody who's going to get you killed, no matter which side he's on.

—JOSEPH HELLER, *CATCH-22*

The statistics always come too late. They measure everything, but they explain very little and predict even less. Every season, baseball tries to teach us that the game has a human, unpredictable heart. And is the richer for it. Yet, every year, we insist the game should be less messy than the world around it.

—TOM BOSWELL, *THE HEART OF THE ORDER*

You'd Better Watch Out: Reconstitution Is Going to Get You

Why should the rest of the nation care about the San Francisco Unified School District (SFUSD)? For starters, what happened in San Francisco heralds what No Child Left Behind will bring to your school district. San Francisco put together reconstitution as the school reform of the day. *Reconstitution* means operating all schools on a reward-and-punishment system based on test scores; it means vacating those schools whose scores don't measure up. *Vacating* is quite a term. Keep the building; eliminate the staff.

Reconstitution was introduced as part of settling a 1978 NAACP segregation lawsuit. In the 1983 settlement, known as the Consent Decree, the presiding judge, William Orrick, cautioned NAACP lawyers that they'd better settle and not go to trial because they would not be able to prove that the SFUSD *intentionally* promoted or maintained segregated schools. Judge Orrick suggested that the points of contention be resolved by a settlement team of the nation's leading experts on school desegregation and education policy.[1] As a result, the

NAACP lawyers could demand only what the SFUSD and the California Department of Education (CDE) were willing to concede, thus forestalling any community influence on school reform. Thus, once again, *reform* became the weasel word of education.

The concessions gained by the San Francisco NAACP came at a heavy political price. By accepting a place at the negotiating table, the NAACP acquiesced to excluding teachers, Latinos, and Asian Americans from that table. These three groups filed lawsuits demanding that they, too, be parties to the settlement, but Judge Orrick denied their claims, insisting that the NAACP was able to represent Latino and Asian American interests and that the district office could represent teacher interests.

What a notion. You don't need deep familiarity with San Francisco social structures and politics to guess how Latinos and Asian Americans felt. And is there a teacher alive who believes that the central office represents her interests?

It gets worse. Here's how the SFUSD described reconstitution in a court document: "[W]hile the building remain[s] open and the students stay at the site through the transition, the staff [is] 'vacated' and hiring beg[ins] for new staff."[2] One wonders if these fellows are channeling leftover military press releases from the Vietnam conflict. *The staff is vacated* has a certain militaristic nuance, making reconstitution sound like pacification—or maybe a kind of neutron bomb; it obliterates all adults while leaving the buildings intact. You have to wonder what you've got when you've got an intact building empty of teachers and principals. For starters, it's a building with no culture, no history; you have lots of new inexperienced teachers with no longtime staff mentors available. At Mission High School, one reconstitution manifestation was a new principal removing all the photographs of generations of graduates lining the hallway. It was a deliberate attempt to undermine the power of the community.

The reconstruction plan wasn't just about getting rid of teachers and principals; at its core sit eleven exceedingly earnest Philosophical Tenets. The principle here seems to be Talk New Age but carry a big stick. Here's a sample: *"All individuals want to learn and should be recognized for their achievements; All individuals can learn; All individuals are potential learners and potential teachers. . . ."*[3] One tenet calls for a codicil and a visit with an attorney: *"If individuals do not learn, then those assigned to be their teachers will accept responsibility for this failure and will take appropriate remedial action to ensure success."*

Sure. At some deep, psychic level, every teacher should—and must—subscribe to a positive, pro-kid attitude, but nonetheless, one has to question the practical, in-the-classroom value of such global tenets. *All students can learn.* So can your cat. The no-nonsense, workaday question is *Learn what?* Where the rhetoric meets the kid, we must ask: Can—and should—all students learn quadratic equations? Can—and should—all students write research papers? Deconstruct Shakespearean sonnets? Read *Moby Dick*? Instead of acting as an

echo chamber for Business Roundtable rhetoric, educators need to thi.
what these questions mean to students. All students. They need to
because traveling along with these Philosophical Tenets are *specific student
outcomes for each grade*. Nationwide, such outcomes, to use an appalling Stan-
dardisto term, become an ideological battlefield, littered with the broken spir-
its of students labeled as failures when they don't learn, say, commas in first
grade and the entrepreneurial characteristics of early explorers (e.g., Christopher Columbus, Francisco Vásquez de Coronado) and the technological developments that made sea exploration by latitude and longitude possible (e.g.,
compass, sextant, astrolabe, seaworthy ships, chronometers, gunpowder) in
fifth.[4] It is one thing to say that all students can learn; it is quite another to insist that they must all learn the same things at the same pace—*and* to declare
that teachers are to blame if they don't. But, anticipating criticism, the SFUSD
addressed such issues. For example, for the Philosophical Tenet "All individuals can learn," there are ten subgoals, including *"all teachers will provide learning experiences that will enable students to think critically and creatively and to
solve problems and exercise judgment as they learn new skills and knowledge"*
(emphasis added). Whew! And there are nine more. At each school, principals
are responsible for keeping a professional growth profile on these goals for
each staff member. Problem solved.

We can wonder, though, just how a busy principal charts this professional
growth. Ask ten people what *to think critically and creatively* means. Ask them
to tell you the last time they did it. Ask ten married people if their spouses *exercise judgment as they learn new skills and knowledge*. And then consider how
a principal figures out which students in each teacher's classroom are making
growth in learning to think critically and creatively. It easy to see that in practical terms, such a philosophical tenet is about as useful as a bucket of warm
spit. We'd be more impressed if one of the subgoals were *Talk less and listen
more*. As is, the tenets seem to indicate that school policy is like political campaigns: spin trumps reality.

More than three decades ago, James Herndon, who taught seventh graders
on the outskirts of San Francisco, wrote a couple of books that should be required reading by people who issue orders about philosophical tenets, professional growth profiles, and subgoals—and by people who obey those orders:
The Way It Spozed to Be and *How to Survive in Your Native Land*.[5] Herndon's
comments on both bureaucratic cant and classroom nuance are kid-centered,
irreverent, funny, and, even three decades later, still astonishingly on target.
For starters, Herndon points out, "If anyone thinks the trouble with public
schools comes from incompetent teachers, they are crazy as hell."[6]

Maybe the beginning of a solution to schools' problems would be to stop
blaming teachers for poverty and do something about that poverty. Modest
proposal: Give a few years' reconstitution money directly to the families in the

neighborhoods in question. See how *that* affects the average daily attendance and test scores of the children. This remedy isn't tried because poverty programs are always set up to pay the high costs and overhead of the middle-class people administering them. Not to mention the pile of money that goes to experts.

Following the advice of those who say education should be more like medicine, let's take a page from a study designed by Harvard professor of medicine, renowned infectious-disease specialist, anthropologist, and MacArthur genius award recipient Paul Farmer.[7] Dr. Farmer set up two groups of TB patients in Haiti. Each group got the same free medical treatment, but one also received additional services: regular visits from community health workers and small monthly cash stipends. Cure rates for the two groups were dramatically different. The group receiving only free medical services had a 48 percent cure rate. *All* of those receiving cash stipends were cured. One hundred percent. And whether a patient believed that TB came from germs or from sorcery didn't seem to make any difference in the cure rate.

If we identified poverty as the problem—and gave the parents of children in poor schools cash stipends—then evaluators could track attendance rates, the number of books checked out of libraries, the number of personal journal pages written, the length of entries, the number of parent contacts with the school, and so on. We wouldn't have to pay someone $300 an hour to count the number of books checked out of the library, and the money paid out would stay in the neighborhood where it's needed—instead of flying out on a jet.

For $300 an Hour, You Get an Expert

Reconstitution money is at the core of the San Francisco story. Every year since the Consent Decree, the SFUSD has received megamoney for agreeing to participate in the decree, and, as we'll see later, how it spent the money eventually triggered an FBI probe. On May 17, 2000, the forty-sixth anniversary of *Brown v Board of Education*, San Francisco children became plaintiffs in a lawsuit to get rats out of their classrooms. Civil rights groups and attorneys, coordinated by the American Civil Liberties Union, filed *Williams et al. v State of California et al.*, a landmark suit in San Francisco Superior Court, on behalf of about one million California students. The suit charged that California failed to provide the "bare minimum necessities" required for an education to one in six kids. The list of missing necessities includes lack of certified teachers, lack of textbooks, not enough desks and seats, extremely hot or cold classrooms, filthy toilets, unrepaired, hazardous facilities, vermin infestations, leaky roofs, and mold.

The defendants' experts list is a who's who of advocates for high-stakes testing, charters, year-round schools, and vouchers: Charles E. Ballinger,

Richard Berk, Thomas G. Duffy, Russell M. Gersten, Eric Hanushek, Caroline M. Hosby, John J. Kirlin, Susan E. Phillips, Michael Podgursky, Margaret E. Raymond, Christine H. Rossell, Anita A. Summers, and Herberg J. Walberg. Some of these experts apparently make their livings being experts. Their reports and depositions are available at *Decent Schools for California: Williams v State of California*.[8]

Experts on both sides have been paid from $100 to $500 an hour—to testify in depositions that so far have lasted from two to eleven days and to write expert reports. The state spent $305,808 on written reports by its experts; ACLU and MALDEF (Mexican American Legal Defense and Educational Fund) spent $127,651 on theirs.[9] Dr. Thomas Sobol, former commissioner of education for New York, was one of four experts for the students who donated their time and their expertise, without fee. Lawyers for the defense gave Sobol a hard time for drawing on his own experience in his expert report.

Q: Would you agree that your expert report in this case does not cite to any studies of what conditions and resources are minimally required for any school or what role the state should play in ensuring the provision of educational essentials to students?

A: The report does not cite formal studies of those matters. I based my opinion on a lifetime of work in the schools in a variety of roles.

Q: Would you agree that your report in this case does not cite to any studies showing that the state role you described will better ensure the provisions to students of educational essentials?

A: The report is not based on studies. It's based on my experiences over a long period of time in a variety of roles.

Several more times, a lawyer for the state asked essentially the same question about Sobol's report not citing studies, hammering home the state's point that one's personal day-to-day work in the schools has no value—even if that work included being a teacher, a superintendent, and a state commissioner of education.

How many experts can dance on the head of a pin? How many expert studies would a man on the street need to hear to know that it's not good for kids to go to vermin-infested schools loaded with mold and hang out in classrooms lacking enough chairs for everybody?

Writing in the *San Francisco Chronicle*, Nanette Asimov and Lance Williams described the lawyers' tactics in taking depositions from children as "browbeating," scaring some children, making others cry.[10] Eleven-year-old Carlos Ramirez of San Francisco, who had once fainted in a ninety-degree classroom with a perennially broken air conditioner, asked to have a substitute testify on his behalf after his mother was shot to death just weeks before the deposition. The state's lawyers refused because the substitute's name wasn't on the original complaint. Several children dropped out of the case, which was the apparent purpose of the lawyers' tactics.

Needless to say, children, not regarded as experts, weren't paid $300 an hour for their testimony. Children are dismissed as anecdotals unless and until an expert puts them into a controlled study—and then only their test scores are counted.

The team representing low-income students has fourteen experts arguing that children who are denied basic school resources suffer a permanent disadvantage in life. Thirteen other experts are working for the State of California, testifying that low-income students wouldn't do any better if they had the same educational benefits as middle-class kids. Between May 2000 and May 2003, the state spent nearly $18 million for the right not to rid poverty schools of vermin and mold. Lawyers for the children aren't taking a fee, hoping to recoup costs if they win the suit. The trial is set to start in August 2004.

The lawsuit has special relevance in San Francisco, not just because children in some of the rat-infested schools are plaintiffs, but because officials in San Francisco and even the FBI are asking questions about where the Consent Decree money that might have fixed the buildings was spent.

Where Has All the Money Gone?

In the annual evaluation of the Consent Decree in 2001, the court appointed monitor questioned the accounting practices of the San Francisco Unified School District. The monitor found it remarkable that 8.5 percent of the Consent Decree budget, listed as *indirect costs*, "simply disappears": that's $3.5 million.[11]

Writing for Salon.com in February 1999, San Francisco parent-of-a-child-in-public-school and writer specializing on issues of urban poverty Joan Walsh reflected, "The consent decree represented the best and worst of 1960s-style liberal social engineering."[12] As is the case across urban America, fully 50 percent of San Francisco kids attend private schools. Eighty-eight percent of SFUSD students belong to an ethnic minority, with 46 percent receiving free or reduced lunch. Of course even to mention poverty earns one castigation by *No Excuses* commandos.

During the NAACP lawsuit, the school district agreed that there was de facto segregation and that a disproportionate number of African American students were not succeeding in school. The solution rested on a single shared assumption: teachers were responsible for the failure of students in school. No mention of lack of community participation or power in controlling what was happening within the school. With teachers identified as the problem, reconstitution became the solution. And reconstitution, San Francisco–style, meant emptying the school of faculty and staff—everybody. Then, new teachers and administrators were hired if they could demonstrate fealty to high standards. Four schools were physically renovated, the new staff was given six days of training, brochures welcoming new students were distributed, and the reconstituted school doors opened. According to plan, parents from all over the city should have rushed to send their kids through these doors, producing a racially diverse school whose success rates and reputation of academic rigor would place it among the most prestigious schools in the district. Should have.

It didn't quite happen that way. As part of the Consent Decree, the district conceded that there were nineteen racially segregated schools and it agreed to launch what it called targeted programs. Not surprisingly, these programs zeroed in on academic performance, attendance, and dropout, expulsion, and suspension rates. To address segregation issues, the district agreed to a 45 percent cap for any of the nine specified racial/ethnic groups in nineteen regular schools and a 40 percent racial/ethnic cap for the sixteen elite alternative schools. An independent, court-ordered monitor annually checked district compliance with the more than forty major stipulations required by the Consent Decree. Since the district was never in full compliance, the NAACP lawyers periodically sued for expansion of the settlement in an attempt to apply more of the stipulations to more schools.

When, by 1990, racial balance had not happened, the NAACP requested that the judge appoint another panel of experts to investigate why. Judge Orrick appointed Gary Orfield to chair a panel of experts (Robert Green, Gordon Foster, David Tatel, and Barbara Cohen).[13] From November 1991 to June 1992, the panel gathered its data. Its interviews with district administrators "and other parties" were deemed "confidential private discussions."

> The goal of the committee was . . . to recommend ways to improve the desegregation plan. Our goal was to examine issues fully so that it would be possible to find evidence sufficiently convincing to win the agreement of experts chosen by all of the parties.[14]

Agreement of experts. Note that the goal was *not* to win the agreement of teachers, parents, students, and other interested members of the community. Experts are what counts. Experts talk to other experts. Institutional elimination of obstacles in the way of integration doesn't require the knowledge or cooperation of the community. The experts' report did call for the cooperation of "other basic community institutions and for increased parental involvement." But these are the very groups excluded by the decision-making process. The experts "urge[d] the decision makers to . . . keep a strong focus on the needs of African American and Hispanic youth" but never invited these youth to help the experts understand why they dropped—or were pushed—out in disproportionate numbers.

Instead, the experts relied on district data and interviews with NAACP lawyers to arrive at their conclusions. And thus they concluded that reconstitution worked.

> The implementation of the Bayview-Hunters Point model of school reconstitution—with staff selection and training built around a philosophy of opportunity for all children—did work [in terms of integrated schools, higher test scores, and lower dropout rates]. Reconstitution, under the first phase of the Consent Decree, involved selecting a new principal and recruiting an entire new staff at a school, committed to the goals of the Consent Decree. . . . We recommend that more schools be required to undergo fundamental transformations like those that occurred in the Bayview-Hunters Point area. There should be deadlines for schools receiving Consent Decree funds to produce clear gains for student outcomes. When schools succeed they should be rewarded with increased flexibility in managing their educational program. If a school fails, after adequate notice and special training assistance, a new principal and a newly recruited faculty should be appointed.[15]

In 1992, Orfield's committee of experts submitted a report to Judge Orrick, concluding that the district was in compliance with the racial caps but had not closed the achievement gap between whites and African Americans. Many of the recommendations ended up in a compromise document, *Second Joint Report*.[16] When the teachers union protested its lack of participation, the judge observed that, based on his previous decisions, the union had no legal right to do so. Concerned that the needs of limited English speakers were not being met, attorneys representing the Chinese American Democratic Club and Multicultural Education, Training, and Advocacy, Inc. (a Latino nonprofit organization), argued to be part of the overseeing committee.[17] Their motion was also denied. Among the more than seventy specific recommendations in the Orfield report was one that the newly appointed San Francisco superintendent, Waldemar (Bill) Rojas, would pursue diligently: *reconstitution*. Orfield recommended that the district ratchet up the reconstitution program, reconstituting three schools each year. The three parties agreed, and from 1993 to 1998, reconstitution became Rojas' signature issue.

But as Jennifer Goldstein points out in a paper presented at an American Educational Research Association meeting, it is not clear that vacating adults led to improved student performance.[18] There were seven other components in the reforms. "The experts did not and cannot isolate which of the reforms actually caused the improved achievement." Goldstein also observes that "reconstitution was expanded as a remedy for failing schools . . . without a firm understanding of the educational illness."[19]

In 1998, Orfield told *Catalyst*, a journal that runs with the subtitle *Voices of Chicago's School Reform*, that reconstitution isn't about clearing out bad teachers; it's about creating a new school culture with a common vision and a plan for tackling the problems that "burnt out or overwhelmed" the last group. "Not just the faculty, but the community has to go through a very tough change," Orfield said. "All the relationships have to be rebuilt." And he concluded, "Any fundamental reform like this is likely to be disruptive in the short run. You have to see it as a long-term process."[20]

Middle school teacher Brad Stam described it another way: "The My Lai approach to school reform: You destroy the village in order to save it."[21] Plenty of teachers have pointed out that this carpet bombing of shame is the way they are trained *not* to treat children.

An unaddressed question is, Just how does the community enter this relationship, when it is denied a place at the table?

Alignment of District and State Policy

With top-down, punitive, data-driven reform in San Francisco toppling desegregation efforts, it was probably no coincidence that state legislators decided the time was ripe to adopt reconstitution statewide. On January 19, 1999, California state senator Dede Alpert introduced the first draft of the Public School Accountability Act. Stuart Biegel, the Consent Degree monitor, had noted that since the spring of 1997, the San Francisco teachers union had been negotiating with Rojas to shift the emphasis of his accountability system (Comprehensive School Improvement Program [CSIP/reconstitution]) away from test scores and toward site plans and school portfolios.[22]

> Negotiations between the district and the teachers in the School Accountability Process were unofficially terminated in the fall of 1999 as SFUSD officials chose instead to buy into California's new Immediate Intervention/ Underperforming Schools Program (II/USP). These shifts of direction initially resulted in an additional level of tension between the district and the teachers' union, but by the end of the 1999–2000 academic year a Labor Management Community Advisory Committee had begun work toward developing a process that would hopefully lead to improved II/USP collaboration.[23]

Biegel's expectation that teachers would cooperate more readily with state reconstitution (II/USP) rather than district reconstitution was tempered a few pages later when he expressed a certain frustration with Rojas' focus on test scores and then noted the direction in which reform was heading on the state level.

> As we have pointed out year after year, research in the area of educational assessment and evaluation points unequivocally to the centrality of a basic principle in this area: relying on *one* standardized test to measure anything

is at best inappropriate and at worst a very dangerous practice.[24] (Emphasis in original.)

Cutting against these research-based imperatives, however, is the state's ongoing effort to tie a growing number of programs and policy decisions to the results on only one test—the STAR test (a.k.a. SAT-9). . . . The monitoring team has found that as a result of this increased focus on the scores of this one test, individual school sites in San Francisco have understandably begun to devote more time to test preparation exercises and activities. To the extent that these activities help build basic skills, they can serve a valuable purpose. But at a certain point, test preparation crosses the line and ceases to be a valuable educational activity. At a certain point, it serves only a narrow cognitive function, taking away from time that can and should be spent developing the student's writing skills, problem solving skills, higher order thinking skills, and creative abilities in general. Thus we urge members of the SFUSD community to monitor closely the nature and extent of test preparation activities in individual schools and supplement this monitoring with relevant staff development so that an important curricular balance continues to be maintained.[25]

The monitoring team ignored the fact that no forum existed in the SFUSD community for defining and exploring test-preparation activities; the point became even more moot when accountability was moved to the state level. Given such a finding, it is difficult to see why the monitoring team was hopeful that the district's negotiations with teachers would lead "to improved II/USP collaboration." Too bad the teachers union didn't raise the issue.

Whatever ambitions Rojas had, he seemed to overstep them on March 17, 1999, the deadline for districts to report their fiscal condition to the state and the day before the assembly was scheduled to vote on extra funding for SFUSD. Rojas announced his plan to cut $17 million from the district's budget. The San Francisco Assembly representatives were furious, immediately adding an amendment authorizing an audit of SFUSD finances to the funding bill.[26] Less than a month later, on April 22, the Dallas school board stunned San Francisco by announcing that Rojas was its first choice to replace a superintendent who had pleaded guilty to fraud and embezzlement. Two San Francisco school board members called for Rojas to resign immediately "on the grounds that he violated his contract by interviewing for a job without telling the board."[27]

The Legacy of Rojas and Reconstitution

Although Rojas could make a legitimate claim to expect the state to reimburse the district for the $17 million it had spent from 1993 to 1997 on Consent Decree programs, his March 17 announcement unleashed a firestorm of criticism of his fiscal practices. Here's how one observer described Rojas' explanation of budget shifts: "Former San Francisco Unified boss Wally Rojas slimed into City Hall this week. . . . He turned up the volume. He denied responsibility. He threw in a massive blame-shift. He blustered and ignored all time limits and parliamentary procedure. He had not lost his edge."[28] Other press-ascribed adjectives indicate the strong feelings Rojas inspired: *Education Week* called him *peppery*, the *San Francisco Chronicle* and SchoolWisePress.com called him *Wild Bill*; DallasArena.com dubbed him *Lounge Lizard*; Salon.com said he was *visionary, autocratic,* and *widely-loathed.* The *Dallas Business Journal* said that although he went by the title Doctor, he seemed to be angling for emperor.

The conclusions of the state audit indicate why Rojas might have been eager to leave San Francisco. Auditors found that many of the problems leading to fiscal mismanagement dated back "five years or more," about the time Rojas fired a conservative budget manager and replaced him with one of his New York colleagues. The audit found that information provided by the district offices was "unreliable and untimely." Auditors also concluded that it was likely that "fraud and abuse" occurred, as well as possible "violations of laws and regulations."[29]

The auditors expressed concern that, in addition to leaving the school district vulnerable to fiscal "fraud and abuse," Rojas' bureaucracy at the district level was not "receiving the level of service they need[ed] to support adequately the educational programs." So they put a radical plan like reconstitution into place without even funding the administrative support to let it function.

The monitoring team also noted that it was unclear how the support from Consent Decree funds was being spent.

> Once the Department of Integration approves a school's budget, the Department appears to have no further monitoring function to ensure that the school in fact spends its funds as it promised or to ensure that the programs funded lead to improvements in the academic performance of the school or toward other Consent Decree goals (e.g., improved attendance).[30]

It took more than budget discrepancies for the *San Francisco Chronicle* to fall out of love with Rojas. The June 1999 postmortem headline trumpeted: "Rojas' Record Can't Be Denied: Scores, Graduation Rates Rose During His Tenure as San Francisco Schools Chief."[31]

> Even a critic such as school board member Dan Kelly still glows when talking about the educational state of the district today. . . . [He] praised the district's focus on low achievers and non-English speakers, its interest in expanding the variety of schools and programs, and its overall emphasis on

student progress. . . . "If we say that what really counts in a school district is student achievement, then Bill Rojas gets an 'A,'" state Superintendent Delaine Eastin said, noting that San Francisco's numbers have gone up faster and higher than in such cities as Los Angeles, New York, and Chicago.[32]

Funny thing: The reported numbers went up and up. But official figures today indicate that the schools in question still score abysmally. One difficulty in explaining this is apples and oranges. Tests changed, so it is impossible to make comparisons. All we can tell is that by the state's rating system, despite years of progress trumpeted by Rojas' press releases, certain schools are still at the bottom.

Even as *San Francisco Chronicle* education reporter Nanette Asimov admitted that the cornerstone of Rojas' reform package—reconstitution—showed little benefit, and "did not always help raise scores," she offered the upbeat conclusion that "the chaotic environment at some schools eased"; a quote from NAACP attorney Peter Cohn "praised Rojas as being more committed to minority student achievement than any previous superintendent"; Pedro Noguera, then-professor of education at Berkeley, concluded that Rojas improved the district because he "challenge[d] the orthodoxy and tr[ied] new things." Asimov explained that the fiscal problems of the district were the responsibility of the school board, who "did nothing, for example, when Rojas stopped giving members budget previews that might have provided early warning of fiscal problems" and "did not forbid him" from using the same evasive tactics again and again.[33] So, it seems, the focus on rising test scores concealed a multitude of sins, and it worked for Rojas' own reputation. His promises to eliminate the achievement gap, to hold teachers accountable, and to provide high standards for all led to the hijacking of desegregation funds and the elimination of even the appearance of democratic decision making. The school board did nothing to hold Rojas accountable because the Consent Decree gave him the right to ignore school board members' request for information. The sloppy, if not illegal, manipulation of the budget and the lack of structural support for Rojas' drastic changes were hidden from public view under the umbrella of the Consent Decree, whose protective coverage was spread out districtwide by the experts' promotion of the BRT agenda. Ironically, in the name of accountability, systemic reform relieved Rojas from being held accountable by the people of San Francisco. With the emphasis on test scores as the end, other indicators of institutional health were made invisible.

Welcome to school governance in the twenty-first century. Similar tales are being played out across America. Districts may not have consent decrees, but they have at-large school board members with no ties—or responsibilities—to neighborhood needs. Plus autocratic superintendents whose mandate is to raise test scores—no matter what the cost. The difference between visionary and autocratic usually depends on where you're standing.

Teachers were upset but in an awkward position: To criticize Rojas was to criticize the Consent Decree, thereby taking a stand against equity and excellence. This necessarily pitted the mostly white teachers against the NAACP and its allies. Nevertheless, many teachers persisted in asserting that Rojas' public descriptions of what was going on in the schools had little to do with the reality. One teacher told the *San Francisco Chronicle*,

> "[W]e don't have nearly adequate counseling staff in the district. Teachers are so overworked that we barely have time to say 'hi' to the kids. We don't even have a phone number that we can count on to be answered in case of emergency. . . ." Other [teachers] complained that Rojas eliminated a number of vocational electives such as wood shop, home economics, and auto mechanics classes that had kept many students coming to school.[34]

Across the country, teachers face a similar problem when trying to confront No Child Left Behind. The U.S. Department of Education and Congress have framed the case so that to argue against No Child Left Behind is to argue against excellence for all, and the *all* is minorities. Speak against mandated algebra for all and in favor of vocational courses, and you are put in the camp of leaving some children without access to a full academic program.

In San Francisco, Peter Cohn, NAACP attorney, spoke for many when he applauded the elimination of vocational electives and the substitution of academics. But teachers pointed out that this change actually resulted in dumbed-down academics because a Rojas edict required that middle and high schools maintain at least a C average for all racial and ethnic groups. Rojas also decreed that high schools should either maintain a B average for all college-preparatory courses or improve grades in classes required for University of California admission. The result was documented grade inflation at Balboa High and anecdotal reports at other schools. Under Rojas' direction, the district also began highlighting the scores of fewer students each year in its reports, eventually putting into its primary report only the scores of the English-speaking students who had been in the district at least two years. It was all part of the superintendent's push for higher graduation rates and better numbers overall. Such an approach means teachers and principals are not asked what should be done but are told what must be done.[35]

Although it is impossible to determine to what degree the numbers indicating better academic achievement were accurate, the educational establishment, and even the publishers of standardized tests themselves, all agree that no important decision should ever be made on the basis of one test score alone. Yet Rojas, Cohn, members of the San Francisco Chamber of Commerce, the

California Business Roundtable, and the editorial board of the *San Francisco Chronicle* dismissed the pleadings of community leaders, parents, teachers, and students that higher test scores not be used as the sole indication of educational excellence in the schools.

Rojas pioneered the state's high-stakes accountability system—the 1999 Public School Accountability Act—by using Comprehensive Test of Basic Skills (CTBS) test scores to determine whether a school was either high- or low-performing. Low-performing schools were, in lip service, anyway, given support to help raise their scores. When the scores did not go up within one or two years, the schools were reconstituted. We now see a similar scheme in No Child Left Behind.

The California Business Roundtable is currently lobbying state legislators to streamline teacher credential programs and reorient the courses to focus on training teachers on how to use test scores to develop their instructional methodology—even though using test scores in this way is probably less useful than reading tea leaves. So many variables affect test-score results that the test score itself must be confirmed by other means. But such confirmation defeats the ostensible purpose of using standardized tests in the first place—to make assessment cost-effective.[36] That supporters of the BRT agenda are not concerned with this issue of test validity suggests that they are either willfully and stubbornly ignorant or determined to use tests first, to undermine community influence in curricula and instruction and, ultimately, to weaken, even destroy, public education.

Bill Rojas, Won't You Please Fess Up

We've seen how the hostility of the San Francisco NAACP lawyers toward district teachers allowed Rojas to use the rhetoric of the BRT agenda to eliminate the debate over the complex benefits of diversity. Rojas and his supporters succeeded in replacing discussion and debate over the multiple and legitimate goals of education (and an examination of the budget) with a false dichotomy: one is either for *high standards for all* or for allowing poor and minority students to continue to fail. There was no question, until the last two years of his term as superintendent, about the authenticity, validity, or reliability of the test scores he was using to justify the elimination of community participation in policy making.

Rojas was congratulated for raising expectations but, as the reports of the Consent Degree monitor showed, he never managed to close the achievement gap.[37] Within-school segregation began to get worse after 1998.[38] From 1996 to 2000, there was no progress in disproportionate suspensions and dropouts of African American students, and in 2000, Biegel reported that the situation was "getting worse."[39] African American students continue to have the lowest mean GPA in all twelve of the district high schools and the lowest percentage attending 96 to 100 percent of their classes at every level.[40]

What the Rojas record reveals is that he used test scores to maintain control in his top-down reform and to distribute patronage. This patronage system absorbed and co-opted systemic, data-driven reform, something that should penetrate the hard-shelled consciousness of even the Business Roundtable. Autocracy trumps data every time. For that matter, so does hubris. This is why Deborah Meier, for one, argued in *Will Standards Save Public Education?* that "[i]mportant decisions regarding kids and teachers should always be based on multiple sources of evidence that seem appropriate and credible to those most concerned."[41]

Equally important, sanctions must remain under the control of the local community and be determined by people who have intimate knowledge of each school, each child. If all politics is local, so, too, should be all education decisions.

In spite of evidence suggesting the ineffectiveness of Rojas' policies, his claim that CTBS test scores were "going up"—announced periodically in press conferences from the board rooms of Pacific Bell and the San Francisco Chamber of Commerce—allowed him to advance his own career goals. He gained a Ph.D., a national reputation, access to state senator Gary Hart's team, election to the presidency of the Council on Great City Schools, and a 41 percent increase in salary when he moved to Dallas. Rojas pursued the Business Roundtable's agenda of *high standards for all* and was rewarded for it. That such policies left havoc in their wake did not seem to bother the CEOs of the California Business Roundtable since the ultimate effect—and maybe the real purpose—was to eliminate community-based reform.

As we have seen, this havoc didn't seem to bother the city's media either. Or the court system. Or the experts.

In the end, Rojas was used and discarded in the same way he used and discarded others. Given the larger context in which he was a player, this seems more predictable than surprising.

Postscript

Rojas' successor, Arlene Ackerman, has continued down the free-for-all test-prep highway, decreeing that those who score below 40 percent on the SAT-9 (approximately one-third of the SFUSD student population) must go to summer school and Saturday classes—to be drilled from test-prep materials. The claim is that such drill gives students a better chance of passing the state's high school exit exam. The next step is to force teachers to "teach at high enough standards." Get that? One more example of media mendacity is its failure to acknowledge that posing the hypothetical question of when teachers stopped teaching to high enough standards is as twisted as the wife-beating saw.

The district gets teachers marching to these high standards by creating end-of-course exams. One plan brought forward at a Secondary Task Force meeting by Elois Brooks is that district administrators, not teachers, will write the final exams for courses.[42] Brooks, chief academic officer for the San Francisco district, was described by Loose Lips, an alternative press political source in Washington, D.C., as Ackerman's "strong-willed deputy": "Although Ackerman set school policy during her two-year tenure, it was Brooks who implemented that policy. It was Brooks who took the flak from disgruntled parents at community meetings. It was Brooks who returned the flak with a snarling mien that cleared an egress for her when the meetings were over." The commentary writer noted that, in the face of Brooks' departure, all the new D.C. superintendent would have to do to "look like a model of cordiality and openness" is smile.[43] Ackerman brought Brooks with her when she took the San Francisco job. Brooks reiterates the party line in an interview with *School Board News*, pointing out that in Ackerman's three-year tenure, the district has seen two-thirds of its 117 schools make gains in both reading and math. "It really wasn't an issue of resources," she told *School Board News*. "In these schools it was an issue of attitude."[44]

Attitude. That sends chills down a teacher's spine. The *Washington City Paper* reported that during their tenure in Washington, D.C., Ackerman and Brooks "whipped their subordinates into a totalitarian panic, fed by threats, finger-wagging, and wanton use of the superintendent's unchecked power over the school system." The reporter added, "Forcing a code of silence onto her underlings is just one piece of Ackerman's PR effort."[45] Four years later, a *San Francisco Chronicle* headline read "Ackerman Is Accused of 'Gag Order.'" Heather Knight wrote that some board members complain that school principals are instructed not to speak to them, and teachers complain that speaking up at board meetings or to members of the press earns a reprimand. Ackerman insists that charges that she doesn't allow people to speak and offers a top-down management style couldn't be further from the truth.[46]

Ackerman's five-year plan, called Excellence for All, is closely linked to the state's Public School Accountability Act. The school board, however, passed a resolution in January 2002 requiring the superintendent to accompany the announcement of all major policy initiatives with a "racial/ethnic impact study." The resolution came out of a school board meeting on October 30, 2001, at which dozens of teachers, students, and community leaders testified to the increasing segregation and alienation in the district's schools. Shortly after the passage of the board's resolution, Ackerman announced the closing of one the poorest-performing comprehensive high schools. When a board member asked her for the impact study, she replied that she had not done one.

In 1999, after six months as superintendent of the Dallas, Texas, public schools, Rojas was fired. In 2002, Rojas was an invited participant at the Broad Foundation third strategic planning retreat, wherein a "distinguished group of leaders in public education assembled to discuss the launch of several initiatives incubated at previous retreats." Most specifically, he was invited to advise the Broad Foundation on "how best to scale-up current Foundation investments and develop new high-impact policy initiatives."[47] The invitees were a premier list of Standardistas. We met the group already in Chapter 5's discussion of the Broad Foundation's wide reach. But it is useful to take another look at the bedfellows list. It shows who's running things, and it reminds us that change is one thing, progress another.

Arlene Ackerman, who by virtue of the alphabet tops the Broad participant list, was hired by the San Francisco school board in 2000. The board based its decision on Ackerman's reputation for implementing standards-based accountability in the Washington, D.C., school district. Systemic reform, ironically, came to San Francisco in the guise of desegregation. Yet while systemic reform planted deep roots from 1984 to 1998, desegregation disappeared as an issue, leaving the San Francisco NAACP defending the new black superintendent's five-year, standards-based accountability plan titled Excellence for All.

In his preface to *The Activist's Handbook*, San Francisco attorney and longtime activist for urban issues Randy Shaw comments that of late, the power of activism to achieve social change has gained new respect.[48] "Once-invulnerable targets ranging from the National Rifle Association to the World Bank are taking citizen action more seriously." His book profiles grassroots campaigns led by activists who used "the strategies and tactics necessary for success." In some cases this meant nontraditional alliances, such as Hasidic Jews and Puerto Rican Catholics forming a coalition to defeat a proposed incinerator at the Brooklyn Navy Yard. The problem, Shaw observes, is that these successes get little publicity: so *"few activists across the country learned of such victories, and certainly had no 'behind the scenes' information regarding the keys to success. Activists thus continued to lack the confidence that they too could succeed against similar odds"* (emphasis in original). The Internet is changing this. What's needed now are teachers willing to become activists.

San Francisco's story is being repeated in urban centers across the country, where hyped rhetoric trumps every wisp of reality—and hides the real agenda. Roxbury, Massachusetts, first-grade teacher Jane Ehrenfeld could have been commenting on any urban center in the United States when she wrote, "It is cheaper to test than to commit the dollars to fix decrepit classrooms, lower class sizes, and pay teachers decent salaries."[49]

Parents and teachers have to get up every morning asking, "Amid the static, whom do I trust?" For starters, we all need to look very closely at what the corporate-politico alliance is doing: not what these people are saying, what they're doing. Parents and teachers would do well to read Barbara Kingsolver's account of the eighteen-month strike against the Phelps Dodge Copper Corporation.[50] A group of mostly Latino women whose culture had limited their roles, women who describe themselves as "just housewives," took on corporate America. They became strategists, leaders, forces to be reckoned with. Kingsolver, a young reporter at the time, watched and listened. In her words, "I tracked my subjects' changes of heart and mind as they held the line with their hearts in their throats." *Holding the line.* This is what teachers and parents need to learn to do.

Notes

1. Judge Orrick appointed as cochairs of the settlement team "two of the best educators in the country," Harold Howe (chair of the board of the Institute for Educational Leadership) and Gary Orfield (professor of political science, public policy, and education at the University of Chicago). The NAACP lawyers appointed Gordon Foster (professor of education at the University of Miami) and Robert Green (dean of urban affairs at Michigan State University). The district appointed Barbara Cohen (administrative assistant to the superintendent of SFUSD and previously employed by Far West Laboratories) and Fred Leonard (associate superintendent for instructional support services of SFUSD). The state appointed Ples Griffin (chief of office of intergroup relations for the California Department of Education and formerly a special consultant to the Rand Corporation) and Thomas Griffin (lecturer in a graduate student law course at the University of California at Berkeley).

2. San Francisco Unified School District. 1992. Findings and Recommendations on Consent Decree Implementation, Report to Judge William H. Orrick. SFUSD, July.

3. Rojas, Waldemar, and Assembly Education Committee, California Legislature. 1998. "Accountability in the SFUSD." 4 February. Accessed at *www.sfusd.k12.ca.us/news/account.pdf.*

4. When you write about education, you never have to make anything up: here's the source declaring this knowledge essential to fifth graders: *www.cde.ca.gov/standards/history/grade5.html.*

5. Both books have been reissued by Heinemann.

6. Herndon, James. 1985. *Notes from a Schoolteacher.* New York: Simon and Schuster.

7. Kidder, Tracey. 2003. *Mountains Beyond Mountains: The Quest of Dr. Paul Farmer, a Man Who Would Cure the World.* New York: Random House, 34.

8. See *www.decentschools.org.*

9. Asimov, Nanette. 2002. "Bitter Battle over Class Standards." *San Francisco Chronicle*, 5 May.

10. Asimov, Nanette, and Lance Williams. 2001. "High-Priced Legal Team Browbeats Youths About Shoddy Schools." *San Francisco Chronicle*, 2 September.

11. Biegel, Stuart. 2001. *San Francisco Unified School District Desegregation, Paragraph 44 Independent Review* (18). Los Angeles: University of California, Los Angeles.

12. Walsh, Joan. 1999. "A New Racial Era for San Francisco's Schools." Salon.com. Accessed at *www.salon.com/news/1999/02/18news.html*.

13. At the time, Orfield was a professor at the University of Chicago. Currently he heads the Harvard Civil Rights Project.

14. Orfield, Gary. 1992. *Desegregation and Educational Change in San Francisco: Findings and Recommendations on Consent Decree Implementation*. Research. San Francisco: U.S. District Court, 15.

15. Ibid., 5–6.

16. Orfield, G. 1992. *Desegregation and Educational Change in San Francisco: Findings and Recommendations on Consent Decree Implementation*. Research. San Francisco: U.S. District Court.

17. Fraga, L. R., B. A. Erlichson, and S. Lee. 1998. "Consensus Building and School Reform: The Role of the Courts in San Francisco." In *Changing Urban Education*, ed. C. Stone, 79. Lawrence: University of Kansas Press. The concerns of MALDEF and other Latino advocacy groups were to some degree incorporated into the parties' *Second Joint Report*. The report made specific recommendations to the district regarding bilingual and LEP instruction. Yet these recommendations were never implemented. For example, the time LEP students spent in segregated classes was not "minimized." Those in bilingual programs who developed English proficiency were rarely placed out even after official redesignation (Biegel, Stuart. 2000. San Francisco Unified School District Desegregation, Paragraph 44 Independent Review. Los Angeles: University of California, Los Angeles, 182, 40). When the district was out of compliance, the NAACP had the legal right to file suit. MALDEF and others did not.

18. Goldstein, J., M. Kelleman, and W. Kosaki. 1998. Reconstitution in Theory and Practice: The experience of San Francisco. Paper presented at the American Educational Research Association, San Diego, 13–17 April.

19. Goldstein et al. 1998, 9–10.

20. Duffrin, Elizabeth. 1998. "Lessons from San Francisco." *Catalyst*. June. Accessed at *www.catalyst-chicago.org/06-98/068wmm09.htm*.

21. Ruenzel, David. 1997. "Do or Die." *Teacher Magazine*, March.

22. Biegel. 2000, 9.

23. Ibid.

24. Ibid., 11.

25. Ibid., 13.

26. The bill "set aside $48.3 million to reimburse 14 districts for desegregation expenditures. San Francisco's share would be $12.7 million . . . perceived by some as a pork barrel bill for San Francisco" (Asimov, Nanette. 1999. "San Francisco Schools Shaken by Deep Budget Cuts." *San Francisco Chronicle*, 1999, 18 March).

27. Asimov, Nanette. 1999. "Rojas Set to Bolt San Francisco for Dallas School Job." *San Francisco Chronicle*, 23 April. It would not be the first time that Rojas took a job while under a cloud. When hired by the San Francisco school board in 1992, the district was sued for allegedly violating the Brown Act. This act was passed to stop backroom dealing. One of the concerns that the public had but did not get a chance to explore during the hiring process was Rojas' DUI record.

28. Brown, H. 2001. "Watching City Hall." *San Francisco Call*, 21 May. Accessed at *www.sfcall.com/issues%202001/5.21.01/watching_city_hall.htm*.

29. Fiscal Crisis and Management Assistance Team. 2000. *Comprehensive Fiscal Assessment of the San Francisco Unified School District*. San Francisco: San Francisco Unified School District. Just as a point of history: the Arthur Anderson firm did the audit on the SFUSD books.

30. Biegel. 2000, 57.

31. Asimov, Nanette. 1999. "Rojas' Record Can't Be Denied: Scores, Graduation Rates Rose During His Tenure as San Francisco Schools Chief." *The San Francisco Chronicle*, 21 June.

32. Ibid.

33. Ibid.

34. Ibid.

35. Ibid.

36. The misuse of testing, that is, the use of testing for high-stakes accountability and systemic reform, has led James Popham, a longtime developer and defender of such tests, to express his frustration with their current usage: current "policymakers' actions reflect their ignorance of the reality of educational testing. Even worse, they don't know what they don't know" (35). Popham argues that the only thing in a test that seems of value to policy makers is its ability to reliably result in a "substantial score spread, enough to distinguish between 83rd and 84th percentile." The reason the strongest correlation is between test scores and socioeconomic status is because socioeconomic status is "a nicely spread out variable that isn't easily altered" (53). This allows the test to function as a sorting device for many years, thereby saving districts and states the cost of having to purchase a new test once teachers learn how to teach to it. Popham, James. 2001. *The Truth About Testing: An Educator's Call to Action*. Alexandria, VA: Association for Supervision and Curriculum Development.

37. Biegel. 2000, 51.

38. Ibid., 73.

39. Ibid., 110.

40. Ibid., 133.

41. Meier, Deborah et al. 2000. *Will Standards Save Public Education?* Boston: Beacon, 16.

42. Brooks, Elois. 2002. Secondary Task Force meeting. 11 April.

43. Loose Lips. 2000. "Mea Maxima Culpa." *Washington City Paper*. 1–7 September.

44. "San Francisco's STAR Program Turns Around Low-Performing Schools." 2003. *School Board News*, 15 April. Accessed at *www.nsba.org/conference/daily/040503-4.cfm*

45. Loose Lips. 1999. "No More Teachers' Dirty Looks." *Washington City Paper*, 19–25 February. Accessed at *www.washingtoncitypaper.com/archives/lips/1999/lips0219.html*.

46. Knight, Heather. 2003. "Ackerman Is Accused of 'Gag Order.'" *San Francisco Chronicle*, 16 October.

47. The Broad Foundation. n.d. "Our History." Accessed at *www.broadfoundation.org/about/history-net.shtml*.

48. Shaw, Randy. 2001. *The Activist's Handbook*. Berkeley: University of California Press, ix.

49. Ehrenfeld, Jane. 2001. "The Trouble with Testing." *Education Week*, 24 October.

50. Kingsolver, Barbara. 1996. *Holding the Line: Women in the Great Arizona Mine Strike of 1983*. New York: ILR.

10

Up Close with Teachers, Tests, and Technology

In the elementary and middle schools of Rockingham County, N.C., a rural district north of Greensboro, administrators have to discard as many as 20 test booklets on exam days because children vomit on them. "Kids [are] throwing up in the middle of the tests," says Dianne Campbell, the district's director of testing and accountability. "They cry. They have to be removed. The stress is so much on the test that they can't handle it."[1]

This opening to a powerful article by Lawrence Hardy, an associate editor of *American School Board Journal*, could describe Anytown, North Carolina. Hardy comments, "In numerous interviews with professionals in education and mental health—including school nurses, counselors, and psychologists—*ASBJ* found near-unanimous agreement that too many students are suffering from intolerable levels of stress."

Across the country, even six-year-olds know where they stand in class academic rankings—who's the best in reading and who's the worst. If the feds have their way with preschool tests, we can have screaming headlines about failing three-year-olds. Not failure to provide housing and health care to three-year-olds, but their literacy and math skills deficiencies—as measured by quite loony tests. Schoolchildren have always known whether they were bluebirds or buzzards, but the old reading group caste system has gotten a whole lot meaner. DIBELS (Dynamic Indicators of Basic Early Literacy Skills) has ravaged classrooms across the land. The tester (in plenty of schools, this is not the child's teacher) shows the five-year-old pictures of carnival bumper cars, a grasshopper, a refrigerator, and a roller skate, saying, "This is bump, insect, refrigerator, skate. Which picture begins with /sk/? Which picture begins with /r/? Which picture begins with /b/? What sound does *insect* begin with?" The testee has to sort out that the tester is calling the grasshopper an insect, and so on.

A number of the pictures are, at best, problematic. But there's no time for lollygagging over definitions or wondering how many urban kindergartners have ever seen bumper cars: testees are scored on how many correct sounds they produce in sixty seconds. There's lots more to DIBELS. You can check it out at <*http://dibels.uoregon.edu*>.

Every child's so-called reading ability is tested and reported out with a precision that infects every moment in school. Instead of nurturing children for who they are and for what they can do, instead of fostering a joy in reading, schools now make kids afraid they aren't good enough; they make kids vomit. How did we get to this point where parents send their children off to a place that makes them vomit?

For starters, parents and teachers are locked out of any of the decisions made about children. Take North Carolina, where an interlocking network of Business Roundtable allies promotes systemic reform. The board of directors of the Public School Forum (PSF), established in 1985 and headquartered in Raleigh, North Carolina, is loaded with state legislators and other politicos, business and industry representatives, and fifteen education administrators, mostly postsecondary. There is one teacher and one representative from the state parent teacher organization. PSF describes itself as an "independent public school policy think-tank and best practices organization whose mission is to contribute to a statewide system of schooling second to none." PSF's staff of fourteen oversees a wide variety of programs and publications dedicated to advancing an education agenda aligned with that of the Business Roundtable. This agenda is no secret, as the PSF website states:

> The Forum was also a founding member of the Education: Everybody's Business Coalition, a six-year-old coalition that is the national Business Roundtable's North Carolina conduit for school improvement effort. Linking major educational and business groups, the Coalition has strengthened the bridge between elected officials, educators and business leaders committed to school improvement.[2]

When this statement was written, the Charlotte-Mecklenburg website boasted that a national finance magazine had rated the community as having the "number one pro-business attitude" in the nation.[3]

Here's a description of PSF's ability to influence legislation:

> Because the study group process is so thorough and collaborative and its members are key stake-holders, the groups' reports are influential on state policy. The study groups give policy makers an opportunity to examine complex issues *away from partisan arena* and build consensus on educationally sound strategies to address them. In large part because of this consensus,

every study group has resulted in the introduction of legislation that includes all or most of the group's recommendations.[4] (Emphasis added.)

You can guess who the partisans are.

PSF's 2000 report *Things That Matter* argues that state funding formulas for public schools should not try to narrow the gap between amounts spent on rich and poor districts, but should "ensure that all young people have a 'sound basic education.'" [5] To this end, PSF lobbied the North Carolina legislature in 1999 to provide $86 million in extra funds for those schools whose test scores defined them as "under performing." The vicious circle here, as suggested by Linda McNeil's study in Houston, is that such money is spent on test-prep material.

Firsthand reports from North Carolina teachers confirm this. All elementary-grade students take the End of Grade (EOG) tests in North Carolina; the EOGs are mostly multiple-choice and are used to make promotion decisions in grades 3, 5, and 8. As eighth-grade teacher Teresa Glenn recounts in "The Monster in Our Schools," the pressure for high marks on these EOGs is unrelenting: schools post their (good) EOG results on signs on the front lawn; in faculty meetings, the scores of individual teachers' classes—called out by name—are discussed.[6]

Teresa's school mandated a daily thirty-five-minute EOG test-preparation period. Teresa joined a listserv sponsored by the North Carolina Department of Public Instruction (DPI), set up so that teachers and administrators could share ideas. Or so it said. After watching her students struggle with the EOG test, Teresa posted a critical comment to the list, paraphrasing two inappropriate questions. Teresa also expressed her disgust:

> I am personally offended by the EOG tests. I've seen students—good students, A/B students—CRYING because of these tests . . . . I've seen teachers do nothing the last 6–10 weeks of school but work on EOG preparation. I've seen teachers publicly humiliated because they had lower test scores than the year before. I've seen children made fun of, called names and put down based on their EOG scores. . . . The entire spectacle is disgusting.[7]

Teresa also questioned the lack of accountability for test makers, the lack of validity, and the fact that testing specifications aren't released to the public. Two days later, she had more to say: "I wonder if DPI's reluctance to release tests is because they know just how horrendously bad the tests themselves are. We retested our students with a released test and I took it with them. On five questions I couldn't be sure of the answer. These questions required knowledge outside the reading passage. Another five were so poorly worded that I had no idea what the question was asking. In short, 18 of the 65 questions were themselves questionable."

On May 30, 2000, two days after her second email to the listserv set up by the DPI so that educators could communicate with each other, Teresa was summoned to the principal's office. He let her know that DPI thought she had breached the Testing Code of Ethics. Teresa's principal made it very clear that DPI was gunning for her license.

After Teresa's case was bounced to the superintendent, to the testing coordinator, to nameless DPI workers, and then back to the district office, the district decided that the Testing Code of Ethics didn't specifically preclude paraphrasing test questions. The superintendent told Teresa he was going to recommend a two-week suspension and she'd better feel sorry about what she'd done. When Teresa asked whether the test questions would be fixed, he replied, "That's none of your business."

Teresa reflects that instead of picturing clocks in *Persistence of Memory*, Salvador Dali should have painted a wasteland of bubble sheets from EOG tests melting in the desert. She says the experience changed her: "It's made me more determined than ever to speak out about the End of Grade tests and how they injure kids." If Teresa changed, so did the North Carolina Testing Code of Ethics. It now carries a specific warning against paraphrasing test questions.

Kathie Guild, a guidance counselor in a North Carolina elementary school, says that like many school counselors, she is "the designated test coordinator" for her building. One week after students scored nonproficient on their EOG exam, Kathie had to test them again. She reports, "Without exception, all of these children had turned in assignments, completed homework, worked on projects and reports, and had made academic progress during the year." However, their previous 170 days didn't matter; only what they did in the next two hours counted, and they knew it. The students were nervous; some cried as they bubbled in answer sheets.

Kathie worries about the way EOGs harm all children, not just the ones who score nonproficient. "In many schools, eight- and nine-year-old children take six state tests a year. This means twelve hours of test-taking. Translated into real class time, this means 24 lost reading lessons, 24 lost ESL lessons, 24 lost math lessons."[8] Not to mention science labs, computer time, the arts.

And then there are the phone calls. Derek Jennings, columnist at the *Independent Weekly*, writes that his honor-roll daughter's teacher took "the extraordinary step of calling us a few weeks prior to the EOGs to let us know that our daughter had been making a few careless mistakes in math lately, and that she would hate for her to slip up and do less than her best on the test."[8] One can wonder what kinds of calls the parents of kids not on the honor roll received. North Carolina parents can be grateful they are not yet receiving instructions such as those directed at Virginia parents. The Virginia Department of Education posts released Standards of Learning tests on its website, along with parent tips for helping their kids prepare for the tests. Here are a few tips for parents of fifth graders:

- Have your child write a verbal statement for an algebraic expression that you provide.
- Have your child identify pictures of organisms that belong to each of the five kingdoms: monerans, protists, fungi, plants, and animals.
- Have your child identify the functions of cells by drawing a diagram and describing the role of each part of the cell.
- Have your child give a heading to a paragraph from a story you are reading with him/her or he/she is reading.[9]

Only a psychotic Standardista could dream up the imperative to stop reading so a kid can affix a heading to a paragraph. Truly, this is disarranged social functioning.

The Skill Is the Thing

Greg Decker, elementary principal in Lead Mine, North Carolina, insists that the key to raising student performance on high-stakes tests is "continuing assessment and evaluation throughout the school year."[10] Using a data-driven framework, "teachers, students, and parents can see student expectations for each grade level; track student progress; identify student needs; provide focused instruction and interventions; and, ultimately, improve student achievement in the class and on the EOG Test."

This presupposes, of course, that a curriculum is made up of a host of skills. Not just skills, but skills in a prescribed order. At Lead Mine Elementary and at an increasing number of schools across the country, the curriculum map "lists the skills in the order they will be taught in each grade level from kindergarten through fifth grade." At Lead Mine, all students in the school use Pearson Education Technologies' SuccessMaker[11] for thirty minutes a day, three times a week "to strengthen their skills." The results of all this is, writes Decker, are that "the school can now forecast the time a student needs to reach a specific SuccessMaker level and see the relationship of that level to achievement on the EOG Test."

Forecast: At 10:14 A.M. tomorrow, we know where your child will be on SuccessMaker. One can envision schools sending out weekly skills forecasts—of when Johnny and Istheme *will* learn apostrophes, semicolons, and square roots. Then Mom and Dad can phone in at 10:14 to see if things are on schedule. Standardistas call this data-driven decision making. The North Carolina

Department of Public Instruction named Lead Mine a North Carolina School of Distinction with Exemplary Growth.

International Business Machinations[12]

From 1993 to 1996, IBM engineered an ambitious educational project in Charlotte-Mecklenburg, described in fascinating detail by University of North Carolina at Charlotte researcher Roslyn Mickelson, who observes that "the relationship between IBM and the Charlotte-Mecklenburg Schools is instructive for understanding the larger ideological, political, and educational policy significance of corporate involvement in the school reform process more generally."[13] Superintendent John Murphy and Stanley Litow, IBM's vice president of corporate-community relations, designed a four-school complex named Education Village. In 1993, the district paid IBM $6 million for two hundred acres adjacent to IBM corporate headquarters in University Research Park. Then, in the fall of 1994, IBM CEO Louis Gerstner announced that the first of ten national Reinventing Education Grants would be given to Charlotte to support the development of technology in Education Village. Not cash, mind you, but an assortment of computers, software, and consultant and research time. Up to 25 percent of the grant might be in cash, and, as it turned out, the computers might be outdated.

Billed by IBM as "a commitment to corporate citizenship," the Reinventing Education grants form the "centerpiece of IBM's global commitment to education." Through these Reinventing Education grants, IBM modestly claims to be "solving education's toughest problems with solutions that draw on advanced information technologies and the best minds IBM can apply. Our programs pave the way for systematic reform in school systems nationwide."[14]

Beware of the systemic reformer bearing gifts.

Now pay attention: To receive the $2 million grant, the school district was obligated to raise $82 million to pay for construction of the complex, which it did by passing a bond measure.

What a deal: Pay $6 million for property. Then pay $82 million for construction on that property. Do this in order to earn a $2 million grant, 75 percent of which will be paid in services to be determined by the grantor. And there's more: The fellows who give the $2 million will create havoc by demanding an exorbitant share of seats in the school built on that property they sold you. Capitalism at work for America's schoolchildren.

Not until the fall of 1996, with the first of the four schools in Education Village scheduled to open, did the school board finally get wind of the attendance formula cooked up by IBM's Litow and C-M's superintendent, Murphy. The school board began hearing from angry constituents, people outraged at the attendance formula that gave two-thirds of the seats in the new school to

University Park children and children from wealthy adjacent subdivisions, which just happened to be where IBM white-collar workers lived. Mickelson explains that the board regarded this apparent fait accompli as a "usurpation of their statutory rights to make pupil assignment decisions."[15] The newly elected school board cancelled the attendance formula, citing lack of compliance with the 1971 desegregation court decision; it began a process of open forums to come up with a fairer system of enrollment.

The corporate players were furious. The president of University Research Park, Chapel Hill, wrote an editorial in the *Charlotte Observer*:

> These companies [that donate to the school] do not need to have their motives questioned. They do not need to be hassled. . . . They need to be persuaded to offer even more support. . . . If our school board can't understand the grant's purpose, won't honor agreements, and can't act graciously, other companies will think twice before extending new offers of support.[16]

One CEO of a Research Park firm told Mickelson that business leaders "were very upset that the school board got involved. . . . It is business. . . . It was not an issue of quality education, it was an issue of development of University Research Park."[17]

The Technology Fix in Charlotte-Mecklenburg Schools

With much fanfare in 1994, Charlotte-Mecklenburg Public Schools received the very first IBM Reinventing Education grant. Since then, there's been a lot of hoopla about the wonders of technology, but research seems problematic. The Center for Children and Technology/EDC, hired to take a look at IBM's Reinventing Education Grant Partnership Initiative, issued a press release that opens with this line: "EDC today released an independent evaluation of IBM's Reinventing Education Program which indicates that investments in educational technology are yielding gains in student performance, teaching quality, and school management." The research summary accompanying the report is even more effusive,[18] declaring that computers have become essential to the teaching practices of the majority of teachers, that communications (email exchanges, teacher-produced homepages and calendars) between parents and teachers is increasing. Funny thing how summaries sometimes distort the actual research.[19] The full report is not nearly so rosy, noting that "[t]he district needs to encourage teachers to update their homepages on a regular basis and provide training and/or structure for substantive and meaningful homepage content."[20]

Here's a quick look at two schools cited as exemplary. At Nathaniel Alexander Elementary School, a viewer is four times as likely to find an inoperative homepage as an up-to-date one. Running through half the alphabet of faculty names at Vance High School, one finds the ratio more like seven to one.

Nearly every teacher has the homepage template up, with places to enter homework, resources, featured student work, and scholar of the week. But most of these sections are blank. Somewhere between four hundred and five hundred teachers are listed on the Learning Village site. Taking an alphabet letter at random, we find that of twenty-three teachers whose last names begin with that letter, just one teacher's homepage is working. One principal's page that works after a fashion was last updated in July 2001. It had 144 hits between February 2001 and August 2003.

IBM's Reinventing Education (A), available for purchase on the Harvard Business School website, notes: "Professor Rosabeth Moss Kanter prepared this case. HBS cases are developed solely as the basis for class discussion. Cases are not intended to serve as endorsements, sources of primary data, or illustrations of effective or ineffective management."[21] Of six references in Kanter's Harvard Business School case, four are to her own work, one to the Center for Children and Technology/EDC, and one to Gerstner's book (written with Roger D. Semard, Denis Philip Doyle, and William B. Johnston) *Reinventing Education: Entrepreneurship in America's Public Schools*. A point of information: Professor Kanter was a judge for the Ron Brown Award for Corporate Leadership, which went to IBM in spring 2000. Second point of information: Kanter is a senior adviser to IBM's Reinventing Education.

"IBM and Education: A Perfect Match," an interview with Kanter, is available on the IBM website,[22] with links to the Center for Children and Technology. Responding to the unnamed interviewer, Kanter calls IBM a role model and pioneer for "sustained, sweeping long-term" change in schools. She says that each of the Reinventing Education programs operates "the way companies need to operate in the global information age—that is, you need to have local experiments that turn into products or services that can be used anywhere in the world interchangeably." She asserts that Reinventing Education is aimed at this transformation, "a kind of transformation that will bring schools into the same modern internet-enabled digital world that businesses have been getting into." Here's more:

> IBM is awfully smart because IBM isn't saying that the technology will substitute for teachers. What IBM is saying is that we can use the internet to empower teachers, to help them teach more effectively, to develop new curriculums faster, to get access to the World Wide Web with all of its resources, to communicate with parents so we can solve children's problems.

Speeded-up curriculum sounds rather like fast food: mass-produced, cheap, and bad for you. What schools need is slowed-down curriculum: slower, deeper, more diverse, and more thoughtful. Surely it comes as no surprise that researchers committed to high tech sing the praises of the potential of IBM's project. What's missing is skeptical inquiry. Why aren't teachers using their homepages? Is a curriculum based on state standards well served by being tied to computers? Or is the very premise flawed? Fittingly, the *American Heritage Dictionary* illustrative sentence for *hubris* draws on an observation by McGeorge Bundy: "There is no safety in unlimited technological hubris."

A second case study, *IBM's Reinventing Education (B): West Virginia*, was prepared by research associate Daniel Galvin under the supervision of Professor Kanter.[23] Galvin observes that in June 2001, about 150 U.S. national leaders gathered "for a press conference sponsored by the prestigious Hudson Institute,[24] where Stanley Litow, vice president of IBM Corporate Community Relations and president of the IBM International Foundation, affirmed IBM's commitment to a third phase of its Reinventing Education Initiative." But, writes Galvin, "the most exciting revelation on June 12, came from the Center for Children and Technology, a nonprofit research and evaluation organization, which announced the results of a comprehensive evaluation of IBM's Reinventing Education partnerships with K–12 public school systems. Their findings demonstrated that public education could change quickly and that technology could be a major catalyst for raising student achievement. . . ."

Another IBM project, West Virginia Learning Village, features juried lesson plans written by teachers. Posted on the Internet as *Best Practices*, the plans often list four or five coauthors. Although the human dynamics involved in this kind of collaboration are more revolutionary than learning to use high-tech templates, for researchers, the technical whizbang is the thing. As always, the Standardista premise is accepted as a given: nobody looks at whether the premise of tying class curriculum to state standards is itself flawed.

Of the Best Practices lessons posted in the West Virginia Learning Village, 128 are dated 1999, 10 were produced in 2000, with similar small numbers thereafter. Surely, these numbers raise questions about whether the juried lesson is a model that can be replicated and sustained. We need to ask some basic and serious questions not addressed in the reports. Who came up with the templates that drive the lessons? How do these templates both help and hinder lessons? *Can* all lessons be rigged to fit into the same Standardista template? People in IBM's Learning Village sure try.

As we saw in Chapter 3, a serious problem with lesson plans that are data-driven, standards-based, and tied to the Internet is that you can lose the center, lose sight of why you're doing what your doing. The Internet is part of the problem, screaming as it does, *More More More!* In a juried lesson from West Virginia Learning Village titled *Auschwitz: A Literary Approach*, the Internet offers the lure of visiting Anne Frank's home in Amsterdam and the Auschwitz concentration camp; it invites students to listen to the stories of survivors.[25] All this will enhance some students' experience of reading Anne's diary. But some books demand silence. For some readers, all the interruptions might well be a distraction from responding to Anne's words in a deeply personal way. But the template for Learning Village lessons demands that a certain format be observed, and so we get lots of Internet visits, lots of activities, and lots of assessments. The culminating rubric judges students on how well they worked in groups.

Looming over every lesson is the list of state standards. Surely the teacher and the students know that they aren't reading Anne Frank's diary to learn how to use the computer or to trace the surprise ending in a story. But the template demands the listing of all these standards. Apparently, the more, the better. Never mind that the list is jarring and even offensive to the work under consideration. *The Diary of Anne Frank* becomes the delivery system for a workplace skill. We don't know if school districts in West Virginia require the teacher to write on the board each day the standards being addressed.

10.12 (WV-English Language Arts: Grade Ten English Language Arts: Listening/Speaking): read literary works by national and international authors to include but not limited to novels, drama, short story, and poetry for cultural literacy appreciation and application.

10.13 (WV-English Language Arts: Grade Ten English Language Arts: Reading Comprehension): identify and research the influences of historical, cultural, and biographical (author) factors in shaping styles and voice of literary works (e.g., group research via Internet or CD-ROM guest speakers).

10.23 (WV-English Language Arts: Grade Ten English Language Arts: Reading Comprehension): make generalizations from implicit ideas (e.g., trace the implicit ideas that lead to a surprise ending in a short story such as those of O'Henry or Saki).

10.24 (WV-English Language Arts: Grade Ten English Arts Reading Comprehension): read directions necessary to sequentially perform a task then perform the task.

10.82 (WV-English Language Arts: Grade Ten English Language Arts: Computer/Technology): use a variety of audiovisual and multimedia materials to practice and master tenth grade English language arts instructional objectives.

10.82 (WV-English Language Arts: Grade Ten English Language Arts: Study Skills): use outlining to organize text and information by selecting main points and supporting details (e.g., take notes from a text and organize them in outline form; prewrite an essay).

10.86 (WV-English Language Arts: Grade Ten English Language Arts: Study Skills): use appropriate study/review techniques for given materials (e.g., paraphrase paragraphs, mnemonics).

10.86 (WV-English Language Arts: Grade Ten English Language Arts: Computer/Technology): select and use appropriate technologies to locate and use reference sources.

And there's more!

This lesson addresses all of the National Standards for the English Language Arts as delineated by the National Council of Teachers of English and the International Reading Association. A link is provided.

And still more!

Process/Workplace Objectives

PW.9: use correct grammar when speaking and writing

PW.16: understand what it takes to develop an effective team, including team rules, behavior norms, team roles, communications, and decision-making practices

PW.27: demonstrate the ability to operate computer equipment

Understand that the criticism here is of the template. At the same time the lesson template trivializes the profound, it exaggerates the trivial. The *Synonyms and Antonyms* plan is thirty-three pages long—and that's just the bare-bones description—without all the assignments and assessments.[26] Remember, one of the rules of the juried lesson template is that for every activity, there must be an assessment. So one lesson asks, "How would I assess my students after a Hink Pink activity?" Assess? How about watching them laugh? Or frown in puzzlement? Surely there's a tenth ring in hell for people who create tests on hink pinks.

The real problem is that when Standardistas rule, you get this assignment-assessment, assignment-assessment template, and teachers are encouraged, cajoled, and forced to do only those activities that can be assessed. Eighth graders do all this work with synonyms and antonyms to meet West Virginia English Language Arts Standard 8.50: "use writing strategies to write for audiences including peers, teachers, and employers." Again, everything comes back to the Business Roundtable agenda. Remember Marc Tucker's infamous eighteen-page "Dear Hillary" letter, which laid out a plan of systemic reform for the American school system to serve the economy?[27] In the letter Tucker intones, "All students are guaranteed that they will have a fair shot at reaching the standards: that is, that whether they make it or not depends on the effort they are willing to make, and nothing else."

No exceptions.

Train Them Early

In a move to inculcate future teachers into the standards-curriculum axis early on, IBM is infiltrating teacher ed colleges. In June 2002, Riverdeep Interactive Learning and IBM announced a partnership where IBM's Learning Village educational software became a part of the Riverdeep family of products. In the words of a Riverdeep press release, "Riverdeep Learning Village will play a key role in helping school districts leverage technology to meet the national education reform guidelines brought forth by the No Child Left Behind Act of 2001."[28] Two months later, IBM announced its plan to join with schools of education in nine states to develop new teacher training and professional development through its Web-based instructional platform called Riverdeep Learning Village.[29]

Such schemes are buttressed by a press filled with virulent bashing of colleges of education. Funny thing: the press chose not to notice when Reid Lyon, chief of the Child Development and Behavior Branch of the National Institute of Child Health and Human Development, part of the National Institutes of Health, speaking at a "major policy forum" held by the Council for Excellence in Government, titled "Evidence-Based Education Forum with Secretary Paige," expressed his desire to blow up colleges of education: "If there was any piece of legislation that I could pass it would be to blow up colleges of education."[30]

After these remarks, Lyon continued talking and participated in the question-and-answer session. No one indicated in any way that anything unusual or outrageous had been said. No one asked him to explain his rhetoric of terrorism; no one denounced this rhetoric of terrorism. Lyon was safe in saying it because with this group, it's business as usual.

What About the Children?

With the push for systemic reform, a raising of the bar, and a push for world-class students, North Carolina ends up with what it calls the Information Skills Curriculum. Here are the standards for kindergarten.

1.04 Acknowledge ownership of ideas;

1.07 Follow acceptable use policy (AUP/IUP) for electronic resources;

2.01 Identify published criteria of excellence for resources;

2.05 Recognize the power of media to influence;

3.03 Identify bias and stereotypes;

3.05 Describe how information and ideas are influenced by prior knowledge;

4.02 Describe several research models;

4.03 Develop a search strategy which includes the continuous evaluation of the research process and the information gathered;

4.06 Comply with the Copyright Law;

4.07 Credit sources of information.[31]

Read this and either you guffaw or you upchuck. Instead of worrying about copyright laws and research models, kindergartners, of course, should be building with blocks, exploring at sand tables, playing dress up, finger painting, dancing, singing, and learning that school is a joyous, cooperative place for learning new things with friends. But these days, those kindergartners are being interrogated about their "DIBELS," racing the clock while worrying over the initial sound in *insect*.

People who care about public education would do well to read the final report by the Columbia Accident Investigation Board. This report raises fundamental questions about the National Aeronautics and Space Administration's (NASA) increasing dependence on private contractors. In a *Wall Street Journal* summary of the report, we learn that the board expressed concern that "while NASA streamlined the space program during a push toward privatization that began in the mid-1990s, it abdicated much of its responsibilities for overseeing the safety of manned space flight," that mounting pressure to complete the already-overdue International Space Station "contributed to a shift in emphasis to schedules rather than safety."[32] The parallels with public schools are obvious. As the pressure increases to prepare workers for the global economy, teachers feel forced to shift the emphasis to artificial standards and schedules rather than to create a curriculum that meets the needs of children.

In *Earthly Pleasures*, science writer and maple-syrup maker Roger Swain tells us that even where the sap flows best, "the drops form one at a time."[33] Even in our present circumstance of instant everything, you can't hurry maple syrup—or third graders. Neither is a project for the impatient. Chris' change from intransigent, reluctant reader, the child who only scowled at books, to the boy who insisted on copying the entire text of *Peter Rabbit* in longhand because he liked the *feel of the words* didn't happen overnight, nor did it happen from accumulating 14,682 DIBELS. We must recognize that children make great intuitive leaps, but in between times, things often seem impressively slow.

Chris' classmate Charles gets the last word. At age eleven, Charles was mainstreamed from special ed. Conferences with his mother, social worker, and psychologist revealed a history of abuse, upheaval, and retarded development. Charles' third-grade journey was difficult, heartbreaking, joyous, and altogether remarkable. Charles ended third grade still facing very real limitations—not on track to becoming 100 percent proficient on New York

State's standards. But Standardista proficiency does *not* get the last word on Charles' scholastic journey or on his school's competence. Charles gets the last word, not because we're looking for what Education Trust derides as excuses but because third graders can teach us if we learn how to listen. Charles ended the year by writing a nine-page testimony on a book of his choice, a book he'd kept hidden behind other books in the classroom bookcase so it would be ever available when he needed it. Charles wrote about *The Ugly Duckling*. This is his first sentence: "The ugly duckling found out it is okay to be different."

Notes

1. Hardy, Lawrence. 2003. "Overburdened/Overwhelmed." *American School Board Journal* 190 (4). Accessed at *www.asbj.com/2003/040403coverstory.html*.

2. From *www.ncforum.org/programs/ebc*.

3. Johnson, Alvin, et al. 1999. "A Case Study of the Charlotte-Mecklenburg Public Schools School-Based Performance Award Program." *Consortium for Policy Research in Education*, April.

4. Kronley, Robert. 2000. *Southern Synergy: The Columbia Group, Business and Education Reform*. BellSouth Foundation, 7. Accessed at *www.bellsouthfoundation.org/pdfs/synergy/pdf*.

5. Public School Forum, 2000. Accessed at *www.ncforum.org/forumpub.htm*. 3–4.

6. Glenn, Teresa. 2003. "The Monster in Our Schools." In *Silent No More: Voices of Courage in American Schools*, ed. ReLeah Cossett Lent and Gloria Pipkin. Portsmouth, NH: Heinemann.

7. Ibid., 29.

8. Jennings, Derek M. 2003. "Test Stress." *Independent Online*, 28 May. Accessed at *http://indyweek.com/durham/2003-05-28/jennings.html*.

9. From *www.pen.k12.va.us/VDOE/Assessment/release2000/grade5.pdf*.

10. Decker, Greg. 2003. "Using Data to Drive Student Achievement in the Classroom and on High-Stakes Tests." *T.H.E. Journal Online*, January. Accessed at *www.thejournal.com/magazine/vault/articleprintversion.cfm?aid=4310*.

11. See *www.pearsondigital.com/successmaker*.

12. Roslyn Mickelson uses this descriptive phrase in the title of her 1999 article "International Business Machinations: A Case Study of Corporate Involvement in Local Educational Reform" (*Teachers College Record* 100 [3] 476–512).

13. Ibid.

14. From *www.ibm.com/ibm/ibmgives/*.

15. Mickelson. 1999, 488.

16. Seddon "Rusty" Goode Jr. 1996. "Don't Botch the Education Village." *Charlotte Observer*, 29 February.

17. Mickelson. 2000, 144.

18. Spielvogel, Bob. 2001. *IBM Reinventing Education: Research Summary and Perspective*. New York: The Center for Children and Technology/EDC June. Accessed at *www2.edc.org/cct/admin/publications/report/ibmsum.pdf*. IBM is listed as a funder and a partner on the EDC website.

19. For the premier example of this, take a look at Elaine Garan's work on the contradictions between the National Reading Panel report and the summary document. See Garan, Elaine M. 2002. *Resisting Reading Mandates: How to Triumph with the Truth.* Portsmouth, NH: Heinemann.

20. Spielvogel, Bob, et al. 2001. *IBM's Reinventing Education Grant Partnership Initiative: Individual Site Reports.* Center for Children & Technology/EDC. March. Accessed at *www2.edc.org/cct/admin/publications/report/ibmsite.pdf.*

21. Kanter, Rosabeth Moss. 1998. *IBM's Reinventing Education (A).* Cambridge: Harvard Business School Publishing. Revised 10 September 2001.

22. "IBM and Education: A Perfect Match." n.d. Accessed at *www.ibm.com/ibm/ibmgives/grant/education/programs/reinventing/kanter.shtml.*

23. Galvin, Daniel. 2002. *IBM's Reinventing Education (B).* Cambridge: Harvard Business School Publishing. 9 January.

24. When seven education scholars of national reputation were asked to supply an adjective for Hudson Institute, four said "right-wing," two said "fascist," and one said "elitist/repressive/arrogant." Even FrontPagemagazine.com, whose columnists include Ann Coulter and David Horowitz, characterize Hudson as "conservative."

25. See *http://reinvent.k12.wv.us/lt/ltipbp.nsf?OpenDatabase.*

26. See *http://reinvent.k12.wv.us/lt/ltipbp.nsf?OpenDatabase.*

27. See *www.mredcopac.org/tucker.htm.*

28. From *www.riverdeep.net/about_us/press_releases.jhtml?SECTION=AboutUs&HEADING=Press%20Releases.*

29. Participating sites have school districts and universities at each site: Baltimore; the Carolinas; Chicago; Clark County, Nevada; Memphis; Philadelphia; San Jose; Vermont; West Virginia.

30. From *www.excelgov.org/displayContent.asp?Keyword=prppcEvidence.* For a description of the meeting and information about those in attendance, see *http://susanohanian.org/show_research.html?id=3.* On December 27, 2002, the Vermont Society for the Study of Education (VSSE) sent the following open letter to Secretary Rod Paige. Copies were sent to major media and professional organizations as well as congressional representatives. There was no response from Paige or the media.

Dear Secretary Paige:
    Speaking at a major policy forum held by the Council for Excellence in Government, titled "Evidence-Based Education Forum with Secretary Paige," Reid Lyon, Chief, Child Development and Behavior Branch, National Institute of Child Health and Human Development, made the following statement: *If there was any piece of legislation that I could pass it would be to blow up colleges of education.*
    We find Reid Lyon's statement to be terribly chilling, entirely unacceptable and clearly irresponsible. We call for his immediate dismissal.
    Vermont Society for the Study of Education

31. From *www.ncpublicschools.org/curriculum/Information/gradek.htm.*

32. Lunsford, J. Lynn, and Anne Marie Squeo. 2003. "Shuttle Probe Faults NASA for Relying on Contractors." *The Wall Street Journal,* 27 August. Accessed at *http://online.wsj.com/article/0,,SB106190731284649600,00.html?mod=home_whats_news_us.*

33. Swain, Roger. 1981. *Earthly Pleasure: Tales from a Biologist's Garden.* New York: Scribner.

Conclusion

So What Do We Do Now?

They were careless people—they smashed up things and creatures and then retreated into their money or their vast carelessness or whatever it was that kept them together, and let other people clean up the mess they had made.

—F. Scott Fitzgerald, *The Great Gatsby*

In late June 2003, residents of Cayce, South Carolina, expressed concern over the resettling of 120 Somali Bantu refugees in their city of 12,000. The Lutheran Family Services Refugee Resettlement program has plans for English classes and cultural training; it expects the Bantu to be self-sufficient within six months. Local faith groups have pledged support until they are self-sufficient. So why are Cayce residents so worried? They are worried that under the federal No Child Left Behind Act, Bantu children are required to take the state test, the Palmetto Achievement Challenge Test (PACT); their specific concern is that the Bantu children will lower school averages.

On the one hand, one might chide the residents of Cayce and tell them to look at South Carolina's ranking on the Economic and Social Well-Being Index, which rates states according to income and employment, health and social conditions, business activity, human capital, and physical environmental conditions. South Carolina ranks 49 out of 51 (including the District of Columbia). Breaking out one item on this ranking, human capital, which includes ACT and SAT scores, percentage of high school graduates, percentage of college graduates, and percentage of educational expenditure change from 1970 to 1996, South Carolina still ranks 49. Cayce, though, is in one of the highest-ranking counties in South Carolina, so maybe the residents are worried about hanging on to what they have. No Child Left Behind is designed to scare people: Schools whose test-score numbers don't keep going up lose money. So immigrants, instead of being welcomed and helped, are perceived as a threat to those test scores and therefore to the schools.

Nationally normed and criterion-referenced tests have been a central part of the educational sorting system for almost a hundred years. They have always been used as gatekeepers, providing legitimacy for the middle class as parents bequeath their social and economic status to their children. The psychometricians who make the tests as well as those who make important decisions about children based on these tests claim that they are objective measures of ability and achievement. But they are nothing of the kind.[1] And as high stakes have been increasingly attached to standardized tests, the psychometricians have become increasingly uneasy about how their tests are being used. The Business Roundtable and state legislators show no such squeamishness as they steamroll ahead using standardized tests to drive a top-down fundamental restructuring of the nation's public school system—they promise to "stay the course" and "turn up the heat." And plenty of policy makers and administrators have readily agreed to go along with their plan. Good teachers are retiring, new teachers are following the increasingly scripted curricula, struggling students are being pushed out, good students are becoming nervous wrecks, and parents are either confused, angry, or resigned. But mostly, people are scared, and frightened people are not prone to ask their leaders hard questions. Nor support those who do.

When three San Francisco school board members asked for evidence of the effect of the superintendent's policies on students, teachers, and the course of instruction, their request was ignored and instead they were characterized as racist—they were "attacking the superintendent because she is black." When the *New York Times* reported that the Texas Miracle looked like a mirage,[2] Kati Haycock, director of the Education Trust, wrote in response that such criticism is part of a "sad history of treating successes among low-income and minority students with deep suspicion," implying that such suspicion is inherently racist by asking, "Why do we seem unable to accept the fact that these kids actually can learn?"[3] In San Francisco, in Houston, and across the nation, those who question the validity of using a single test score to make decisions about a teacher's abilities, a student's future, the effectiveness of curriculum, and the selection of instructional methods are silenced by the accusation that they must be racist because they don't want high standards for low-performing students.

To many teachers, the purposes of high-stakes testing are not about "high standards for all" or "excellence and equity." Neil Liss writes in response to the *New York Times* exposé of the Houston mirage:

> As a former teacher in the Houston Independent School District, I know that the focus on test scores, at the exclusion of all else in the classroom tells only part of the travesty that has altered schooling. Students are deprived of

pportunity to think critically and openly. Teachers are locked into cur-
ums that deny the freedom to create provocative learning environments. Administrators are shackled to a system that reduces them to
sycophants toward their leadership. The community is silenced from a progressive dialogue about real quality in education.[4]

A caveat: Before high-stakes testing existed, not all students had the opportunity to "think critically and openly" and not all teachers were allowed
the "freedom to create provocative learning environments." But there were
pockets of freedom and creativity. High-stakes testing is having the effect of
eliminating whatever there has been of learning for the joy of it, learning to
develop higher-order thinking skills, or learning something because it is what
one is interested in.

Cynical (and terribly ironic) accusations of racism by supporters of standardista administrators and institutions like Education Trust have been
effective in dividing and quelling proponents of progressive education and
opponents to high-stakes testing. Schools labeled as "low-performing" have
their arts and physical education programs cut and replaced with hours of reading and math drills. Schools labeled as "high-performing" are besieged by
parents fighting to get their children into those schools, turning districts into
battlegrounds of parent fury and futility. Principals who give space to education goals other than higher test scores find themselves looking for another
job. The only role that teachers and parents can play in the new system is to
take responsibility for spending woefully insufficient funds, select curricula that
will improve test scores, and coach the students on the new curricula. At the
same time, business leaders and district superintendents can pat themselves
on the back because they have forced the famously hidebound educational
bureaucracy to adopt fundamental reform that lets them assess a school's
quality at a glance (just one number!), insisting that improved test scores can
be had for less money than was spent on more complicated forms of assessment
and instruction. How convenient. And horrible.

Orwellian doublespeak will continue to silence progressive dialogue over
the goals of education unless currently divided groups start talking to each other
in very specific ways. The "sad history" that Haycock attempts to appropriate
needs to be reexamined and retold, and an authentic debate over what consti-
tutes "real quality in education" must be revived outside the context of high-
stakes testing and its concomitant accountability rhetoric. This is not an easy
task and requires that teachers, parents, nonprofits, and businesspeople look
at their own assumptions about what they believe is equity and quality, look
closely at what is happening in schools because of high-stakes testing, recognize
the legitimacy of multiple goals of education, and then be prepared to make
compromises. Teachers will have to open their doors to parents; parents will

have to spend time in schools; business and middle-class property owners will have to pay more in taxes; nonprofits will have to change their funding strategies from putting out fires to long-term sustainable support of community-based reform efforts, efforts defined by the community, not by corporate foundations. Everyone, including business leaders, must be at the table to debate what the goals of education should be and how best to achieve them. Consensus around the table is a must.

Fundamental and long-term divisions between parents and teachers must be overcome before such a consensus can be achieved. The *high standards for all* rhetoric is effective at obviating consensus since it speaks to these differences. Charles Payne, speaking to a group of urban parent advocates at a national conference, elicited laughter and applause from his audience with the following observations:

> [This is how schools view parents:] If parents don't come into the school, they don't care. If parents do come into the school, they are meddling.
>
> How have schools reacted to accountability issues? They have better test scores. . . . They do more teaching, which is not the same as better teaching . . . and more students are being taught. [This is progress because] mediocrity is better than no teaching.
>
> There is more and more cheating [around accountability requirements] because teachers start with the assumption that kids can't learn.[5]

Parents nodded knowingly, and much cathartic teacher bashing ensued. Parental mistrust and teacher frustration must be addressed. Parents and teachers need to talk; they need to ask the really basic questions of themselves and share them with others before an alliance can be built between teacher unions and parent advocacy groups:[6]

1. What are the biggest concerns you have about your school?
2. What do you like about your school?
3. What kinds of relationships do you want to see among staff, students, and parents?
4. What kind of relationship should there be between the central district administration and each school?
5. What should be the goals or mission of your school?

The answers to these questions are the building blocks of an alternative vision of reform to high-stakes testing. Inherent to this process of reform are two assumptions: (1) each school needs to have both the support of and autonomy from the central district administration in order to implement its vision and (2) experts must be subordinate to the policy-making process by the community. This contrasts sharply with two of the central assumptions of the high-stakes testing agenda: (1) corporate business interests are identical to the interests of the community and (2) a centralized authority made up of middle-class "experts" should administer educational programs with teachers and parents as subordinates, not partners in the process. It is important when discussions occur about the evils of high-stakes testing that people be honest about their assumptions and examine them openly so that they are clear as to what they want to replace high-stakes testing with.

While school boards still exist, they need to be lobbied and supported to pursue alternative and authentic assessments; conduct educational equity impact studies of their district administration's policies; implement school safety policies that rely primarily on supportive services, not punitive police tactics; and introduce measures that encourage more participation by the community in setting educational goals and policies, such as more frequent board meetings and transparency in the decision-making process. Without a swelling of grassroots community support for reform around real equity and real excellence, current opposition to high-stakes testing will not be able to gain much more traction than it already has. The number of push-outs and dropouts will increase. And middle-class suburbs will be transformed into increasingly insular communities defending their high test scores and the privileges that attend to them.

Washington State parent activist Juanita Doyon offers a message of resistance and hope:

> In March 2003, I traveled to Birmingham, Alabama, to help honor the World of Opportunity, a learning community that stands up to test-driven oppression in that city's public schools. While there, thirty education activists from around the country formed a new organization, ACT NOW—Advocates for Children and Teachers National Organizing Workshop. One of our activities at this first annual gathering was to visit the Birmingham Civil Rights Institute. Among the examples of successful activism and life-changing struggle was a small piece of encouragement to our fight here in Washington. On a table, there was a stack of paper, an announcement of a bus boycott. How simple and effective!

Don't ride the bus. Don't drink the tea. Don't give the test. Yes, the world is changed by individuals who have the ability to say "No!" They say they're mad as hell and aren't going to take this any more. Maybe these folks still read and teach Henry David Thoreau's *Civil Disobedience*.

> They hesitate and they regret, and sometimes they petition; but they do nothing in earnest and with effect. They will wait, well disposed, for others to remedy the evil, that they may no longer have to regret. At most, they give only a cheap vote, and a feeble countenance and God-speed, to the right, as it goes

by them. There are nine hundred and ninety-nine patrons of virtue to one virtuous man.

Notes

1. See Thorndike, R. M., and D. F. Lohman, 1990, *A Century of Ability Testing*, Chicago: Riverside; and James Popham, 2001, *The Truth About Testing: An Educator's Call to Action*. Alexandria, VA: Association for Supervision and Curricular Development, Chapters 3 and 4.

2. Front-page story. 2003. *New York Times*, 3 December.

3. Haycock, Kati. 2003. Letters. *New York Times*, 6 December.

4. Liss, Neil. 2003. Letters. *New York Times*, 6 December.

5. Payne, Charles. 2003. School Based Organizing: Analyzing Schools as Places to Change and Places Out of Which to Organize. Talk presented at the Organizing for Educational Excellence Institute, Temple University Sugarloaf Conference Center. Philadelphia, August.

6. The Oakland Community Organizations (OCO) in Oakland, California, has been particularly effective in building an alliance with the Oakland teachers union. Their story is an excellent model of grassroots reform in the face of high-stakes testing.

A
Six Degrees of Separation Cut in Half

The Business Roundtable Education and the Workforce Task Force Links

Achieve

Achieve links to these education organization sites for "their high-quality content": American Association for the Advancement of Science; American Association for Colleges for Teacher Education; American Association of School Administrators; American Educational Research Association; American Federation of Teachers; American Mathematical Association of Two-Year Colleges; American Mathematical Society; Annenburg Challenge; Annenberg Institute for School Reform; Association for Educational Communications and Technology; Association for Supervision and Development; Business Coalition for Education Reform; the Business Roundtable; Center for Children and Technology; the Center for Education Reform; Center for Research on Education, Diversity, and Excellence; Center for Research on Students Placed at Risk; Center for the Study of Teaching and Policy; Center for Workforce Preparation; Consortium for Policy Research in Education; Core Knowledge Foundation; Council for Basic Education; Council of Chief State School Officers; Council of the Great City Schools; Education Commission of the States; Education Excellence Partnership; Education Leaders Council; the Education Trust; Eisenhower National Clearinghouse for Mathematics and Science Education; GOALLINE; Guide to Math and Science Reform—Annenberg/Corp. for Public Broadcasting Project; the Heritage Foundation; Hoover Institution, Stanford University; Hudson Institute; Institute for Educational Leadership, Inc.; International Reading Association; International Society for Technology in Education; International Technology Education Association; Learning First Alliance; Learning Research and Development Center at the University of Pittsburgh; Looking at

Student Work; the Manhattan Institute; Mathematical Association of America; the Milken Family Foundation; Modern Red Schoolhouse; National Academy of Science; National Alliance of Business; National Assessment of Educational Progress; National Assessment Governing Board; National Association of Elementary School Principals; National Association of Secondary School Principals; National Association of State Boards of Education; National Board for Professional Teaching Standards; National Center on Education and the Economy; National Center for Education Statistics; National Center for History in the Schools; National Center for Research on Evaluation, Standards, and Student Testing; National Council for Accreditation of Teacher Education; National Council on Economic Education; National Council for History Education; National Council for the Social Studies; National Council of Teachers of English; National Council of Teachers of Mathematics; National Education Association; National Education Goals Panel; National Governors Association; National Parent Teacher Association; National Partnership for Excellence and Accountability in Teaching; National Research Council; National School Boards Association; National Science Education Standards; National Science Foundation; National Science Teachers Association; New American Schools; New Standards; Performance Assessment Links in Science; Public Education Network; RAND; Regional Labs Home Page; Standards for Success, University of Oregon; Third International Mathematics and Science Study (TIMSS); and U.S. Department of Education, Office of Educational Research and Improvement, National Educational Research Policy and Priorities Board.

Another link on the Achieve site is the American Diploma Project. Sponsored by Achieve, Inc., the Education Trust, the Thomas B. Fordham Foundation, and the National Alliance of Business, the American Diploma Project's partner states include Indiana, Kentucky, Massachusetts, Nevada, and Texas.

Achieve acknowledges the following contributors: Agilent Technologies Foundation; the Annenberg Foundation; the Atlantic Philanthropies; AT&T Foundation; BellSouth Foundation; Bill and Melinda Gates Foundation; the Boeing Co.; Bristol-Myers Squibb Foundation, Inc.; Citicorp Foundation; Eastman Kodak Co.; E. I. DuPont de Nemours and Co.; IBM Corp.; the Pew Charitable Trusts; Phillips Petroleum Co.; the Procter & Gamble Fund; the Prudential Foundation; State Farm Insurance Cos.; State Street Foundation; the UPS Foundation; the Washington Mutual Foundation; the William and Flora Hewlett Foundation; Williams; and the Xerox Foundation.

Ad Council

The "Keep the Promise" advertising campaign is a product of the Advertising Council and sponsored by the Education Excellence Partnership. The partnership's members include

The Business Roundtable
U.S. Department of Education
American Federation of Teachers
National Alliance of Business
National Education Association
National Governors Association
U.S. Chamber of Commerce

Business Coalition for Education Reform (BCER)

Members

American Business Conference
Business-Higher Education Forum
The Business Roundtable
The Chamber of Commerce of the United States
Committee for Economic Development
The Conference Board
Council of Growing Companies
Council on Competitiveness
National Alliance of Business
National Association of Manufacturers
National Association of Women Business Owners
U.S. Hispanic Chamber of Commerce
Utility/Business Education Coalition

Affiliate Members

Achieve
National Association of Partners in Education, Inc.

A state or local organization can become a member at no charge if it

1. has strong business leadership in its activities and/or board of directors and

2. has committed to one or more of the following objectives:
   - raising academic standards for all students
   - ensuring that academic standards reflect the skills needed for personal development and career success in a changing economy
   - publicizing the critical need for world-class academic standards and the changes school systems must make to achieve them

Education Excellence Partnership (EEP)

Members

Achieve
American Federation of Teachers
The Business Roundtable
National Alliance for Business
National Education Association
National Governors Association
U.S. Department of Education

State Roundtables and Business Education Coalitions

You can find all these state links on the Business Roundtable site. Here are a few highlights—just to illustrate how influence, while traveling, always finds its way home.

Georgia

Georgia Partnership for Excellence in Education lists the following education links: Achieve; American Association of School Administrators; Columbia Group; Council of Chief State School Officers; Education Commission of the States; Georgia Association of Educational Leaders; Georgia Association of Educators; Georgia Industrial Technology Education Association; Georgia Learning Connections; Georgia School Boards Association; Georgia School Council Institute; Georgia School Public Relations Association; Georgia School Superintendents Association; Professional Association of Georgia Educators; Project-GRAD; Southeast Center for Teacher Quality; Southern Regional Education Board; Teach for America; the Georgia Closing the Achievement Gap Commission; Georgia Department of Education; HOPE Scholarship; Office of School Readiness; Professional Standards Commission; National Center for Educational Statistics; National Education Association; No Child Left Behind; the Library of Congress; U.S. Department of Education; Business Roundtable; Georgia Chamber of Commerce; National Alliance of Business; *Atlanta Journal-Constitution*; *Education Week*; and *Education World*.

Illinois

Illinois Business Roundtable links with Baldridge. Baldrige links with National Alliance of Business and the American Productivity and Quality Center. APQC was chosen as the original Texas Award for Performance Excellence award administrator, sought after by government, education, nonprofit, and business organizations.

Maryland

Maryland Business Roundtable for Education links to Achieve; Business Roundtable; GetSmarter.org; Legg Mason, Inc.; National PTA; Partnership for Kentucky Schools; Public Agenda; Reading by 9; U.S. Chamber of Commerce; U.S. Department of Education; and Washington Roundtable.

Oregon

Oregon Business Council links to No Child Left Behind; Reality Check 202: Public Agenda's annual nationwide poll; *Education Week*; and Northwest Regional Educational Laboratory. It lists the following organizations as advocating for high standards: Achieve; Business Roundtable; Education Excellence Partnership; Education Trust

Texas

Texas Business & Education Coalition. Anyone who thinks that big money doesn't rule Texas in education should just take a look at the corporate and educational partners for 2002:

$50,000 and above: ExxonMobil Foundation; Houston Annenberg Challenge; ING Financial Services; Verizon

$25,000–$49,999: Citigroup; Dell Computer Corp.; JC Penney; IBM; Shell Oil Company Foundation; Southwestern Bell; Washington Mutual.

$10,000–$24,999: AT&T; H-E-B; Palmetto Partners; State Farm Insurance; TXU

$5,000–$9,999: Akin, Gump, Strauss, Hauer & Feld; Alliance Data Systems; American Electric Power; Apple Computer; Bank of America; CenterPoint Energy; Dow Chemical Co.; Duke Energy; the Anne and C. W. Duncan Jr. Foundation; El Paso Corp.; Flint Hills Resources; Kroger Co.; Lockheed Martin; Medical City Dallas; Motorola; RGK Foundation; Texas Instruments; Waste Management

$250–$4,999: ACT; AIG/VALIC; Akin; AMD; Association of Texas Professional Educators; Austin Industries; Bank One; the Beck Group; Broadway National Bank; Chevron Texaco; Comerica Bank–Texas; Compass Bank; Conceptual Mindworks; Cooper Industries; Dodge

Jones Foundation; Eastman Chemical; *El Paso Times*; Fiesta Mart; Fluor, Graeber, Simmons & Cowan; Greater Austin Chamber of Commerce; Greater Dallas Chamber; Greater Houston Partnership; Holt Cos.; *Houston Chronicle*; Intel Corp.; JP Morgan Chase; Linebarger, Goggan, Blair, Pena & Sampson; Moak, Casey & Associates; Omni-American Credit Union; Padgett Stratemann & Co.; Pier 1 Imports; ProjectGRAD; Quicksilver Resources; Randall's Food Markets; Region IV Education Service Center; Scientific Learning Corp.; Seton Healthcare Network; the William A. and Madeline Welder Smith Foundation; Solectron Texas; Southwest Airlines; TD Industries; Texas Association of School Boards; Texas Association of School Business Officials; Texas Association of Secondary School Principals; Texas Classroom Teachers Association; Texas Federation of Teachers; Texas Computer Education Association; Texas Elementary Principals & Supervisors Association; Texas PTA; University of North Texas; University of Texas at Arlington; University of Texas–Pan American; *USA Today*; USAA Foundation; Walsh, Anderson, Brown, Schulze & Aldridge; XTO Energy

The recommended experts list makes for interesting reading; see *<www.tbec.org/experts.shtml>*.

Washington

The Washington Roundtable links to Washington Research, which has a section titled "Policy Research" that links to Governmental Research Association; Discovery Institute; Citizens for Tax Justice; the Cato Institute; the Council of State Governments; the Independent Institute; National Center for Policy Analysis; Northwest Power Planning Council; the Fiscal Policy Center; National Taxpayers Conference; Evergreen Freedom Foundation; Washington Institute for Policy Studies; Washington Policy Center; and Washington Roundtable.

B

Evidence of Coordination by the National Business Roundtable

In 1990, the Business Roundtable launched a "50-state initiative" in order to persuade each state to adopt the BRT's Nine Essential Components. By 2000, the BRT believed it had made significant progress.

> Policymakers now agree on the need for high standards of academic achievement for all students, meaningful assessment tools to measure progress in meeting those standards and accountability for results applicable to all students, teachers and schools. . . . Now that these policies are beginning to be implemented at the local school and district level, continued leadership and involvement of BRT companies is even more important. There still is a long way to go before we see U.S. education performance that meets or exceeds the best in the world. (*www.businessroundtable.org/document.cfm/466*)

In the BRT's report *The Business Roundtable Education Initiative: 2000 and Beyond*, the CEOs asked their members to exercise their considerable policy influence. The Business Roundtable encourages CEOs to

- Advocate and support the changes required to help all students achieve higher standards, using the Roundtable's [1995] Essential Components of a Successful Education System as a guide.

- Help develop a national consensus around a common core of knowledge and skills that all students need, no matter where they live.

- Align [their companies'] philanthropy to help students and educators reach higher standards. Three areas need special attention: leadership development, teacher quality and learning readiness.

- Inform [their] employees why education reform is a priority issue for [their companies] and how they can contribute to improving schools in their communities.

213

- Ask for high school transcripts.
- Name company education advocate. (*www.businessroundtable.org/ document.cfm/466*)

Column E in the following table is an attempt to identify what these state CEOs have managed to do since 2000. Column E contains updates taken from the states' BRT organizations. Many state organizations have white papers outlining what their state's agenda is for education, or rather, what the states' CEOs are going to persuade state legislatures to do. Financing school reform and altering teacher certification are two of the consistent themes emerging from the state agendas as identified by their publications or press releases.

Many of the state business organizations listed in column B were started by their state's Business Roundtable organization as part of the BRT's 1990 "50-state initiative." States in boldface had passed high-stakes legislation (tests, standards and accountability measures) by 1998. The information in Columns B and C is from the 1999 BRT report *Transforming Educational Policy: Assessing Ten Years of Progress in the States* (7–52). Column D represents the grade that Education Week Online has assigned to each of the state's efforts at developing high-stakes testing. Interestingly, Ed Week uses the American Federation of Teachers' definition of "clear and specific" to rate the content standards of each state. The report cards for each state can be found by going to <*www. edweek.org/context/states/*> , clicking on the desired state, and looking for "Report Card." According to Education Week Online,

> A strong state accountability system has three main components: state-developed standards in the core subjects at all grade levels, state tests that are aligned with those standards, and methods of holding schools accountable for results, based in part on test scores. (*www.edweek.org/sreports/qc04/ state.cfm?slug=17ia.h23*)

Ed Week gave more points (toward a higher grade) if the state's assessment instruments included more than just multiple-choice exams. Ed Week looked for "five types of student-assessment instruments (multiple-choice, short-answer, extended-response in English, extended-response in other subjects, and portfolio) [and whether or not they were used] at each grade span (elementary, middle, and high school)." Also calculated into the grade was the degree to which the state tests were aligned with the standards. Five areas of accountability "were graded. . . : report cards, ratings (based on AYP [*Annual Yearly Progress*] or state criteria), assistance, sanctions, and rewards."

It seems that the state BRT organizations no longer need (as they did in 1998) to report directly to the national organization. Instead, the national Business Roundtable members can keep tabs on the progress each state is making by accessing several sources in addition to Education Week Online. The

National Conference of State Legislatures has a handy Education-Related Legislative Tracking Database (*www.ncsl.org/programs/educ/educ_leg.cfm*). Education Commission of the States has State Policy Developments in the Last Month (*www.ecs.org/ecs/ecscat.nsf/WebTopicMonth?OpenView&Start=1&Count=1000&Expand=1#1*). The Center on Education Policy provides updates on its website, under "From the Capitol to the Classroom: State and Federal Efforts to Implement the No Child Left Behind Act." The interlocking network of organizations is working smoothly to provide updates on the status of state legislation as well as provide reports—reports whose research becomes circular because of the degree of coordination among these organizations.

A	B	C	D	E
STATE	BUSINESS COALITION (DATE ESTABLISHED)	STATUS OF SYSTEMIC REFORM LEGISLATION (1999)	2004	2004 UPDATE FROM CURRENT STATE'S BRT-AFFILIATED ORGANIZATION (SAME AS IN COLUMN B UNLESS OTHERWISE NOTED)
AL	A+ Education Foundation (1991)	Systemic reform passed in Senate but defeated in the House	B–	• State-mandated testing with "levels of academic status" attached to a school's test results (changes pending) • Alabama Reading Initiative served as basis for $102 million federal "Reading First" grant (based on **DIBELS**) (*www.aplusala.org/libr/ ednews/2002/en02-jun28.asp*)
AK	Arkansas Business and Education Alliance (1990)		C+	Arkansas Scholars program: Slide show to eighth-grade students that "provides information on employment trends, achievement expectations and income potential for different jobs." More than half of the state's eighth graders saw this in 2000. Participating local employers agree to request high school transcripts and recognize the Arkansas Scholars designation on student's school records . . . [So this] becomes a factor in employment decisions. (*www.arkbea.org/scholars/default.html*)
AZ	1994-Established site councils, school report cards, open		B	• P-20 program: Seamless transition from K through postgraduate work (*www.gplinc.org/CommunityIssue.aspx?IssueID=16 ProgramID=3*)

	Arizona Business Leaders for Education (1991–1994); Motorola, Inc.	enrollment and charter schools, state standards, state test (AIMS) as pilot program 1998–Teacher Certification Standards		• Arizona Business & Education Coalition (ABEC) • Arizona Department of Education–AIMS fully in place (*www.ade.state.az.us/standards/*)
CA	California Business Roundtable (1976); California Business for Education Excellence (1998)	1999–High-stakes testing, high school exit exam	B	• Strengthening academic standards and implementing an academic assessment program to make certain these standards are achieved • Reducing class size while allowing school districts adequate flexibility • Integrating technology into classrooms • Financing new school facilities, repairing/modernizing older schools • Improving teacher preparation and credentialing (*www.cbrt.org/education.html*)
CO	Public Education and Business Coalition (early 1980s)	1993–State standards and development of state test (CSAP)	B–	• Partnered with Just for the Kids • On-site teacher training by PBEC staff • Supported HB 1160: "Under-performing or at-risk low-income students from eleven school districts eligible to use public money to attend nonpublic schools [**vouchers**]" (*Quick Facts, www.pebc.org/ourwork/policy/QuickFactsBooklet.pdf*)

A	B	C	D	E
STATE	BUSINESS COALITION (DATE ESTABLISHED)	STATUS OF SYSTEMIC REFORM LEGISLATION (1999)	2004	2004 UPDATE FROM CURRENT STATE'S BRT-AFFILIATED ORGANIZATION (SAME AS IN COLUMN B UNLESS OTHERWISE NOTED)
CT	Connecticut Business for Education Coalition (1990)	Individual schools must provide annual performance profiles to public	B–	Connecticut Business and Industry Association created the CBIA Education Foundation to develop public-private sector partnerships in education and job training (School-to-Career Program); **implement NCLB**; focus on getting schools to develop workforce skills, especially retraining. (*www.cbia.com/gov/Issues/Education.htm*)
DE	Business/Public Education Council (1990)	State standards and tests	B+	On January 21, 2003, the Delaware Business Roundtable created an Education Committee (*www.findarticles.com/cf_dls/m4PRN/2003_Jan_21/9665427/p1/article.jhtml*). B/PEC works closely with the Delaware Chamber of Commerce and the Delaware BRT to implement the National BRT agenda. See time line at *www.doe.state.de.us/sbe/timeline%202002.pdf*.
FL	Business/Higher Education Partnership (1994)	1999–"Significant advances in the state's standards and accountability systems"	A	• **FCAT fully in place** • K–20 Pipeline (*www.flboe.org/arm/*) • K–20 Accountability Project (*www.fldoe.org/K20AccAdv Counc/July_15_02/default.asp*) • HB 915 (2003) **K–20 system must comply with NCLB,**

				and performance-based funding to be in place by December 2004 (*www.sreb.org/main/LegAction/legrept/2003Reports/2003_Final_Actions.pdf*)
GA	Georgia Partnership for Excellence in Education (1990)	1993–Next Generation School Project programs	B+	A Plus Education Reform Act of 2000: Courts can fine parents for failing to attend parent-teacher conferences; requires financial reports to state by local superintendents; instructional care teams can be requested by underperforming schools; school site councils mandated; reduced class size; reduction of salaries for administrators of failing schools; **mandates criterion-referenced tests in grades 1–8 and the development of end-of-course exams for all high school courses (to replace high school exit exam)**; alternative education is for suspended students (*www.gpee.org/IssueActionDB.lasso?StoryID=0092*)
HI	Hawaii Business Roundtable (1990)	Site-based management in 90% of schools	C+	• Good Beginnings Alliance: Elementary school preparation • Collaborative Action for Public Education: Train principals for "leadership" *www.bizjournals.com/pacific/stories/2001/03/19/editorial3.html* • HBR received grant to develop and implement **Just for the Kids** database model *http://pacific.bizjournals.com/pacific/stories/2003/10/13/daily15.html*
ID	Idaho Boise Chamber of Commerce	(no BRT report)	C+	Legislative Agenda: Implement education achievement standards; assessment programs and accountability systems (*www.boisechamber.org/gov/legislative_agenda.htm*)

A	B	C	D	E
STATE	BUSINESS COALITION (DATE ESTABLISHED)	STATUS OF SYSTEMIC REFORM LEGISLATION (1999)	2004	2004 UPDATE FROM CURRENT STATE'S BRT-AFFILIATED ORGANIZATION (SAME AS IN COLUMN B UNLESS OTHERWISE NOTED)
IL	Illinois Business Roundtable (1989); Illinois Business Education Coalition (1994)	1996–High-stakes testing, prohibition of social promotion 1997–Rewritten teacher certification requirements	A–	• Expand the influence of the Lincoln Foundation for Business Excellence • Encourage teachers to become nationally board certified • Work to make student transcripts useful to potential employers (state test scores added) (*www.ilbusinessroundtable.com/education/initiatives.asp*)
IN	Indiana Chamber of Commerce (c. 1900)	"Accountability legislation that holds schools and students accountable for meeting achievement standards"	A–	• Develop vocational education programs targeted at high-demand, high-wage, and high-skilled occupations • Increase parental choice • Privatize to allow for alternative school management • Think K–16: Higher achievement standards for high school curriculum and the use of these criteria as minimum admissions criteria by Indiana colleges and universities; end remediation at postsecondary level; reduce training that is targeted to low-demand, low-skill, and low-wage occupations • State only regulates performance standards, incentives, school rehabilitation measures, instructional time, and performance reporting

	Organization	Action	Grade	Notes
				• End social promotion • Education research must be scientifically based (does it increase test scores?) (*www.indianachamber.com/pdf/legislative_business_issues.pdf; www.indianachamber.com/pdf/BizVoice/Jan_03_vocational.pdf*)
IO	Iowa Business Council (1986)	Work Keys–A workplace skills assessment test implemented in early 1990s	F	"Iowa receives the lowest grade of any state for its standards and accountability system, because it leaves most such decisions up to local districts."–Ed Week state report card on Iowa
KS	Kansas Business Education Coalition (1995)		B–	• High-stakes testing in place • Reality 101: Employers visit classrooms and share workplace expectations with students and teachers • School-to-Career opportunities (*www.kckacc.com/bec/BEChome1.html*)
KY	Partnership for Kentucky Schools (1991)	High-stakes testing	A	Education 2020 designed to ensure continuous improvement: Strengthen existing support; socialize new legislators; disseminate successful programs and research to educators and lawmakers (*www.pfks.org/edu/work_00s.html*)
LA	Council for a Better Louisiana (1962), member of Columbia Group	State standards and test Accountability Commission to create a statewide accountability system	A	• Forum for Education Excellence to focus on improving teacher quality • **School Accountability System** is leading to "improved scores . . . and a reduction of the dropout rate . . . continues to monitor its implementation while steadfastly protecting its standards and components . . . Education Week recognized Louisiana's school accountability plan as one of the top four in the nation" (*www.cabl.org/default.aspx?pane_0=education_content&pane_2= education_menu&pane_3=education_submenu&pane_4=education_mai n_image&pane_5=education_rightmenu*)

A	B	C	D	E
STATE	BUSINESS COALITION (DATE ESTABLISHED)	STATUS OF SYSTEMIC REFORM LEGISLATION (1999)	2004	2004 UPDATE FROM CURRENT STATE'S BRT-AFFILIATED ORGANIZATION (SAME AS IN COLUMN B UNLESS OTHERWISE NOTED)
ME	Maine Coalition for Excellence in Education (1991)	1997–State standards	C	Report of the Task Force to Review the Status of Implementation of the System of Learning Results: Local assessments not in place, but some districts "well along with the implementation of the *Learning Results* even though they were not necessarily . . . spending more than the state average per pupil . . . " It is important to find out how they did that. (*www.state.me.us/education/lres/LR%20Final%20Report%203–24.pdf*)
MD	Maryland Business Roundtable for Education (1992)	1991–Standards and tests	A	Goals: • High school diploma signifies achievement of high standards • The public carries the banner for educational excellence • The system of continuous school improvement is self-sustaining Programs: • Inventory of technology resources in public schools • 2002–2005 Technology Plan • Speakers Bureau: Presentations to ninth graders • Parents Count: Monthly letter/fact sheets to employees (*http://mbrt.org/new.htm#Events*)

			Grade	
MA	Massachusetts Business Alliance for Education (1988)	1993–High-stakes testing (MCAS)	B+	• Just for the Kids partnership to provide school report cards • Plan for Under-performing Schools • Amici curiae to defend MCAS as a high school graduation requirement (*www.mbae.org/news/default.asp?catid=#2*) • School Finance Forum Project: Town hall meetings across Massachusetts
MI	Michigan Business Leaders for Education Excellence (1990)	GAP Analysis Reports (1992, 1995, 1998): MI system v. BRT's Nine Essential Components	B	• Focus on implementing NCLB requirements • January 27, 2003: "Tough Financial Times Offer Great Opportunity for No Child Left Behind" *www.michamber.com/channews/jan03.asp#nochild* • NCLB "builds on the work started in the states and provides new accountability measures and resources to help raise achievement." • P.A.S.S. program, Education Yes! and Just for the Kids provide accountability (from MBLEE report *Education Now 2002*)
MN	Minnesota Business Partnership (1977)	1996–High school exit exam	C	• New state standards will allow the state to implement NCLB and "measure . . . individual schools based on student performance" • "As part of Minnesota Charter School Coalition, we helped defeat efforts to impose a moratorium on" charter school grants (*www.mnbp.com/ATC-Agenda.cfm*) • Bottom Half initiative: Focus foundation support of education "on helping at-risk, under-performing students and promoting systemic change in our public education system"
MS	Public Education Forum of Mississippi (1989)	High-stakes testing	B–	• Teacher Quality Task Force Report (February 2003) • Make Accountability Count (2002) (*www.publiceducationforum.org/*)

A	B	C	D	E
STATE	BUSINESS COALITION (DATE ESTABLISHED)	STATUS OF SYSTEMIC REFORM LEGISLATION (1999)	2004	2004 UPDATE FROM CURRENT STATE'S BRT-AFFILIATED ORGANIZATION (SAME AS IN COLUMN B UNLESS OTHERWISE NOTED)
MO	Missouri Partnership for Outstanding Schools (1994)	1993–High-stakes testing (to be implemented in stages)	B+	• MAP has five achievement levels • Public Education Evaluation Report: Recommends that schools be clustered according to SES, so there can be different curricula for each cluster (*http://pfos.missouri.org/*) • *www.goalline.org*: A website for parents "offers an eight-step process for creating and attaining high academic standards in schools" (January 2000 PFOS newsletter)
MT	Montana Chamber Foundation	(no BRT report)	D	High School Business Challenge
NE	OMAHA 2000 (1991)	1994–Pilot testing of Work Keys tests (workplace skills assessment) 1998–State standards	D	• Community Progress Annual Report • Increased number of nationally certified teachers • Expansion of school-to-work program • "[No] exams based on state content standards . . . gets credit only for having a state writing test. Instead, this strong local-control state has left it up to local school systems to devise their own standards-based exams. That policy significantly affects the state's grade . . . state does not impose sanctions on low performing or Title I schools." –Ed Week's Nebraska report card

NV	Nevada Manufacturers Association (adopted education as issue in 1992)	1998–State standards	B–	• NMA works through the Nevada Public Education Foundation • The purpose of NPEF is to focus local, state, and federal funding on the following programs: school to careers; training educational leaders; replicate systemwide the successful magnet and charter schools in the state • High-stakes testing in place, though not all grades and subjects tested
NH	New Hampshire Business Roundtable on Education (1993)	1994–Standards and assessment	C–	• Josiah Bartlett Center for Public Policy • NH Reading First Plan accepted by U.S. Department of Education • No rewards or sanctions program
NJ	Business Coalition for Educational Excellence (1996)		B–	• Three position papers calling for high-stakes testing, based on national summit of 1999 (*www.bcee.org/*) • No rewards or sanctions program, not all tests aligned with standards.–Ed Week report card for New Jersey
NM			B	• New Mexico Business Roundtable for Educational Excellence • **Computerized Learning System Grant program:** Able to align "curricula to the Terra Nova and state standards-based tests, state standards and benchmarks and adopted textbooks, diagnosing students' skill deficiencies and automatically preparing lesson plans to address those deficiencies and measure objectives by grade level. . . ."—New Mexico Public Education Department press release (*www.sde.state.nm.us/press/2003/dec/12.18.03.htm*)

A	B	C	D	E
STATE	BUSINESS COALITION (DATE ESTABLISHED)	STATUS OF SYSTEMIC REFORM LEGISLATION (1999)	2004	2004 UPDATE FROM CURRENT STATE'S BRT-AFFILIATED ORGANIZATION (SAME AS IN COLUMN B UNLESS OTHERWISE NOTED)
NY	The Business Council of New York State, Inc. (1980)	Tests and standards *High school exit exam*	A	Draft 2004 Legislative Program: Education and Job Training: "[M]aintain strong support for the higher standards and graduation requirement . . . require neighboring school districts to accept students from schools designated as in need of improvement under NCLB . . . support expansion of NY state's charter school law . . . tax credits for [vouchers] . . . course work" leading to technical education concentration and more. (*www.bcnys.org/inside/legprog/2004/04education.htm*)
NC	Education: Everybody's Business Coalition (1994)	High-stakes testing	B	• High Priority Schools Initiative (2001): 36 elementary schools in state identified (over 80% free or reduced lunch; less than 55% performed at or above grade level) for class size reduction, 5 extra days of professional development, and add 1 additional instructor per school (from evaluation, *www.ncforum.org/doclib/news/*) • Ed Week points out that NC best known for its strong accountability system but notes that not all standards and tests are in place yet (NC report card)

State	Organization		Grade	Notes
ND			C–	• Not all subjects have state-aligned tests and a limited accountability system, according to Ed Week's ND report card • Statewide Talent Pool Strategy • Primary focus is on higher education, but 2002 strategic plan includes creating a "research corridor to help define new career opportuties"
OH	Ohio Business Roundtable (1992)	Tests	A	• In 2001 established **Battelle for Kids** to advance its educational agenda • In 2003, foreign languages, the arts, and technology standards presented for adoption by the state board of education • From 2002 onward, advocating for the state system to be aligned with NCLB (*www.battelleforkids.com/b4k/rt/reform/sbr/ohio_timelines*)
OK	Business Council on Education (1994)	1990–Reform package 1999–Three of four proposals passed	B+	• Oklahoma Business and Education Coalition (est. 2002) areas of focus: Teacher instruction, preparation, credentialing, professional development, and school funding (*www.obecinfo.com/areas_of_focus.html*) • May 2003: "Catalyst" for adoption of Just for the Kids (*www.obecinfo.com/obec_initiatives.html*)
OR	Oregon Business Council (1990)	Standards and assessment	B–	• Employers for Education Excellence (E3) is "holding the line on high expectations and standards despite diminishing resources." Initiatives include small schools, community outreach and employer engagement strategies. (*www.e3oregon.org/*) • *Oregon Business Plan White Paper: Building High Performance K–12 Education*, January 2003 (*www.orbusinesscouncil.org/fs_policydoc.html*)

STATE	BUSINESS COALITION (DATE ESTABLISHED)	STATUS OF SYSTEMIC REFORM LEGISLATION (1999)	2004	2004 UPDATE FROM CURRENT STATE'S BRT-AFFILIATED ORGANIZATION (SAME AS IN COLUMN B UNLESS OTHERWISE NOTED)
	B	C	D	E
PA	Pennsylvania Business Roundtable (1979)	1999–Standards and assessment frameworks	B	2004 Legislative Priorities of Pennsylvania Chamber of Commerce: • Accountability provisions for teachers • Innovative educational programs such as charter and magnet schools • Additional funding *only if* teacher accountability for outcomes is implemented (*www.pachamber.org/ba/legislativepriorities/Education AndWorkforce/edu_policies.asp*)
RI	Business Education Roundtable (1998)		D	• "Education Is Everybody's Interest" • The Principal Residency Network • BER providing strategic planning assistance to three school districts • Retreat planning for RI Association of School Principals
SC	South Carolina Chamber Excellence in Education Council (1998)	1998–High-stakes testing	A	*Skills That Work III: Bridging the Gap Between Work and School*, 2003: The third state survey of employers' assessment of the K–16 curriculum. Conclusions are to drive lobbying efforts. (*www.scchamber.net/Education/Education.htm*)

SD	unknown	unknown	C+	unknown
TN	Tennessee Business Roundtable (1983)	1992–High-stakes testing 1994–Standards and high school exit exam	B	• Tennessee Tomorrow, Inc., participant in Just for the Kids Best Practices Study, and a member of TNP-16 Council • Tennessee P–16 Council's Guiding Principles: • Improve student learning at all levels and strengthen the connections between Pre–K–12 and higher education • Ensure that all students have access to competent, caring, and qualified teachers • Increase public awareness of the link between an educated citizenry and a healthy economy (*www.tntomorrow.org/p16council/index.htm*)
TX	Texas Business and Education Coalition (1989); Texans for Education (1989)	1993–Testing & accountability 1997–Standards ("most of the objectives in the BRT's nine-point agenda")	C+	• Some TBEC policy results for 2001: • Legislature established math content training for fifth-through eighth-grade teachers • Recommended High School Program became default graduation plan for sixth graders (college tuition for eligible students completing program) • Fiscal Accountability system to begin in 2003–04 school year (*www.tntomorrow.org/p16council/index.htm*) • Ed Week observes that the standards are not clear enough and the state assessment system "relies heavily on multiple-choice." (Texas report card)

A STATE	B BUSINESS COALITION (DATE ESTABLISHED)	C STATUS OF SYSTEMIC REFORM LEGISLATION (1999)	D	E 2004 UPDATE FROM CURRENT STATE'S BRT-AFFILIATED ORGANIZATION (SAME AS IN COLUMN B UNLESS OTHERWISE NOTED)
			2004	
UT	Utah Partners in Education (1990)	Statewide School-to-Careers Initiative	C+	The Utah Partnership for Education and Economic Development appoints a partnership coordinator for each of the state's forty school districts. Each district is also assigned a work-based learning coordinator. "Partners" help districts develop curriculum for each grade, resulting in "significant measured increases in student achievement." (*http://utahpartnership.utah.org/benefits.htm#*)

VT	Vermont Business Roundtable (adopted education as issue in 1989)	High-stakes testing	C	• Education Working Group's priorities for 2003–04:
				  • Medallion School Award Program
				  • Early Care and Education
				  • Higher Education
				  • School Performance
				  • Collaboration with State Board of Education (*www.vtroundtable.org/TB1+RL+I+C.asp?SiteAreaID=605*)
				• Ed Week complains that the AFT has deemed Vermont's standards "clear and specific only in science." (Vermont report card)

VA	Virginians for a World Class Education (1993)	1995–Standards Assessment	B	Virginia Business Council
WA	Washington Roundtable (1983); Partnership for Learning (1994)	1993—High-stakes testing 1999–New accountability system	C+	Washington Roundtable's 2004 policy agenda: • High school exit exam by 2008 • Use NCLB to strengthen state's assessment and accountability efforts • Enact state intervention of low-performing schools • Authorize use of charter schools • Merit career ladder for teachers • focus postsecondary school funding in "high demand areas" (*www.waroundtable.com/policy/04%20policy%20agenda.htm#Reg*)
WV	The Business Council for Education (1991)	High-stakes testing	A	• West Virginia Business Roundtable • Intellectual Infrastructure in the 21st Century Committee • *What We're Looking For: Business Defines Its Workforce Training Needs* (July 2000) (*www.wvbrt.org/infrastructure.asp*)
WI	Wisconsin Manufacturers & Commerce (1911) WMC Foundation est. 1980	Standards and testing	C+	• Wisconsin Chamber of Commerce Foundation is "a clearinghouse of information on high-performing school districts, innovative programs, and outstanding partnerships." It issues awards to recognize successful schools and districts. (*www.wischamberfoundation.org/SchoolImprovement/index.cfm?ID=8*) • Ed Week complaints: "[A]bsence of clear and specific standards for science and social studies" and "does not impose sanctions on [low-performing schools]."—Wisconsin report card

A	B	C	D	E
STATE	BUSINESS COALITION (DATE ESTABLISHED)	STATUS OF SYSTEMIC REFORM LEGISLATION (1999)	2004	2004 UPDATE FROM CURRENT STATE'S BRT-AFFILIATED ORGANIZATION (SAME AS IN COLUMN B UNLESS OTHERWISE NOTED)
WY			D	Clear and specific standards only in math. No help or sanctions for low-performing schools.—Ed Week report card for Wyoming

C

Institute for Educational Leadership Connections

It can be instructive to look at the connections between and among groups. Here are the organizations IEL lists as resources. When available, links and associations for these resources are given.

American Association of School Administrators Links: American Enterprise Institute; Annenberg Public Policy Center; Ballot Watch; Brookings Institution; Cato Institute; the Center for Democracy & Technology; Center for Labor Education and Research; Center for Media and Public Affairs; Center for Responsive Politics, Child Trends; the Center for Information and Research on Civic Learning and Engagement; Economic Policy Institute; Education Policy Studies Laboratory; the Heritage Foundation; Hudson Institute; Institute for Public Accuracy; Institute for the Study of Knowledge Management in Education; National Legal and Policy Center; Public Agenda; RAND; Taxpayers for Common Sense; the Thomas B. Fordham Foundation; the Vanishing Voter

American Institutes for Research Clients: Abbott Laboratories; AKSYS Ltd.; Alfred P. Sloan Foundation; Almond Board of California; American Association of Occupational Health Nurses; American Association of School Administrators; American Cancer Society; American Council on Education; American Dental Associates; American Federation of Teachers; American Institute of Certified Public Accountants; American Psychological Association; American Red Cross; Ameritech Services Co.; Apple Computer, Inc.; Asian Development Bank; Association of American Medical Colleges; Association of State and Territorial Directors of Health Promotion and Public Health; A.T. Cross Co.; AT&T Corp.; Baxter Healthcare Corp.; BBN, Inc.; the Bell Foundation; Bell

South Cellular; Biblioteca di Documentazione, Pedagogica, Italy; Bill and Melinda Gates Foundation; Brazilian Ministry of Education and Sports; Bureau of Indian Affairs; California Commission on Teacher Credentialing; Carnegie Corporation of New York; Center for Applied Linguistics; Central Intelligence Agency; Charles C. Mott Foundation; Chase Manhattan Bank; Cisco Systems; Citibank; Coalition of Essential Schools; the College Board; COMSAT; the Council for Exceptional Children; Council of Administrators of Special Education; Council of Chief State School Officers; Council of Great City Schools; DATEX Medical Instrumentation, Inc.; David and Lucile Packard Foundation; Deloitte & Touche; Design Continuum, Inc.; Digital Equipment Corp.; Eastman Kodak Co.; Edison Electric Institute; the Education Trust; Educational Testing Service; Fannie Mae; Federal Emergency Management Agency; Fundaçao Luis Eduardo Magalhes; the Gallup Organization; GE Information Services, Inc.; General Services Administration; Geological Survey; George Soros Open Society Institute; George Washington University; Graduate School of Education and Human Development; GTE Corp.; Harcourt Educational Measurement; Harvard University; Health Care Financing Administration; Herbst LaZar Bell, Inc.; Hewlett-Packard Co.; Hill-Rom Co. Inc.; IBM Corp.; Internal Revenue Service; John S. and James L. Knight Foundation; Johns Hopkins University; Kaiser Foundation Research Institute; Kodak; KPMG Consulting LLP; Library of Congress; Lilly Endowment, Inc.; Lotus Development Corp.; Luke B. Hancock Foundation; Lyle M. Spencer Foundation; MathSoft, Inc.; Microsoft Corp.; MicroTouch Systems, Inc.; Motorola Corp.; National Association of Elementary School Principals; National Association of Secondary School Principals; National Aeronautics and Space Administration; National Assessment Governing Board; National Education Association; National Safety Council; National Science Foundation; National Skill Standards Board; NEW-MED Corp.; New York Stock Exchange; New York University; net.Genesis; Northern Telecom Canada Ltd.; Northwestern University; Nova Biomedical; nView Corp.; Office of Personnel Management; Ohmeda, Inc.; Oracle Corp.: Organization for Economic Cooperation and Development; Pew Charitable Trusts; Pew Internet and American Life Project; Polaroid Corp.; Postal Service; Price Waterhouse; Robert Wood Johnson Foundation; San Francisco Foundation; School District of Philadelphia; Simon Wiesenthal Center; Social Security Administration; George Soros Open Society Institute; Sprint Corp.; Stanford University Medical Center; Alabama, Alaska, Arizona, Arkansas, California, Connecticut, Delaware, Florida, Georgia, Illinois, Indiana, Iowa, Kentucky, Kansas, Louisiana, Maryland, Massachusetts, Minnesota, Missouri, Montana, New Jersey,

New York, North Carolina, North Dakota, Ohio, Oregon, Pennsylvania, Rhode Island, Utah, Virginia, and Wyoming State Departments of Education; Minas Gerais and Parana, Brazil; Susan G. Koman Breast Cancer Foundation; Thomson Consumer Electronics; Temple University; United Nations Children's Fund; United Nations Educational, Scientific, and Cultural Organization; University of California, Office of the President; UNUM Life Insurance Corp.; U.S. Agency for International Development; U.S. Department of Defense, Air Force, Army, Defense Advanced Research Projects Agency, Marine Corps, Navy; U.S. Department of Education, National Center for Education Statistics, Office of Educational Research and Improvement, Office of Special Education Programs; U.S. Department of Health and Human Services, Agency for Healthcare Research and Quality Centers for Disease Control and Prevention, Centers for Medicare and Medicaid Services Head Start Bureau, Health Resources and Services Administration, National Cancer Institute, National Heart, Lung, and Blood Institute, National Institute for Health Care Management, National Institute of Child Health and Human Development, National Institute of Mental Health, Office of Minority Health; U.S. Department of Housing and Urban Development; U.S. Department of Justice, Federal Bureau of Prisons; U.S. Department of Labor; U.S. Department of State; U.S. Department of Transportation; U.S. Department of Veterans Affairs; U.S. Information Agency; Walter S. Johnston Foundation; Waters Chromatography; William and Flora Hewlett Foundation; William T. Grant Foundation; W. K. Kellogg Foundation; the World Bank; Xerox Corp.

American Youth Policy Forum Funders: Carnegie Corp. of New York; Charles S. Mott Foundation; DC Action for Children; Ford Foundation; Ford Motor Fund; General Electric Fund; George Gund Foundation; McKnight Foundation; W. K. Kellogg Foundation; Wallace-Reader's Digest Fund; Walter S. Johnson Foundation; William T. Grant Foundation

Brown Center on Education Policy (part of Brookings Institution)

Center on Education Policy Funders: the Atlantic Philanthropies; The George Gund Foundation; the Joyce Foundation; the Hewlett Foundation; the Gates Foundation; the Ford Foundation; Phi Delta Kappa International

Coalition for Community Schools (part of IEL)

Council for Basic Education Major Funders: Achieve, Inc.; AOL Time Warner; AT&T Foundation; Jacob and Hilda Blaustein Foundation; Carnegie Corp. of New York; Circuit City Foundation; ExxonMobil

Foundation; the Ford Foundation; GE Fund; the Joyce Foundation; John S. and James L. Knight Foundation; Leon Foundation; Lockheed Martin Foundation; Lucent Technologies Foundation; John D. and Catherine T. MacArthur Foundation; Metropolitan Life Foundation; Milken Family Foundation; New American Schools; the New York Community Trust; the Pew Charitable Trusts; the Proctor & Gamble Fund; the Rapides Foundation; the Rockefeller Foundation; Sodexho Marriott; the Spencer Foundation; the Starr Foundation; State Farm Cos. Foundation; the UPS Foundation; Wallace-Reader's Digest Funds; Whirlpool Foundation; Cleveland Municipal School District; District of Columbia Public Schools; East Allen, Indiana, County Schools; Maryland State Department of Education; Montgomery County, Maryland, Public Schools; National Council of Chief State School Officers; National Science Foundation; North Carolina Department of Instruction; State of Florida; State of Nevada; State of South Carolina; Temple University Laboratory for Student Success; U.S. Department of Education; U.S. Department of State, Office of Overseas Schools; University of Georgia Board of Regents; University System of Maryland

Council of Chief State School Partnerships

Heritage Foundation Mission: To formulate and promote conservative public policies based on the principles of free enterprise, limited government, individual freedom, traditional American values, and a strong national defense

National Center for Education Statistics

National Clearinghouse for Comprehensive School Reform Partnership: the George Washington University; the Council for Basic Education; and the Institute for Educational Leadership

National Conference of State Legislatures

National Education Association

National Partnership for Reinventing Government (formerly National Performance Review)

OMB Watch

The Urban Institute

D

Ten-Point Framework of the Local Education Fund Network and Corporate Funders

The Public Education Network (PEN) is partnered with state BRT organizations and exists to support Local Education Fund. These LEFs are the vehicles through which local business groups pursue standards-based Reform in their cities. Following is the Ten Point Framework that guides the work of LEFs as well as a list of those corporations who contribute to PEN. Note how closely this framework aligns with NCLB.

Ten-Point Framework

1. **Commitment:** Everyone in the community must believe, and act as if they believe, that all children can learn at high levels.
2. **Standards and Outcomes:** We must measure educational outcomes, rather than just inputs.
3. **Assessments:** In order to reach these outcomes, we must have appropriate assessments in place to measure students' progress.
4. **Accountability:** We must establish "consequences of success." If we don't have consequences, no one will take seriously the striving for success.
5. **School-Based Management:** If we intend to hold school staff accountable, we must move decision-making down to the school level.
6. **Good Teachers:** Recruitment, Licensing, and Continued Learning Teachers' licensure should be based on what children need to know, not on outdated credentialing programs.

7. **School Readiness:** We must establish quality, developmentally appropriate pre-kindergarten programs for all children.
8. **School Community Links:** Health and social services must be a part of any quality school reform.
9. **Technology:** Technology must be included in teaching, special education, and information management.
10. **Public Engagement and Support:** Public engagement is critical. Significant change can only be achieved with the understanding, agreement, and participation of a broad base of community members.

(*From www.publiceducation.org/about/ten2.htm*, viewed on 20 August 2002.)

In 2004, the funder's list had changed a little bit but not much.

American Express Foundation

The Annenberg Foundation

BP Foundation, Inc.

Carnegie Corporation of New York

Chevron Texaco Corporation

Discovery Communications, Inc.

Edna McConnell Clark Foundation

Ford Foundation

The J. P. Morgan Chase Foundation

Kirkpatrick & Lockhart LLP

MetLife Foundation

Microsoft Corporation

New York Life Foundation

The New York Times Company Foundation

The Prudential Foundation

Schott Center for Public and Early Education

The Sulzberger Foundation

The UPS Foundation

U.S. Department of Education. Office of Educational Research and Improvement

U.S. Department of Health & Human Services

Washington Mutual Foundation

William & Flora Hewlett Foundation

Working Assets Youth Focus Fund

Corporate Donors to PEN

(From *www.publiceducation.org/about/funder.htm*; viewed 20 August 2002.)

ABC, Inc., Foundation

Alabama Power Foundation

American Express Foundation

Annenberg Foundation

Bet Holdings, Inc.

BP Amoco Foundation

Centers for Disease Control and Prevention

Chevron Products Co.

Citigroup Foundation

Edna McConnell Clark Foundation

Epson America, Inc.

Ford Foundation

Harcourt Educational Measurement

Heinz Family Foundation

James Irvine Foundation

JP Morgan Chase Foundation

Metropolitan Life Foundation

Microsoft Co.

New York Times Co. Foundation

Pew Charitable Trusts

Prudential Foundation

Qwest Foundation

Rapides Foundation

Joseph E. Seagram & Sons

Sulzberger Foundation

Tides Foundation

UPS Foundation

U.S. Department of Education

U.S. Department of Health and Human Services

Wallace-Reader's Digest Funds

Washington Mutual

William and Flora Hewlett Foundation

Working Assets

E

Texas Just for the Kids Funding

The following groups are listed as contributing to Just for the Kids in Texas: American Airlines; American Income Life Insurance Co.; Arter & Hadden; AT&T; Atlantic Philanthropies; Austin Community Foundation; Austin Industries, Inc.; Baker & Botts, LLP; Baylor Health Care System; Bernard and Audre Rapoport Foundation; Bosque Foundation; Broad Foundation; Buford Foundation; Cardinal Investment Co., Inc.; Carl B. and Florence E. King Foundation; Central and South West Corp.; Compaq Computer Corp.; Constantin Foundation; Crowley-Carter Foundation; Dallas Foundation; Dell; Dell Foundation; Denitech Corp.; Dodge Jones Foundation; EDS; Education Commission of the States; Elkins Interests; Enserch Corp.; Galloway-James, Inc.; Goldman, Sachs & Co.; H. E. Butt Grocery Co.; HCB Contractors; Hicks, Muse, Tate, & Furst; Hillcrest Foundation; Hobby Family Foundation; Hoblitzelle Foundation; Houston Endowment; Hunt Oil Co.; IBM; International Bank of Commerce; J. McDonald Williams Fund of the Dallas Foundation; J. F. Maddox Foundation; Jack and Dee Willome Fund; James R. and Judy C. Adams Fund; Jim Deatherage & Associates, P.C.; John Castle Fund of the Episcopal Foundation; John T. and Margaret Sharpe Fund; Lucent Technologies; Marilyn Augur Foundation; McClanahan & Clearman, LLP; Meadows Foundation; Meridian Advisors, Ltd, Michael and Susan Dell Foundation; Microsoft; Moody Foundation; Mort Meyerson Family Foundation; NationsBank; O'Donnell Foundation; Perot Systems; Pier One Imports, Inc.; Priddy Foundation; Public Strategies, Inc.; Ray Ellison Charitable Fund; Reliant Energy; RGK Foundation; Robert and Janice McNair Foundation; Rockefeller Foundation; San Francisco Chamber of Commerce; Saxon Publishers, Inc.; SBC Foundation; Shell Oil Co.; Sid Richardson Foundation; Silicon Graphics Computer Systems; Solectron Corp.; Sterling Software; TDK USA Corp.; Temerlin McClain; Temple Inland, Inc.; Texas Commerce Bank; Texas Instruments Foundation; Texas Instruments, Inc.; Texas Utilities/ENSERCH Corp.; Luce, Tom, Trammell Crow Co.; TU Services; United Way of the Bay Area; Valero Management Co.; Vinson & Elkins, LLP; Washington Mutual Foundation; Wells Fargo Bank; William and Gay Solomon Fund; Williamson Printing Corp.

References

Abbey, Edward. 1977. *The Journey Home: Some Words in Defense of the American West.* New York: E. P. Dutton.

"The Achievement Gap." 2001. Editorial. *St. Louis Post-Dispatch*, 19 March, E6.

Align to Achieve. n.d. "The Academic Standards e-Library." Accessed at *www.aligntoachieve.org/e_library.html*.

———. n.d. "Aligning Standards for Student Achievement." Accessed at *www.aligntoachieve.org/educators.html*.

———. n.d. "FAQs: What Is the Purpose of the Concept Vocabulary?" Accessed at *www.aligntoachieve.org/faqs.html#Q5*.

American Association of School Administrators. 2001. "Preparing Leaders for the New Economy." *School Administrator*, March. Accessed at *www.aasa.org/publications/sa/2001_03/broad.htm*.

American Productivity and Quality Center. 2001. "The Broad Foundation Announces Public School Districts Chosen for Excellence in Leadership and Principal Development: Chicago's School District Selected as a National Model." American Productivity and Quality Center Press Release, 31 August. Accessed at *http://old.apqc.org/about/press/dispPressRelease.cfm?ProductID=1431*.

Annenberg Institute for School Reform. 1998a. "New Directions." Providence, RI: Annenberg Institute. Accessed at *www.aisr.brown.edu/publications/pubops.html*.

———. 1998b. "Reasons for Hope, Voices of Change." Providence, RI: Annenberg Institute. Accessed at *www.aisr.brown.edu/publications/pubops.html*.

Annie E. Casey Foundation. n.d. "Success in School: Education Ideas That Count; Ideas in Action." Aecf.org. Accessed at *www.aecf.org/publications/success/family.htm*.

Arnstine, Donald. 1995. *Democracy and the Arts of Schooling.* Albany, NY: State University of New York Press.

Aschenbrener, Mary. In press. *Reconstitution at Any Cost: When School District Policies Prevail at the Expense of Student Success: The Story of Mission High School: September 1995–June 1997.*

Ascher, Carol. 1991. "The Changing Face of Racial Isolation and Desegregation in Urban Schools." *Eric Digest.* Accessed at *http://eric-web.tc.columbia.edu/digests/dig91.html*.

Asia-Pacific Economic Cooperation. 1992. "Foreword and Overview of the Ministerial Education Standards for the Twenty-First Century: Opening Statements of the Ministers at the Asia-Pacific Economic Ministerial." In *First APEC Education Forum.* Washington, DC: Asia-Pacific Economic Cooperation. Accessed at *www.apec.edu.tw/ef3.html*.

———. 2000. "Education for Learning Societies in the Twenty-First Century." In *Second APEC Education Ministerial Forum.* Singapore: Asia-Pacific Economic Cooperation. Accessed at *www.apecsec.org.sg/apec/ministerial_statements/sectoral_ministerial/education/2000_education.html*.

Asimov, Nanette. 1999a. "Rojas Record Can't Be Denied: Scores, Graduation Rates Rose During His Tenure as S.F. Schools Chief." *San Francisco Chronicle*, 21 June.

———. 1999b. "Rojas Set to Bolt S.F. for Dallas School Job." *San Francisco Chronicle*, 23 April.

———. 1999c. "S.F. Schools Shaken by Deep Budget Cuts." *San Francisco Chronicle*, 18 March.

———. 2003. "Bitter Battle over Class Standards." *San Francisco Chronicle*, 5 May.

Asimov, Nanette, and Lance Williams. 2001. "High-Priced Legal Team Browbeats Youths About Shoddy Schools." *San Francisco Chronicle*, 2 September.

Barber, Benjamin R. 1984. *Strong Democracy: Participatory Politics for a New Age.* Berkeley: University of California Press.

———. 1991. "A Mandate for Liberty: Requiring Education-Based Community Service." *The Responsive Community* 1 (2): 46–55.

———. 1992. *An Aristocracy of Everyone: The Politics of Education and the Future of America.* 1st ed. New York: Ballantine.

———. 1998a. *The Conquest of Politics: Liberal Philosophy in Democratic Times.* Princeton, NJ: Princeton University Press.

———. 1998b. *A Passion for Democracy: American Essays.* Princeton, NJ: Princeton University Press.

———. 1998c. *A Place for Us : How to Make Society Civil and Democracy Strong.* 1st ed. New York: Hill and Wang.

Bastian, Ann. 1986. *Choosing Equality: The Case for Democratic Schooling.* Philadelphia: Temple University Press.

Bay Area School Reform Collaborative (BASRC). 1999a. "Initiatives." BASRC, Accessed at *fwl.org/basrc/initiatives.html*.

———. 1999b. "What's Working." BASRC. Accessed at *fwl.org/basrc/whats_working/index.html*.

Bazeley, Elsie Theodora. 1969. *Homer Lane and the Little Commonwealth*. New York: Schocken.

Bediner, Robert. 1969. *The Politics of Schools: A Crisis in Self-Government*. New York: Harper and Row.

Berliner, David, and Bruce Biddle. 1995. *The Manufactured Crisis: Myths, Frauds, and the Attack on America's Public Schools*. New York: Addison-Wesley.

Berman and Weiler, Associates. 1983. *Improving Student Performance in California: Analysis of First Year's Education Legislation*. Berkeley: California Roundtable, 85.

———. 1988. *Restructuring California Education: A Design for Public Education in the Twenty-First Century*. Berkeley: California Business Roundtable, 295.

Bernbaum, Brian. 2003. "Monkey Theory Proven Wrong." CBS News.

Biegel, Stuart. 1997. *San Francisco Unified School District Desegregation, Paragraph 44 Independent Review*. Los Angeles: University of California, Los Angeles, 118.

———. 1998. *San Francisco Unified School District Desegregation, Paragraph 44 Independent Review*. Los Angeles: University of California, Los Angeles, 145.

———. 1999. *San Francisco Unified School District Desegregation, Paragraph 44 Independent Review*. Los Angeles: University of California, Los Angeles, 55.

———. 2000. *San Francisco Unified School District Desegregation, Paragraph 44 Independent Review*. Los Angeles: University of California, Los Angeles, 182.

———. 2001. *San Francisco Unified School District Desegregation, Paragraph 44 Independent Review*. Los Angeles: University of California, Los Angeles.

Blum, John, et al. 1985. *The National Experience*. New York: Harcourt Brace Jovanovich.

Blume, Howard. 1999. "The Best School Board Money Can Buy." *LA Weekly*, 9–16 April.

Bode, Boyd Henry. 1950. *Democracy as a Way of Life*. New York: Macmillan.

Bolon, Craig. 2000. *Education Reform in Massachusetts*. Brookline, MA: MassParents, 4. Accessed at *www.massparents.org/easternmass/brookline/ed_reform_bolon.htm*.

Broad Foundation. 2003a. "The Broad Foundation Taps Young MBAs to Transform Urban Public Education." *Media Center*, 7 August. Accessed at *www.broadfoundation.org/med-news/2003–0807.shtml*.

———. 2003b. "President Bush Announces Partnership Between the Broad Foundation and the U.S. Department of Education to Improve Our Country's Public Education System." *Media Center*, 9 September. Accessed at *www.broadfoundation.org/med-news/index-net.shtml*.

Broad Foundation. n.d. "Our History." Accessed at *www.broadfoundation.org/about/history-net.shtml*.

Broad Foundation and Thomas Fordham Institute. 2003. "Better Leaders for America's Schools: A Manifesto." Accessed at *www.broadfoundation.org/med-pubs/BetterLeadersforAmericasSchools.pdf*.

Brown, David, W. McIntire, and C. Perry. 1996. *Systemic Change and the Role of School Boards*. ERIC ED 399105. Paper presented at the American Educational Research Association, New York, April.

Brown, H. 2001. "Watching City Hall." *San Francisco Call*, 21 May. Accessed at *www.sfcall.com/issues%202001/5.21.01/watching_city_hall.htm*.

Business Roundtable. 1995. "Continuing the Commitment: Essential Components of a Successful Education System." Business Roundtable. Accessed at *www.businessroundtable.org/pdf/130.pdf*.

———. 1996. "A Business Leader's Guide to Setting Academic Standards." Business Roundtable. Accessed at *www.businessroundtable.org/pdf/80.pdf*.

———. 1998. "Building Support for Tests That Count." Business Roundtable. Accessed at *www.businessroundtable.org/pdf/225.pdf*.

———. 1999. "Transforming Educational Policy: Assessing Ten Years of Progress in the States." Business Roundtable. Accessed at *www.businessroundtable.org/pdf/326.pdf*.

———. 2001. "Assessing and Addressing the 'Testing Backlash': Practical Advice and Current Public Opinion Research for Business Coalitions and Standards Advocates." Business Roundtable. Accessed at *www.businessroundtable.org/pdf/525.pdf*.

California State Board of Education. n.d. "Donald Fisher." In *Members' Biographical Information*. Accessed at *www.cde.ca.gov/board/bio.htm#fisher*.

California, State of. 1983. *Statutes of California and Digests of Measures*. Vol. 2. Ed. Bion Gregory.

Callahan, Raymond. 1962. *Education and the Cult of Efficiency*. Chicago: University of Chicago Press.

———. 1975. "The American Board of Education 1789–1960." In *Understanding School Boards*, ed. Peter J. Cistone, 19–46. Lexington, MA: Lexington (D. C. Heath).

Caruaba, Alan. 2002. "It's Not 'Leave No Child Behind,' It's Leave No One Alone." *The Fan Mountain Almanac and Trout Wrapper*, February. Accessed at *www.troutwrapper.com/archive/feb2002-warningsigns.htm*.

———. 2003. "The Subversion of Education in America." The National Anxiety Center, 25 November. Accessed at *www.anxietycenter.com/subversion.htm*.

Chandler, Louis. 1997. "Forced Busing: A Staff Report of the Allegheny Institute for Public Policy." Pittsburgh, PA: Allegheny Institute for Public Policy, 25.

Chase, Bob. 1999. "The New NEA: Reinventing

Teacher Unions." In *Transforming Teacher Unions: Fighting for Better Schools and Social Justice*, ed. Bob Peterson and Michael Charney, 66–67, 107–10. Milwaukee: Rethinking Schools.

Coalition for Evidence-Based Policy. 2003. *Meeting of Key State/Local Officials*. Washington, DC: The Council for Excellence in Government. Accessed at *www.excelgov.org/displayContent.asp?Keyword=prppc Evidence*.

Coker, Brett. 2001. "Donor Profile: Donald G. Fisher (with Doris F.)." MotherJones.com. Accessed at *www.motherjones.com/news/special_reports/mojo_ 400/184_fisher.html*.

"Committees Wrong on MCAS." 2002. Editorial. *The Boston Herald*, 2 November.

Connor, Kim, and Melinda Melendez. 1994a. *Education Reform Briefing Book. Volume I, First Edition. Education Reform in Review and Emerging Education Issues in California*. ERIC ED 373437. Sacramento: California State Legislature, Senate Office of Research, 138.

———. 1994b. *Education Reform Briefing Book. Volume II, First Edition. Excerpts from Selected California Education Studies and Reports, 1983–Present*. ERIC ED 373438. Sacramento: California State Legislature, Senate Office of Research, 252.

Crews, Colby. 1996. Untitled. San Francisco State University *Golden Gator*, 2 May.

Cuban, Larry. 1972. *Youth as a Minority: An Anatomy of Student Rights; Teaching Social Studies in an Age of Crisis No. 4*. Washington, DC: National Council for the Social Studies.

———. 1988. *The Managerial Imperative and the Practice of Leadership in Schools*. SUNY Series in Educational Leadership. Albany: State University of New York Press.

———. 1999. *How Scholars Trumped Teachers: Change Without Reform in University Curriculum, Teaching, and Research, 1890–1990*. New York: Teachers College Press.

Cuban, Larry, National Institute of Education (U.S.), and Dingle Associates. 1983. *Transforming the Frog into the Prince: Effective Schools Research, Policy, and Practice at the District Level*. Washington, DC: Dingle Associates.

Daily News. 2003. "Young for L.A. School Board: Reformer Is LAUSD's Best Hope for Progress." DailyNews.com, 25 February. Accessed at *www. dailynews.com/Stories/0,1413,200~25405~ 1204294,00.html*.

Danzberger, Jacqueline, Twentieth Century Fund Task Force on School Governance, and Danforth Foundation. 1992. *Facing the Challenge: The Report of the Twentieth Century Fund Task Force on School Governance*. New York: Twentieth Century Fund.

Danzberger, J. P. 1994. "Governing the Nation's Schools: A Case for Restructuring Local School Boards." *Phi Delta Kappan* 75 (5): 367–73.

Danzberger, J. P., and Michael Usdan. 1994. "Local Education Governance: Perspectives on Problems and Strategies for Change." *Phi Delta Kappan* 75 (5): 366.

Davis, Gray. 1999. "Schools on the Road Back." *San Francisco Chronicle*, 4 October.

Decker, Greg. 2003. "Using Data to Drive Student Achievement in the Classroom and on High-Stakes Tests." *T.H.E. Journal Online*, January. Accessed at *www.thejournal.com/magazine/vault/articleprintversion.cfm?aid=4310*.

DeLeon, Richard. 1997. "Progressive Politics in the Left Coast City: San Francisco." In *Racial Politics in American Cities*, ed. Rufus Browning, Dale Marshall, and David Tabb. New York: Longman.

DeLeon, Richard, Elisa Barbour, Kevin Carew, Will Aarsheim, and José Mauro Barrón. 1995. *San Francisco's Changing Demography and Social Needs: Maps and Analyses for Community Development Strategic Planning*. San Francisco: San Francisco State University Public Research Institute, 36.

DeLeon, R. E. 1992. *Left Coast City, Studies in Government and Public Policy*. Lawrence: University Press of Kansas.

Dewey, John. 1944. *Democracy and Education: An Introduction to the Philosophy of Education*. New York: Macmillan.

———. 1946. *The Public and Its Problems: An Essay in Political Inquiry*. Chicago: Gateway.

———. 1963. *Liberalism and Social Action*. Ed. Page-Barbour Foundation, Lecture Series. New York: Capricorn.

———. 1989. *Freedom and Culture*. Buffalo, NY: Prometheus.

———. 1998. *Experience and Education*. 60th anniversary ed. West Lafayette, IN: Kappa Delta Pi.

———. 1999. *Individualism Old and New, Great Books in Philosophy*. Amherst, NY: Prometheus.

Dornan, John. 2001. Email to authors, 2 January.

Durland, Forest. n.d. "The Communist/Socialist/UN Takeover of American Education Falls into Four Parts." *Education List: Truth for our children*. Accessed at *www.uhuh.com/education/list-ed.htm*.

Easton, David. 1965. *A Framework for Political Analysis*. Englewood Cliffs, NJ: Prentice-Hall.

EdSource. 1995. *California's K–12 School Finance System*. Menlo Park, CA: EdSource.

Education Commission of the States. 1999a. "ECS History." Education Commission of the States.

———. 1999b. "ECS Priorities." Education Commission of the States.

———. 1999c. "ECS Spotlight: Members Named to

1999–2000 Committees." Education Commission of the States.

Education Place. 2003. *MathSteps for Parents: Level 2; Introducing the Concept: Addition and Subtraction with Regrouping.* Houghton Mifflin. Accessed at *www.eduplace.com.*

Education Reporter. 1998. "Education Conference Explores Standards and School-to-Work." *Education Reporter,* March. Accessed at *www.eagleforum.org/educate/1998/mar98/conference.html.*

Education Trust. 1999. "Ticket to Nowhere." *Thinking K–16* 3 (2): 5, 31.

Engel, Adam. 2003. "A Conversation in Medieval America with Sam Smith." Counterpunch, 11–14 November. Accessed at *www.counterpunch.org/engel11142003.html.*

Fair Test. n.d. "Who We Are." Accessed at *www.fairtest.org/Who%20We%20Are.html.*

Farrell, Dick. 1997. " 'School to Work'—A Stupid Idea." *The Times Reporter,* 16 March.

Feldman, Sandra. 1999. "Whither Public Education." In *Transforming Teacher Unions: Fighting for Better Schools and Social Justice,* ed. Bob Peterson and Michael Charney, 111–14. Milwaukee: Rethinking Schools.

Fiscal Crisis and Management Assistance Team. 2000. *Comprehensive Fiscal Assessment of the San Francisco Unified School District.* San Francisco: San Francisco Unified School District.

Flanagan, Kathleen. n.d. "Straight 'A's' Deserves an 'F'." Education Reform. Accessed at *www.learn-usa.com/er031.htm.*

FORCES Duluth. 2002. "School to Work." FORCES Duluth. Accessed at *www.forcesduluth.com/stw.html.*

Fraga, Louis Ricardo, Bari Anhalt Erlichson, and Sandy Lee. 1998. "Consensus Building and School Reform: The Role of the Courts in San Francisco." In *Changing Urban Education,* ed. Clarence Stone, 66–92. Lawrence: University of Kansas Press.

France, Mike, and Andrew Osterland. 1999. "State Farm: What's Happening to the Good Neighbor." *Business Week Online,* 8 November. Accessed at *www.businessweek.com/1999/99_45/b3654189.htm.*

Franck, Matthew. 2001. "City Schools Get Generally Good Grades but Test Scores Lag . . ." *St. Louis Post-Dispatch,* 6 March.

Freire, Paulo. 2000. *Pedagogy of the Oppressed.* Trans. Myra Bergman Ramos. New York: Continuum.

Funkhouser, Janie, and Miriam R. Gonzales. 1997. *Family Involvement in Children's Education: Successful Local Approaches: An Idea Book.* Washington, DC: U.S. Department of Education. Accessed at *www.ed.gov/pubs/FamInvolve/title.html.*

Galvin, Daniel. 2002. "IBM's Reinventing Education (B)." Harvard Business School Publishing Online.

Gates, Jeff. 2000. *Democracy at Risk: Rescuing Main Street from Wall Street.* New York: Perseus.

Gelberg, Louis. 1997. *The "Business" of Reforming American Schools.* Albany: State University of New York Press.

Gerstner, Louis. 2000. *Reinventing Education: Entrepreneurship in America's Public Schools.* New York: Dutton.

Giroux, Henry A., and Peter McLaren. 1989. *Critical Pedagogy, the State, and Cultural Struggle, Teacher Empowerment and School Reform.* Albany: State University of New York Press.

Gittell, Marilyn. 1979. "Institutionalizing Community Participation in Education." In *Community Participation in Education,* ed. Carl Grant, 46–66. Boston: Allyn and Bacon.

Glenn, Teresa. 2003. "The Monster in Our Schools." In *Silent No More: Voices of Courage in American Schools,* ed. ReLeah Cossett Lent and Gloria Pipkin. Portsmouth, NH: Heinemann.

Goldstein, J., M. Kelleman, and W. Kosaki. 1998. Reconstitution in Theory and Practice: The Experience of San Francisco. Paper presented at the American Education Research Association, San Diego, 13–17 April.

Gonsalves, Sean. 2003. " 'The Devil's Dictionary' Revisted." Alternet.org, 14 July. Accessed at *www.alternet.org/story.html?StoryID=16393.*

Goode, Seddon. 1996. "Don't Botch the Education Village." *Charlotte Observer,* 29 February.

Goodman, Paul. 1960. *Growing Up Absurd: Problems of Youth in the Organized System.* New York: Random House.

———. 1966. *Compulsory Mis-education, and the Community of Scholars.* New York: Vintage.

Goodman, Paul, and Taylor Stoehr. 1977. *Drawing the Line: The Political Essays of Paul Goodman.* 1st ed. New York: Free Life.

Gottlieb, Rachel, and Robert A. Frahm. 2002. "Mastery Test Grilling Heats Up." *Hartford Courant,* 19 September.

Grant, Carl. 1979. "A Proposal to Minimize the Practical Constraint of Community Participation in Education." In *Community Participation in Education,* ed. Carl Grant, 116–33. Boston: Allyn and Bacon.

Grant, Joanne, ed. 1968. *Black Protest.* New York: Fawcett Premier.

Gray, Dave, and Colleen Carroll. 1998. "The Desegregation Debate." *St. Louis Post-Dispatch,* 8 February.

Greenberg, Polly. 1969. *The Devil Has Slippery Shoes: A Biased Biography of the Child Development Group of Mississippi.* London: Collier-Macmillan.

Greer, Colin. 1972. *The Great School Legend: A Revisionist Interpretation of American Public Education.* New York: Basic.

Grissmer, David, and Ann Flanagan. 1998. "Exploring Rapid Achievement Gains in North Carolina and Texas." National Education Goals Panel. Document Number 1800. November.

Groopman, Jerome. 2003. "The Reeve Effect." *The New Yorker*, 10 November.

Guth, Gloria Deborah Joltzman, Steven Schneider, Lisa Carlos, James Smith, Gerald Hayward, and Naomi Calvo. 1999. "Evaluation of California's Standards-Based Accountability System." Evaluation final. Menlo Park and Davis, CA: WestEd and Management Analysis and Planning, 240.

Gutmann, Amy. 1987. *Democratic Education*. Princeton, NJ: Princeton University Press.

Gutmann, Amy, and Dennis F. Thompson. 1996. *Democracy and Disagreement*. Cambridge, MA: Belknap Press of Harvard University Press.

Haney, Walt. 2000. "The Myth of the Texas Miracle in Education." Education Policy Analysis Archives. 19 August.

Hardy, Lawrence. 2003. "Overburdened/Overwhelmed." *American School Board Journal* 190 (4). Accessed at *www.asbj.com/2003/040403coverstory.html*.

Harmon, Theresa. 2003. "A New and Improved Socialism?" *Federal Observer*, 25 November. Accessed at *www.federalobserver.com/archive.php?aid=2304*.

Hatton, Barbara. 1979. "Community Control in Retrospect." In *Community Participation in Education*, ed. Carl Grant, 2–21. Boston: Allyn and Bacon.

Havighurst, Robert. 1979. "Local Community Participation in Educational Policy Making and School Administration." In *Community Participation in Education*, ed. Carl Grant, 22–45. Boston: Allyn and Bacon.

Haycock, Kati. 2003. Letter to the Editor. *New York Times*, 6 December.

Hayes, Edward C. 1971. *Power Structure and Urban Policy: Who Rules in Oakland? Policy Impact and Political Change in America*. New York: McGraw-Hill.

Hays, Samuel. P. 1983. "The Politics of Reform in Municipal Government in the Progressive Era." In *American Vistas*, ed. Leonard Dinnerstein and Kenneth T. Jackson, 102–29. New York: Oxford University Press.

Herndon, James. 1985. *Notes from a Schoolteacher*. New York: Simon and Schuster.

Hiatt, Fred. 2002. "What's So Sacred About a School Board?" *The Washington Post*, 6 May.

Hill, Paul, Kelly Warner-King, Christine Campbell, Meaghan McElroy, and Isabel Munoz-Colon. 2002. *Big City School Boards: Problems and Options*. Seattle, WA: Center on Reinventing Public Education and Annie E. Casey Foundation. Accessed at *www.crpe.org/pubs/pdf/schoolBoard_Final.pdf*.

Hill, Paul, Arthur Wise, and Lesie Shapiro. 1989. *Educational Progress: Cities Mobilize to Improve Their Schools*. Santa Monica, CA: Rand.

Hofstadter, Richard. 1973. *The American Political Tradition and the Men Who Made It*. New York: Knopf.

Holland, Robert. 1998. "Illegal End Run." *Richmond Times-Dispatch*, 16 September.

Hovenic, Ginger. 2002. "Are School Boards Making the Grade?" *San Diego Daily Transcript*, 30 October. Accessed at *www.thechamberfoundation.org/supports/TranscriptColumn/2002/Are_School_Boards_Making_the_Grade_10_31_46.htm*.

Huggins, Judy, and Susan Alkire. 1999. "Auschwitz: A Literary Approach." Ed. the Learning Village. East Charleston, WV: West Virginia Department of Education and IBM. Accessed at *http://reinvent.k12.wv.us/lt/ltipbp.nsf/77be74f004edafda8525668a00638f66/8525669800638e138525684600798ac2?*

Hutchins, Robert Maynard. 1953. *The Conflict in Education in a Democratic Society*. New York: Harper.

———. 1954. *Great Books, the Foundation of a Liberal Education*. New York: Simon and Schuster.

Hyde, Henry. 1997. "Congressional Record (excerpt)." Constitution Party of Texas, 15 May. Accessed at *www.cptexas.org/articles/OBEGoals2000.shtml*.

Institute for Educational Leadership. 1998. "Together We Can." Institute for Educational Leadership. Accessed at *http://togetherwecan.org/*.

———. 1999a. "Engaging Americans in Education Reform." Washington, DC: Institute for Educational Leadership.

———. 1999b. "EPFP Activities." Washington, DC: Institute for Educational Leadership.

———. 1999c. "Hand in Hand: Parents, Schools and Communities United for Kids." Washington, DC: Institute for Educational Leadership.

———. 1999d. "IEL Grants and Contributors." Washington, DC: Institute for Educational Leadership.

———. 1999e. "IEL's EPFP at a Glance." Institute for Educational Leadership. Accessed at *www.iel.org/about/services.html*.

———. 1999f. "Manufacturing Industries Career Alliance." Washington, DC: Institute for Educational Leadership.

———. 1999g. "School Board Effectiveness Program." Institute for Educational Leadership. Accessed at *www.iel.org/about/services.html*.

———. 1999h. "Superintendents Prepared." Institute for Educational Leadership. Accessed at *www.iel.org/about/services.html*.

———. 1999. *Together We Can: A Guide for Crafting a Profamily System of Education and Human Services*. Washington, DC: ERIC Clearinghouse on

Urban Education. Accessed at *eric-web.tc.columbia. edu/families/TWC/profsch.html.*

International Business Machines. n.d. "IBM and Education: A Perfect Match." In *Reinventing Education.* International Business Machines. Accessed at *www. ibm.com/ibm/ibmgives/grant/education/programs/ reinventing/kanter.shtml.*

———. n.d. "IBM's Central Commitment: Education (Reinventing Education)." In *Community Relations.* International Business Machines. Accessed at *www. ibm.com/ibm/ibmgives.*

Iserbyt, Charlotte Thompson. 2002. "Cold War Myth: An Exercise in the Use of the Dialectic." News WithViews.com, 23 November. Accessed at *www. newswithviews.com/iserbyt/iserbyt2.htm.*

———. n.d. "No Child Left Behind, No American Left Alone." *Property Rights Research.* Accessed at *www.cptexas.org/articles/OBEGoals2000.shtml.*

Issel, W. 1973. "Modernization in Philadelphia School Reform." In *Education in American History: Readings on the Social Issues,* ed. Michael B. Katz, 181–97. New York: Praeger.

Jacobson, Louis. 2003. "The Roundtable's Turnaround." *The National Journal,* 28 June, 2110. Accessed at *www.brt.org/pdf/njroundtableturnaround. pdf.*

Jennings, Derek. 2003. "Test Stress." *Independent Online,* 28 May.

Johnson, Alvin, et al. 1999. *A Case Study of the Charlotte-Mecklenburg Public Schools School-Based Performance Award Program."* Philadelphia: Consortium for Policy Research in Education.

Johnson, Bob L. 1988. *Sacrificing Liberty for Equality: The Erosion of Local Control in American Education.* ERIC ED 356531. LA: LEAD.

Kahlenberg, Richard. 1999. "Economic School Desegregation." *Education Week.* Accessed at *www.ed-week.org/ew/vol-18/29kahlen.h18.*

Kanter, Rosabeth Moss. 1998. "IBM's Reinventing Education (A)." *Harvard Business School Publishing Online.*

Katz, Michael B. 1971. *School Reform: Past and Present.* Boston: Little, Brown.

———. 1973. "The 'New Departure' in Quincy, 1873–81: The Nature of Nineteenth-Century Educational Reform." In *Education in American History: Readings on the Social Issues,* ed. Michael B. Katz, 68–84. New York: Praeger.

———. 1975. *Class, Bureaucracy, and Schools: The Illusion of Educational Change in America.* Expanded ed. New York: Praeger.

———. 1987. *Reconstructing American Education.* Cambridge, MA: Harvard University Press.

———. 1990. *The Undeserving Poor: From the War on Poverty to the War on Welfare.* 1st ed. New York: Pantheon.

———. 1997. *Improving Poor People: The Welfare State, the 'Underclass,' and Urban Schools as History.* 1st paperback. ed. Princeton, NJ: Princeton University Press.

Kidder, Tracy. 2003. *Mountains Beyond Mountains: The Quest of Dr. Paul Farmer, a Man Who Would Cure the World.* New York: Random House.

Kingsolver, Barbara. 1996. *Holding the Line: Women in the Great Arizona Mine Strike of 1983.* New York: ILR.

Kirp, David. 1976. "Race, Politics and the Courts: San Francisco Desegregation." *Harvard Educational Review* 46: 572–611.

———. 1979. "Race, Schooling and Interest Politics: The Oakland Story." *School Review* 87 (4): 355–97.

Kirsch, Steve. n.d. "Rod Paige Page." Steve Kirsch's Political Home Page. Accessed at *www.skirsch.com/ politics/rodpaige/rod_paige_page.htm.*

Kirst, Michael. 1994. "A Changing Context Means School Board Reform." *Phi Delta Kappan* 75 (5): 378–81.

———. 2000. "Bridging Education Research and Education Policymaking." *Oxford Review of Education* 26 (3–4).

Kirst, M., and C. Mazzeo. 1996. "The Rise, Fall and Rise of State Assessment in California, 1993–6." Paper presented at the American Educational Research Association, New York, April.

Knight, Heather. 2003. "Ackerman Is Accused of 'Gag Order.' " *San Francisco Chronicle,* 16 October.

Kozol, Jonathan. 1986. *The Night Is Dark and I Am Far from Home: A Political Indictment of the U.S. Public School System.* New York: Continuum.

Kronley, Robert. 2000. "Southern Synergy." Columbia Group, 56. Accessed at *www.columbiagroup.org/ pdfs/all.pdf.*

Kunnen, James. 1996. "The End of Integration." *Time* 29 April.

Kurtz, Michele. 2003. "Pressured Communities Threaten to Defy State on MCAS: Students Failing Test." *The Boston Globe.* 2 March.

LaFeber, Walter. 1985. *America, Russia and the Cold War, 1945–84.* New York: Alfred A. Knopf.

Landgraf, Kurt. 2003. "International Education: The Best Defense Against Terrorism." *ETS on the Issues.* Accessed at *www.ets.org/aboutets/issues13.html.*

Lane Homer, Tyrrell. 1969. *Talks to Parents and Teachers.* New York: Schocken.

Larson, Joseph. 2001. "Count Down to Socialism in America." RestoringAmerica.org. Accessed at *www. restoringamerica.org/archive/larson/countdown_to_ socialism_p2.html.*

Lazar, Kay. 2003. "Rogue Schools Get Lesson in MCAS Laws." *The Boston Herald*, 1 June.

Learning Research and Development Corporation. 2000a. "About US." Learning Research and Development Corporation. Accessed at *www.lrdc.pitt.edu/about.htm*.

———. 2000b. "AFT Honors Two LRDCers." Learning Research and Development Corporation. Accessed at *www.lrdc.pitt.edu/award_details.htm#mm-aeri*.

Levering, Robert, Michael Katz, and Milton Moskowitz. 1999. *Everybody's Business: A Field Guide to the 400 Leading Companies in America*. 1st ed. New York: Doubleday/Currency.

Liss, Neil. 2003. Letter to the editor. *New York Times*, 6 December.

Logan, John R., and Harvey Luskin Molotch. 1987. *Urban Fortunes: The Political Economy of Place*. Berkeley: University of California Press.

Loose Lips. 1999. "No More Teachers' Dirty Looks." *Washington City Paper*, 19–25 February. Accessed at *www.washingtoncitypaper.com/archives/lips/1999/lips0219.html*.

Lowham, Jim. 1995. "Evolution of Intentions: Two School Districts in a Sparsely Populated Mid-Western State." In *Case Studies in Educational Change: An International Perspective*, ed. D. S. G. Carter and M. H. O'Neill, 100–34. Washington, DC: Falmer.

Lunsford, J. Lynn, and Anne Marie Squeo. 2003. "Shuttle Probe Faults NASA for Relying on Contractors." *The Wall Street Journal*, 27 August. Accessed at *http://online.wsj.com/article/0,,SB106190731284649600,00.html?mod=home_whats_news_us*.

Lutz, Frank W. 1975. "Local School Boards as Sociocultural Systems." In *Understanding School Boards*, ed. Peter J. Cistone, 63–76. Lexington, MA: Lexington (D. C. Heath).

MacNamara, Mark. 2001. "The Lesson of Bill Rojas." *San Francisco Magazine*, September.

Mahlburg, Bob. 2003. "Firm to Crunch FCAT Scores." *Orlando Sentinel*, 16 August.

Maier, Cornell. 1989. "American Survey." *Economist* (UK edition), 26 August.

Main Event Management Corporation. n.d. "What Is Model-Netics?" Accessed at *www.maineventmanagement.com/model-netics_what.html*.

Makarenko, Anton Semenovich. 1973. *The Road to Life: An Epic in Education*. New York: Oriole.

Malonson, Roy. 2002. "Dr. Paige Created Aramark Food Service Monster." *African-American News and Issues*, 3–9 July. Accessed at *www.aframnews.com/archives/2002-07-03/lead1.htm*.

Mann, Dale. 1975. "School Boards and Power in Local Communities." In *Understanding School Boards*, ed.

Peter J. Cistone, 161–70. Lexington, MA: Lexington (D. C. Heath).

Marquand, Barbara. 1998. "As Approval Nears, Science Standards Still Draw Flak." *Sacramento Business Journal*, 12 October.

Mass Insight. n.d. "About Mass Insight Education: Working to Improve Student Achievement in Public Schools." In *Building Blocks Initiative*. Accessed at *www.buildingblocks.org/about.htm*.

———. n.d. "Campaign for Higher Standards: Public and Leadership Engagement to Build Support for Higher Standards." Mass Insight. Accessed at *www.massinsight.org/campaign.htm*.

MassINC. 1997. "Are Schools Improving?" Massachusetts Institute for a New Commonwealth, 14. Accessed at *www.massinc.org/events/forum_education97.html*.

MassINC. 2000a. "Initiatives." Massachusetts Institute for a New Commonwealth. Accessed at *www.massinc.org/mission/initiatives.html#Lifelong Learning*.

———. 2000b. "MassINC's Mission." Massachusetts Institute for a New Commonwealth. Accessed at *www.massinc.org/mission/index.html*.

———. 2000c. "Sponsors." Massachusetts Institute for a New Commonwealth. Accessed at *www.massinc.org/about/sponsors.html*.

Mattel. 1999a. "Hand in Hand TIPS Brochure: Tips for parents, Families and Teachers." Institute for Educational Leadership. Accessed at *hand in hand/org/tips.html*.

———. 1999b. "What's Working." Institute for Educational Leadership. Accessed at *hand in hand/org/whatsworking.html*.

McAdams, Donald. 2000. *Fighting to Save Our Urban Schools . . . and Winning! Lessons from Houston*. New York: Teachers College Press.

McCarthy, Larry. 1998. "Business Cranks Up Volume on Public Education." *San Francisco Business Times*, 28 December. Accessed at *www.bizjournals.com/sanfrancisco/stories/1998/12/28/editorial/4.html*.

McElhenny, John. 2001. "State to Launch Pro-MCAS Ads." *South Coast Today*. Accessed at *www.s-t.com/daily/10-01/10-10-01/a13sr126.htm*.

McLamb, Jack. n.d. "Bush Signs on to Speed Up Indoctrination of Our Children." Patriotamerica.com. Accessed at *www.patriotamerica.com/News%20Items/BUSH%20SIGNS%20ON%20TO%20SPEED%20UP%20THE%20INDOCTRINATION%20OF%20OUR%20CHILDREN.htm*.

McNeil, Linda. 2000. *Contradictions of School Reform: Educational Costs of Standardized Testing*. New York: Routledge.

Meier, Deborah, et al. 2000. *Will Standards Save Public Education?* Boston: Beacon.

Merchant, Carolyn. 1990. *The Death of Nature: Women, Ecology and the Scientific Revolution.* San Francisco: Harper San Francisco.

Mickelson, Roslyn A. 1999. "International Business Machinations: A Case Study of Corporate Involvement in Local Educational Reform." *Teachers College Record* 100 (3): 476–512.

———. 2000. "Corporations and Classrooms: A Critical Examination of the Business Agenda for Urban School Reform." In *The Challenges of Urban Education: Sociological Perspectives for the Next Century,* ed. K. McClafferty, C. A. Torres, and T. R. Mitchell, 127–74. Albany: State University of New York.

Miller, Victor, and Jeanne Hallacy. 1992. "Teen's Tragic Death Will Not Be Forgotten." *New Mission News,* February.

Minar, David W. 1966. "The Community Basis of Conflict in School System Politics." *American Sociological Review* 31 (6): 822–35.

Missouri State Legislature. 1998. SB 781. Accessed at *www.senate.state.mo.us/98info/billtext/ tat/sb781.htm.*

Moore, Solomon, and Doug Smith. 2002. "Broad Denies Gift Was Improper." *Los Angeles Times,* 2 November.

Morain, Dan. 2002. "Davis Appointees Give $12 Million to Campaign." *Los Angeles Times,* 13 October. Accessed at *www.latimes.com/news/local/politics/cal/ la-101302appoint,0,6970002.story.*

Morison, Samuel Eliot, Henry Steele Commager, and William Leuchtenburg. 1983. *A Concise History of the American Republic.* New York: Oxford University Press.

Morrison and Foerster, LLP. 2003. "Experts." In *Decent Schools for California.* Accessed at *www.decentschools. org/experts.php.*

Mosco, Moira. 2000. "How Albany Failed English." *The New York Times,* 5 February.

Murphy, Bruce. 2001. "How Michael Joyce Sold Himself to George W. Bush." *Milwaukee World.* Accessed at *www.milwaukeeworld.com/html/mlaw/ml010625 front.php.*

National Alliance of Business. 1998. " 'Knowledge Supply Chain': Managing K–80 Learning." *Work America* 15 (5).

National Center for Educational Accountability. 2003. "About Us: Founding Organizations." Accessed at *www.nc4ea.org/index.cfm?pg=about_use&subp=fo.*

Neill, Alexander Sutherland. 1960. *Summerhill: A Radical Approach to Child Rearing.* New York: Hart.

Nelson, Ken. n.d. "Statement Before the Appropriations Subcommittee on Labor, Health and Human Services, and Education, U.S. House of Representatives." Washington, DC: National Education Goals Panel. Accessed at *www.negp.gov/page1-15.htm.*

Neubert, Sandra. 1995. "Texas Educational Reform." In *Case Studies in Educational Change: An International Perspective,* ed. D. S. G. Carter and M. H. O'Neill, 43–61. Washington, DC: Falmer.

New Democracy. 2003. "A Call for Mass Refusal." MassRefusal. 23 December. Accessed at *www.mass refusal.org/.*

"New Era at School Board." 1999. Editorial. *Los Angeles Times,* 15 April.

New York State. n.d. "Directions for Teachers: Listening Section Comprehensive Examination in English." NYSEDregents.org. Accessed at *www. nysedregents.org/testing/engre/engs1100.pdf.*

New York State United Teachers. 1999. "Regents Exams Standards Setting: The Cut Scores." *NYSUT Information Bulletin,* May. Accessed at *www.nysut. org/research/bulletins/9905regents.htm.*

Noguera, Pedro. 1996. "Confronting the Urban in Urban School Reform." *Urban Review* 28 (1): 1–19.

Norden, Eric. 1972. "Interview with Saul Alinsky, Concluded." Progress.org. Originally appeared in *Playboy* magazine. Accessed at *www.progress.org/ 2003/alinsky14.htm.*

North Carolina Department of Public Instruction. n.d. "Information Skills Curriculum: Grade Kindergarten." Raleigh: North Carolina State Board of Education. Accessed at *www.ncpublicschools.org/ curriculum/Information/gradek.htm.*

Northwest Regional Educational Laboratory. 1999. "Stepping Up the Rigor, Part 3." *Northwest Education Magazine,* fall. Accessed at *www.nwrel.org/nwedu/ fall99/article6c.html.*

O'Brien, Keven. 1998. "Deep-Cover Bureaucrats Shun the Light." *Cleveland Plain Dealer,* 26 July.

Ogbu, John. 1995. "Cultural Problems in Minority Education: Their Interpretations and Consequences—Part Two: Case Studies." *The Urban Review* 24 (4): 271–97.

Ohanian, Susan. 1999. *One Size Fits Few: The Folly of Educational Standards.* Portsmouth, NH: Heinemann.

———. n.d. "NCLB in Your Face." Susanohanian.org. Accessed at *http://susanohanian.org/show_nclb_ stories.html?id=38.*

———. 2000. "Goals 2000: What's in a Name?" *Phi Delta Kappan,* January. Accessed at *www.pdkintl.org/kappan/koha0001.htm.*

———. 2003. "Capitalism, Calculus, and Conscience." *Phi Delta Kappan,* June. Accessed at *www. pdkintl.org/kappan/k0306oha.htm.*

Orfield, Gary. 1992. *Desegregation and Educational Change in San Francisco: Findings and Recommendations on Consent Decree Implementation.* San Francisco: U.S. District Court, 82.

Orfield, Gary, Jennifer Arenson, Tara Jackson, Christine Bohrer, Dawn Gavin, and Emily Kajejs. 1998.

"Summary of 'City-Suburban Desegregation: Parent and Student Perspectives in Metropolitan Boston,' a Report by the Harvard Civil Rights Project." *Equity and Excellence in Education* 31 (3): 5–12.

Orfield, Gary, and J. T. Yun June. 1999. *The Resegregation in American Schools.* Cambridge: Civil Rights Project at Harvard University.

Orrick, William. 1983. *SF NAACP, et al., Plaintiffs, v. SF Unified School District, et al., Defendents.* Civ. No. C-78-1445 WHO. 576 F. Supp. 34, San Francisco: U.S. District Court ND California, 41.

———. 1999. *Brian Ho et al., Plaintiffs, v. SF Unified School District, et al., Defendents.* Civ. No. C-78-1445 WHO, No. C-94-2418 WHO. San Francisco: U.S. District Court ND California.

Paige, Jeffrey. 1973. *Agrarian Revolution: Social Movements and Export Agriculture.* New York: Free.

Palm Beach County Florida School District. 2003. *Academic Business Plan, FY 2001–2005.* Palm Beach: Palm Beach County School District, 52.

Pateman, Carole. 1970. *Participation and Democratic Theory.* New York: Cambridge University Press.

———. 1989. *The Disorder of Women: Democracy, Feminism and Political Theory.* Cambridge, UK: Polity.

Pateman, Carole, and Mary Lyndon Shanley. 1991. *Feminist Interpretations and Political Theory.* Cambridge, UK: Polity in association with Basil Blackwell Oxford UK.

Payne, Charles. 2003. School Based Organizing: Analyzing Schools as Places to Change and Places Out of Which to Organize. Talk presented at the Organizing for Educational Excellence Institute, Temple University Sugarloaf Conference Center, 6 August. Philadelphia, PA.

Pearson Education. 2002–3. "Success Maker." In *NCLB: Resources for Administrators.* Pearson Education. Accessed at *www.pearsondigital.com/successmaker/.*

Perlstein, Dan. 1999. "If Not Now, When?" In *Transforming Teacher Unions: Fighting for Better Schools and Social Justice,* ed. Bob Peterson and Michael Charney, 86–92. Milwaukee: Rethinking Schools.

Plank, David N., and Paul E. Peterson. 1988. "Does Urban Reform Imply Class Conflict? The Case of Atlanta's Schools." In *The Social History of American Education,* ed. B. Edward McClellan and William J. Reese, 209–32. Chicago: University of Illinois Press.

Pogrow, Stanley. 2000. "The Unsubstantiated 'Success' of Success for All: Implications for Policy, Practice, and the Soul of Our Profession." *Phi Delta Kappan* 81 (April): 596–600.

"The Politics of Teacher Testing." 2000. Editorial. *New York Times,* 24 April, A26.

Popham, W. James. 2001. *The Truth About Testing: An Educator's Call to Action.* Alexandria, VA: Association for Supervision and Curricular Development.

Popkewitz, Thomas. 1979. "Schools and the Symbolic Uses of Community Participation." In *Community Participation in Education,* ed. Carl Grant, 202–23. Boston: Allyn and Bacon.

———. 1991. "Educational Reform as a Discourse of Social Organization and Regulation: The Proposals for the 1980's." In *A Political Sociology of Educational Reform: Power/Knowledge in Teaching, Teacher Education and Research,* 136–55. New York: Teachers College Press.

Portz, John, Lana Stein, and Robin R. Jones. 1999. *City Schools and City Politics: Institutions and Leadership in Pittsburgh, Boston, and St. Louis, Studies in Government and Public Policy.* Lawrence: University Press of Kansas.

Potter, Matt. 2002. "It Was the Biggest Mystery." *San Diego Reader,* 24 October. Accessed at *www.sdreader.com/php/m_potter.php3?mode=article&show-pg=1&id=20021024.*

Progressive Policy Institute. 2000. "About PPI's 21st Century Schools Project." ppionline.org, 29 June. Accessed at *www.ppionline.org/ppi_ci.cfm?contentid=1125&knlgAreaID=110&subsecid=204.*

Public Agenda. 1999. "The Perspectives in Brief." Public Agenda. Accessed at *http:/publicagenda.org/issues/debate_detail2.cfm?issue_type=.*

Public School Forum of North Carolina. n.d. "Education: Everybody's Business Coalition." Raleigh: Public School Forum of North Carolina, 1. Accessed at *www.ncforum.org/programs/ebc/.*

———. 1996. "Things That Matter (review)." Raleigh: Public School Forum of North Carolina, 3. Accessed at *www.ncforum.org/publications.*

———. 2000. "Public School Forum of North Carolina." Public School Forum of North Carolina, 1. Accessed at *www.ncforum.org.*

Ragin, Charles. 1987. *The Comparative Method: Moving Beyond Qualitative and Quantitative Strategies.* Berkeley: University of California Press.

Rebore, Ronald. 1984. *A Handbook for School Board Members.* Englewood Cliffs, NJ: Prentice-Hall.

———. 1997. *Unitary Status: What Does It Mean in the St. Louis Desegregation Case.* ERIC ED 437479. Paper presented at the American Educational Research Association, Chicago, March.

Restoring America. n.d. "Government Education." Restoringamerica.org. Accessed at *www.restoringamerica.org/archive/education_index.html.*

Rewards and Interventions Advisory Committee. 1998. *Steering by Results: A High-Stakes Rewards and Interventions Program for California Schools and Stu-*

dents. Sacramento: California Department of Education.

Roach, Ron. 1997. "Bill Hauck: The Business Roundtable's Man at the Capitol." *Cal-Tax Digest*, May. Accessed at *www.caltax.org/MEMBER/digest/may97/MAY97-7.HTML*.

Rojas, Waldemar. 1996. Reconstitution, Reculturing, and Reform: Adding Options for Urban Education. Ph.D. diss., Teachers College, Columbia University.

——. 1999a. *The Benefits of the San Francisco Unified School District Consent Decree*. San Francisco: San Francisco Unified School District.

——. 1999b. Letter to California state senator Gary Hart. 20 January.

Rojas, Waldemar, and Assembly Education Committee. 1998. "Accountability in the SFUSD." Sacramento: California Legislature, 11. Accessed at *www.sfusd.k12.ca.us/news/ account.pdf*.

Rosenthal, Alan. 1969. *Governing Education: A Reader on Politics, Power, and Public School Policy*. 1st ed. Garden City, NY: Anchor.

Rothstein, Richard. 2000. "How to Create a Skilled-Labor Shortage." *New York Times*, 6 September.

Rousseau, Jean-Jacques. 1979. *Emile*. Trans. Allan Bloom. New York: Basic.

Ruenzel, David. 1997. "Do or Die." *Teacher Magazine*, March.

Ruiz-de-Velasco, Jorge. 1998. The Politics of Education in Court-Ordered School Districts: A Case Study. Paper presented at the Annual Meeting of the American Educational Research Association, San Diego, 3–6 September.

Rust, Edward. 1999. "No Turning Back: A Progress Report on the Business Roundtable." Business Roundtable. Accessed at *www.brtable.org/pdf/312.pdf*.

——. 2001. "Business Views of Assessments and Accountability in Education." In *Hearings, Committee on Education and the Workforce*. Washington, DC: U.S. House of Representatives. Accessed at *http://edworkforce.house.gov/hearings/107th/edr/account 3801/rust.htm*.

Ryan, Clarice. 2002. "Comments on 'A New and Improved Socialism?'" 22 April. Accessed at *www.bitterroot.com/grizzly/socialism.htm*.

Safran, Daniel. 1979. "Preparing Teachers for Parent Involvement." In *Community Participation in Education*, ed. Carl Grant, 94–115. Boston: Allyn and Bacon.

San Francisco Unified School District (SFUSD). 1992. *Findings and Recommendations on Consent Decree Implementation, Report to Judge William H. Orrick*. San Francisco: SFUSD.

Sandalow, Marc. 2001. "Tech-Savvy Bay Area Ranks

No. 1 in New Economy." *San Francisco Chronicle*, 19 April.

Sandel, Michael J. 1996. *Democracy's Discontent: America in Search of a Public Philosophy*. Cambridge, MA: Belknap Press of Harvard University Press.

——. 1998. *Liberalism and the Limits of Justice*. 2d ed. Cambridge, UK, New York: Cambridge University Press.

Sanders, Charlene. 2002. "School-to-Work and Ralph Tyler." Citizenreviewonline.org, 12 August. Accessed at *www.citizenreviewonline.org/august_2002/school_to_work.htm*.

Sassen, Saskia. 1998. *Globalization and Its Discontents*. New York: New.

Schaps, Eric. 2002. "High-Stakes Surveys." *Education Week*, 5 June. Accessed at *www.edweek.org/ew/newstory.cfm?slug=39schaps.h21*.

Schemo, Diana, and Ford Fessenden. 2003. "A Miracle Revisited: Measuring Success; Gains in the Houston Schools: How Real Are They?" *New York Times*, 3 December.

Schlafly, Phyllis. 1997. "The Clinton Master Plan to Take Over Education." Eaglefourm.org, 19 February. Accessed at *www.eagleforum.org/column/1997/feb97/97-02-19.html*.

Schools Not Jails. 2002. "Office of State Superintendent." *SNJ Newswire*, 26 November. Accessed at *http://schoolsnotjails.com/print.php?sid=107*.

Selden, David. 1979. "The Future of Community Participation in Educational Policy Making." In *Community Participation in Education*, ed. Carl Grant, 66–77. Boston: Allyn and Bacon.

Sewell, William. 1990. "Collective Violence and Collective Loyalites in France: Why the French Revolution Made a Difference." *Politics and Society* 18: 527–52.

Shannon, Thomas. 1994. "The Changing Local Community School Board." *Phi Delta Kappan* 75 (5): 387–90.

Shapiro, Svi. 1990. *Between Capitalism and Democracy*. New York: Bergin and Garvey.

Shaw, Randy. 1996. "Rojas to Parents: Keep Quiet!" *The Independent*, 18 June.

——. 2001. *The Activist's Handbook*. Berkeley: University of California Press.

Sherry, Mark. 1992. "Searching for New American Schools." *Education Week*, 6 May.

Shields, James J., and Colin Greer. 1974. *Foundations of Education: Dissenting Views*. New York: Wiley.

Shirley, Dennis. 1997. *Community Organizing for Urban School Reform*. Austin: University of Texas.

Simon, Mark. 1999. "Resisting Resistance to Change." In *Transforming Teacher Unions: Fighting for Better Schools and Social Justice*, ed. Bob Peterson and

Michael Charney, 66–67. Milwaukee: Rethinking Schools.

Sonstelie, Jon, Eric Brunner, and Kenneth Ardon. 2000. "For Better or For Worse? School Finance Reform in California." San Francisco: Public Policy Institute of California.

Southern-Style. n.d. "Warnings from D. L. Cuddy." *World Newsstand.* Accessed at *www.worldnewsstand.net/msc/DLCuddy.htm.*

Speilvogel, Bob. 2001. "IBM Reinventing Education: Research Summary and Perspective." :EDC Center for Children and Technology, 14. Accessed at *www2.edc.org/cct/admin/publications/report/ibmsum.pdf.*

"Spineless: School Boards Beat Shameful Retreat on Standards." 2002. Editorial. *Worcester Telegram and Gazette,* 3 November.

Spring, Joel. 1986. *The American School: 1642–1985.* New York: Longman.

———. 1998a. *Conflicts of Interest.* New York: McGraw-Hill.

———. 1998b. *Education and the Rise of the Global Economy.* Mahwah, NJ: Lawrence Erlbaum.

Steffy, B. E., and F. W. English. 1995. "Radical Legislated School Reform in the United States: An Examination of Chicago and Kentucky." In *Case Studies in Educational Change: An International Perspective,* ed. D. S. G. Carter and M. H. O'Neill, 28–42. Washington, DC: Falmer.

Steinberg, Jacques. 1999. "Academic Standards Eased as a Fear of Failure Spreads." *New York Times,* 3 December.

———. 2001. "Redefining Diversity." *New York Times,* 29 August.

Steinbruner, Maureen. 1999. "Parents, Leadership Disagree over How to Fix Nation's Schools." *San Francisco Chronicle,* 29 September.

Stinchecombe, Arthur L. 1978. "What Theory in History Should Be and Do." In *Theoretical Methods in Social History,* 1–25. New York: Academic.

Stratman, David. n.d. *We Can Change the World.* Boston: New Democracy.

Swain, Roger. 1981. *Earthly Pleasure: Tales from a Biologist's Garden.* New York: Scribner.

Tabscott, Robert. 1999. "Desegregation's Future Could Include Resegregation." *St. Louis Post-Dispatch,* 22 June.

Teachers Fellows. 2000. "Program." NC Teachers Fellows. Accessed at *http://teacher_fellows.org/program.htm.*

Thompson, James D. 1967. *Organizations in Action: Social Science Bases of Administrative Theory.* New York: McGraw-Hill.

Thomson, Susan. 1998. "Desegregation Bill Mandates Many Changes in City Schools." *St. Louis Post-Dispatch,* 5 July.

Tikunoff, William, and Beatrice Ward. 1994. Foreword. In *Teachers, Students, and Language: Multiple Language Settings,* ed. Gary Griffin. Los Alamitos, CA: Southwest Regional Laboratory.

Timar, Thomas, David B. Tyack, and Education Commission of the States. 1999. *The Invisible Hand of Ideology: Perspectives from the History of School Governance.* Denver: Education Commission of the States.

Tucker, Cynthia. 2001. "Ruling on University Got It Wrong." *San Francisco Chronicle,* 30 August.

Tucker, Marc. 1992. "Letter to Hillary Clinton: Entered into the Congressional Record by Representative Bob Schaffer, September 17, 1998." National Center on Education and the Economy, 11 November. Accessed at *www.eagleforum.org/educate/marc_tucker/marc_tucker_letter.html.* Also reprinted at *www.mredcopac.org/tucker.htm.*

Twentieth Century Fund Task Force. 1992. *Facing the Challenge: The Report of the Twentieth Century Fund Task Force on School Governance.* New York: Danforth Foundation.

Tyack, David. 1967. *Turning Points in American Educational History.* Waltham, MA: Blaisdell.

———. 1973. "Bureaucracy and the Common School: The Example of Portland, Oregon." In *Education in American History: Readings on the Social Issues,* ed. Michael B. Katz, 164–80. New York: Praeger.

———. 1974. *The One Best System: A History of American Urban Education.* Cambridge: Harvard University Press.

Tyack, David B., and Larry Cuban. 1995. *Tinkering Toward Utopia: A Century of Public School Reform.* Cambridge: Harvard University Press.

Tyack, David B., and Elisabeth Hansot. 1982. *Managers of Virtue: Public School Leadership in America, 1820–1980.* New York: Basic.

Uchitelle, Louis. 2002. "Answering '800' Calls, Extra Income but No Security." *New York Times,* 27 March.

United Electrical Radio and Machine Workers of America. 2001. "Defending Public Education: Update." *UE Issues Briefing,* summer. Accessed at *www.ranknfile-ue.org/polact_isu_pe.html.*

University of California at Santa Barbara. 1998. "Laurie Olsen [sic]." Accessed at *http://imrinet.ucsb.edu/profdev/2/mrl-conferences/98_conf/conf_bios_1998/olsen_bio.htm.*

University Times. 2000. "Lesgold Named Dean of Education." Pittsburgh: University of Pittsburgh.

Uno, Edison. 1979. "Community Participation in Education: A Minority Viewpoint." In *Community*

Participation in Education, ed. Carl Grant, 162–75. Boston: Allyn and Bacon.

U.S. Conference of Mayors. 2002. "Mayors Lead Efforts to Improve Public Schools Across America." *The United States Conference of Mayors NEWS*, 8 October. Accessed at *www.city.cleveland.oh.us/mayor/press/2002/200210/021008usconfofmayors.pdf*.

———. 2003. "U.S. Conference of Mayors Calls on Administration and Congress to Increase Support for Public Education." *The United States Conference of Mayors NEWS*, 23 September. Accessed at *www.usmayors.org/uscm/news/press_releases/documents/edsummit_092303.pdf*.

Usdan, Michael. 1994. "The Relationships Between School Boards and General Purpose Government." *Phi Delta Kappan* 75 (5): 374–77.

Virginia Department of Education. 2000. *Released Test Items*. Richmond: Virginia Department of Education, 94.

Walsh, Joan. 1999. "A New Racial Era for San Francisco's Schools." Salon.com. Accessed at *www.salon.com/news/1999/02/18news.html*.

Walton, John. 1992. *Western Times and Water Wars*. Berkeley: University of California Press.

Walton, John, and Charles Ragin. 1990. "Global and National Sources of Political Protest: Third World Responses to the Debt Crisis." *American Sociological Review* 55 (December): 876–90.

Warren, Paul. 1999. *K–12 Master Plan: Starting the Process*. ERIC ED 438590. Sacramento: California State Legislative Analyst's Office, 49.

Weiler, Jeanne. 1998. "Recent Changes in School Desegregation." April. Accessed at *http://eric-web.tc.columbia.edu/digest/dig133.html*.   ED419029 ERIC/CUE Digest Number 133.

Weinberg, Neil. 2003. "Educating Eli." Forbes.com, 6 October. Accessed at *www.forbes.com/free_forbes/2003/1006/106.html*.

Welter, Rush. 1962. *Popular Education and Democratic Thought in America*. New York: Columbia University Press.

White, Kerry A. 1998. "Los Angeles Mayor Seeks to Unseat 4 on Board." *Education Week*, 30 September.

White, Patricia. 1983. *Beyond Domination: An Essay in the Political Philosophy of Education, International Library of the Philosophy of Education*. London, Boston: Routledge and Kegan Paul.

———. 1996. *Civic Virtues and Public Schooling: Educating Citizens for a Democratic Society*. Advances in Contemporary Educational Thought Series, Vol. 17. New York: Teachers College Press.

Wiles, David. 1975. "Community Control, Decentralization and School Consolidation: The Impact on the School Board." In *Understanding School Boards*, ed. Peter J. Cistone, 219–34. Lexington, MA: Lexington (D. C. Heath).

Wilgoren, Jodi. 1999. "Credit Given to Failed Education Goals." *New York Times*, 3 December.

Willie, Charles V. 1997. "What We Learned About Urban Education Planning and Governance from the Boston School Desegregation Experience." *Equity and Excellence* 30 (3): 13–20.

———. 1998. "Memorandum to the Boston, Massachusetts, School Committee." *Equity and Excellence* 31 (3): 13–16.

Wirt, Frederick. 1974. "Power in the City: Decision Making in San Francisco." Berkeley: University of California, Berkeley, Press.

———. 1975. "Social Diversity and School Board Responsiveness." In *Understanding School Boards*, ed. Peter J. Cistone, 189–212. Lexington, MA: Lexington (D. C. Heath).

Wirt, Frederick, and Michael Kirst. 1982. *Schools in Conflict*. Berkeley, CA: McCutcheon.

Womack, James, Daniel Jones, and Daniel Roos. 1990. *The Machine That Changed the World*. New York: HarperCollins.

Woodward, C. Vann. 1974. *The Strange Career of Jim Crow*. New York: Oxford University Press.

Wringe, Colin. 1984. *Democracy, Schooling, and Political Education*. London: George Allen and Unwin.

Yu, Corrinne, and William Taylor. 1997. *Difficult Choices: Do Magnet Schools Serve Children in Need? Report of the Citizen's Committee on Civil Rights*. Nashville: Nashville Institute for Public Policy Studies, Vanderbilt University; Spencer Foundation; Pew Charitable Trusts, 113.

Zerchykov, Ross. 1984. *School Boards and the Communities They Represent: An Inventory of the Research*. Boston: Institute for Responsive Education.

Ziegler, L. Harmon. 1975. "School Board Research: The Problems and the Prospects." In *Understanding School Boards*, ed. Peter J. Cistone, 1–16. Lexington, MA: Lexington (D. C. Heath).

Ziegler, L. H., M. K. Jennings, and G. W. Peak. 1974. *Governing American Schools: Political Interactions in Local School Districts*. North Scituate, MA: Duxbury.

Acknowledgments

Above all, I will be eternally grateful to Susan Ohanian for transforming my lengthy and densely written academic dissertation into a compact and compelling critique and call to arms. She has rescued my research from the apparent fate of dissertations and much of educational research—never again to see the light of day. Additionally, she added immeasurably to the existing research, contributing new facts, figures, and stories from schools and teachers across the nation.

I would also like to thank my professors at UC Davis for allowing me to pursue research that questioned the assumptions upon which their professions are based. This was not at all easy for some of them to do (some, in fact, needed to be persuaded by others) and I doubt I would have had such freedom at other institutions.

Without my partner, Sylvia Braselmann, neither dissertation nor book would have been possible. Her rock solid belief in the value of what I was doing gave me the support to continue during all the dark times of self-doubt and uncertainty. She talked me out of quitting many times.

My friend Mary Aschenbrener gave me the gift of her trust and the stories of the Mission High School staff and students both of which revived my faith in the power of truth. It is in the stories of people's lives or how events are made manifest in individual testimony that one can find the truth and know in the marrow of one's bones that it is so.

Thanks to Marian, Suzy, Marisol, Fadia, Lisa, Mara, Marilyn, Kim, John, Karen, and Keith, who cheered me up, picked me up, guided me, housed and fed me.

And thanks goes to all my friends and family that have stood by me, supported me, chastised me, let me cry on their shoulders, let me confide my deepest insecurities, and always loved me for who I am. It is this, my community, that I must thank for all that I ever do.

—Kathy Emery

Index